POSTCARD HISTORY SERIES

Kentucky's Bluegrass

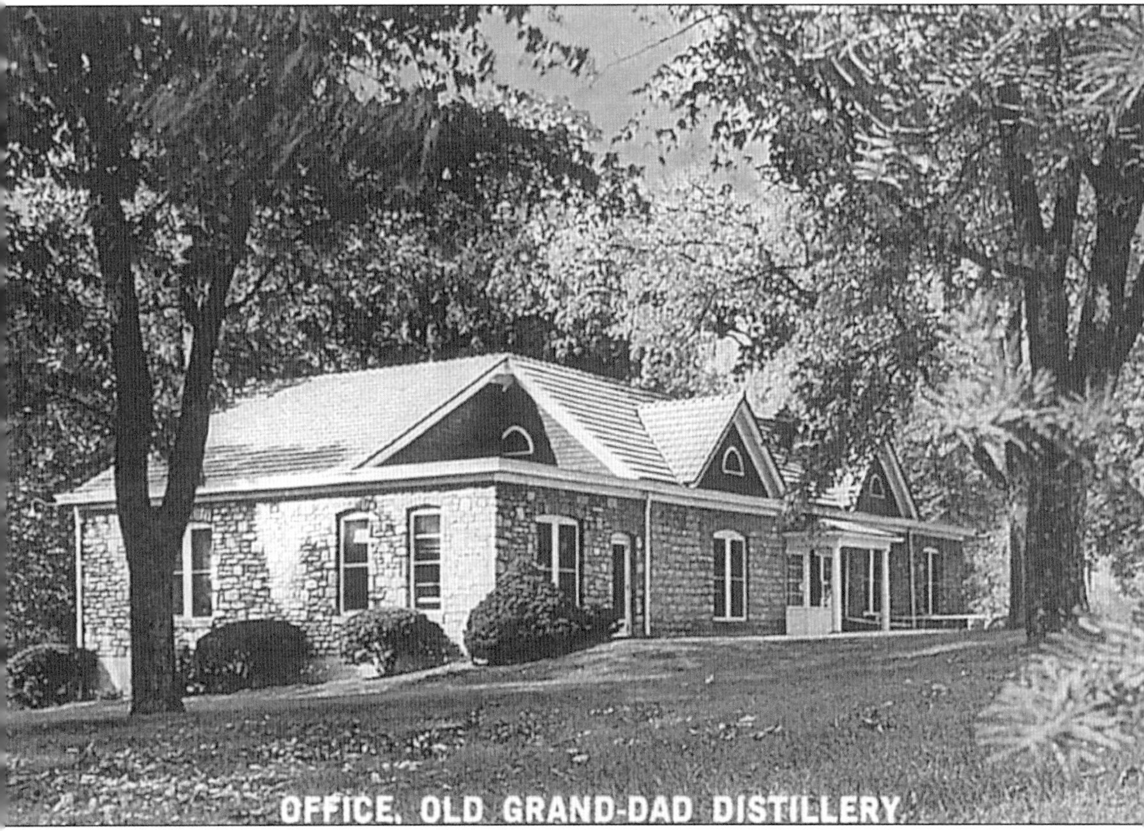

This 1908 postcard with the caption, "A Few Things for which Kentucky is Famous," indicates that Kentucky is known for its natural beauty of the land, the people, early historical roots, hemp or tobacco farming, horse raising or racing, and making whiskey or bourbon. All of these "things" will be discussed and pictured in this book as they relate to the Bluegrass of Kentucky.

POSTCARD HISTORY SERIES

Kentucky's Bluegrass

Wynelle Scott Deese

ARCADIA
PUBLISHING

ISBN 978-0-7385-0565-7

Published by Arcadia Publishing
Charleston, South Carolina

Printed in the United States of America

Library of Congress Catalog Card Number: 00-101914

For all general information contact Arcadia Publishing at:
Telephone 843-853-2070
Fax 843-853-0044
E-mail sales@arcadiapublishing.com
For customer service and orders:
Toll-Free 1-888-313-2665

Visit us on the Internet at www.arcadiapublishing.com

Contents

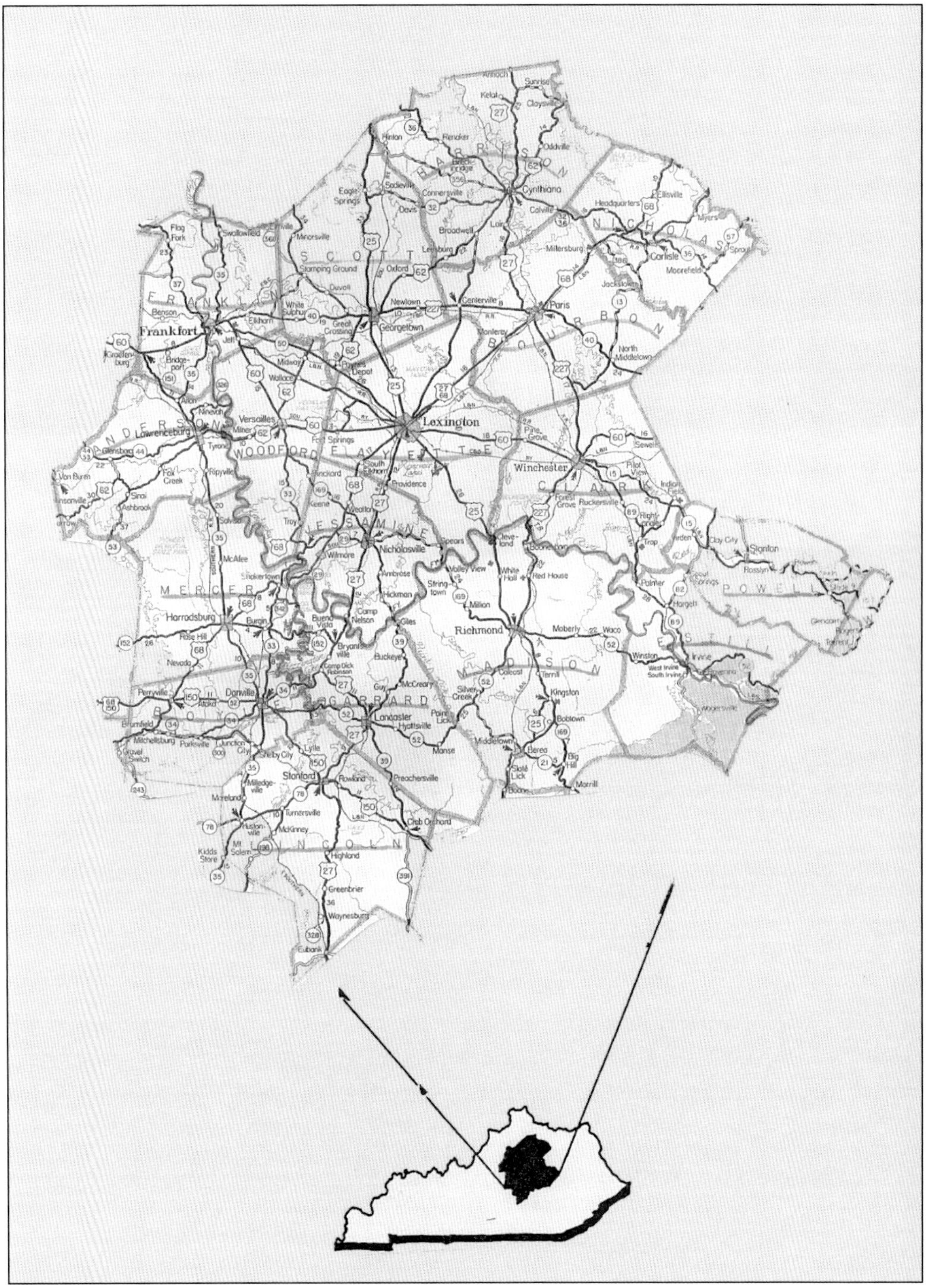

This is a map of the current 17 counties of the Bluegrass Area Development District. This map was published between 1939 and 1944 by the Kentucky State Highway Department "as a concise, serviceable guide to principal Kentucky Highways." These were the Bluegrass roads before the current interstate highways changed the land.

Acknowledgments

Special thanks to Peggy Brown, my previous Kentucky postcard partner, who provided me with copies of postcards needed to complete this book. She was especially helpful with Estill County since her family is from there. Her encouragement and old postcards truly reflect the traditions of the Bluegrass and old postcard friends.

Thanks also go to Harold Barker at the Lexington Fayette Urban County Government Records and Archives in Lexington, Kentucky, for his help and support in obtaining historical records.

Sources

The University of Kentucky Library, Special Archives, Lexington, Kentucky.
The Lexington-Fayette County Library, Lexington, Kentucky.
The Lexington-Fayette Urban County Government Records and Archives, Lexington, Kentucky.

References

Carpenter, J. *Kentucky Courthouses*. Brentwood, Tennessee: JM Productions, 1988.

Collins, L. *History of Kentucky*. Frankfort, Kentucky: Kentucky Historical Society, 1874.

Davis, D. *The Geography of the Blue Grass Region of Kentucky*. Frankfort, Kentucky: The Kentucky Geological Survey, 1927.

Garr, E. *The History of Kentucky Courthouses*. Kentucky: The National Society of the Colonial Dames of America, 1972.

Harrison, L., ed. *Kentucky's Governors: 1792–1985*. Lexington, Kentucky: University of Kentucky Press, 1985.

Kentucky Agricultural Experiment Station. "Farming in the Bluegrass Area of Kentucky." Lexington, Kentucky, 1950, #543.

Kerr, J., ed. *History of Kentucky*. University of Kentucky, Chicago: American Historical Society, 1922.

Powell, R.A. *Historical Sketches of the Kentucky Bluegrass Area*. Lexington, Kentucky: 1990.

Workers of the Federal Writer's Project of the Works Progress Administration of the State of Kentucky. "Lexington and the Bluegrass Country." Lexington, Kentucky: Glass, 1938.

INTRODUCTION

We, who live or have lived in the Bluegrass of Kentucky, may have assumed that counties that constitute the Bluegrass were consistently identified years ago. One county, Fayette County, the seat of Lexington, Kentucky, has always been part of the Bluegrass, but such is not always true of the other counties. When collecting old postcards for this book, I needed specific Kentucky counties identified as part of the Bluegrass. One book, *Historical Sketches of the Kentucky Bluegrass Area*, by Powell (1990), identified 12 "commonly considered" counties of the Bluegrass as the "old Kentucky," but left out counties currently associated with the Bluegrass. Other books about the Bluegrass were less specific as to counties that comprised that area.

Actually, I discovered that the Bluegrass area has evolved over the early 19th and 20th centuries, with shifting county lines contributing to the confusion. As will be discussed with each county, the original three counties in 1780 have multiplied and the existing county lines have changed over many years.

However, still hoping for some definitive criteria of the Bluegrass, I consulted two books about the geographic regions of the area. Both books identified the Inner Bluegrass, the Eden Shale Formations, and the Outer Bluegrass areas, and they described the similarities among the Bluegrass counties in terms of roads, markets, climate, rural conditions, and types of farming. However, when identifying the specific counties, one identified 32 counties, while the other described 30. Obviously, there are too many counties to adequately cover in one book, so I started looking elsewhere.

The Bluegrass Area Development District was formally organized as a regional agency for federal grants in the development of the Bluegrass in 1971. That organization has identified 17 specific counties. Since the Bluegrass Area Development District is a currently recognized authority, those 17 counties were used to compile this book on the Bluegrass. An earlier map showing those counties is on page 6.

This book was written to help preserve the early-20th-century history of the Bluegrass. Each chapter will show, through old postcards from 1900 to 1950, the towns, businesses, and schools in the 17 counties. Each county is arranged in alphabetical order, and depending on the number of postcards used, each chapter may consist of one, two, or three counties. An index of towns can be found on the back page. Old postcards specific to Lexington were published in a previous book, *Lexington, Kentucky: Changes in the early twentieth Century*, in 1998 by this same author and publisher, and it influenced me to write this second book related to Kentucky.

Finding these old postcards has been a life-long project. I started collecting Lexington area postcards 25 years ago and have had a collection of over 1,000 old Kentucky postcards. However, when planning this book, I had hoped to obtain equal numbers of old postcards for each county, but such did not materialize. Smaller areas such as Estill or Powell Counties may have had less postcards made and less to survive. However, this does not hold true for certain areas, such as Estill County, when families or individuals, such as Peggy Brown and her family, have preserved them. This speaks for the "unspoken" influence of those who preserved the old postcards. Without those individuals, old postcards would not be available, and many early histories would be lost. Historical data was obtained from many sources, and accuracy was attempted to my best abilities. Being a retired psychologist, I have difficulty accepting information that cannot be verified. With so much historical data proliferated on the internet, accuracy is difficult to determine. I was constantly drawn between needing data and having data that could not be verified. For example, the I.O. of O.F. Temple in Harrodsburg probably stands for International Order of Odd Fellows, but I could not find proof of that; therefore, I did not include it. Obviously, mistakes will be made with such a large demand for data, but I did attempt to provide accurate information or else, wrote nothing.

The Bluegrass area is really a blend of natural and cultural splendor with historic roots. The inner Bluegrass has exceptionally fertile soils with large farms and the best agricultural land in the state. Lexington, in the 19th century, had prosperity that provided many architecturally significant antebellum mansions. While some mansions have survived into the 20th century, others have not and can be seen in old postcards. This book will show some of those mansions, such as J.B. Haggin's Green Hill (on page 54), which is no longer standing. Some of the old Kentucky farms are still being used, while others are gone. Some can be viewed in the Fayette County chapter of this book.

The 1908 postcard on page 2 shows "a few things for which Kentucky is Famous," specifying the natural beauty and early history. Examples can be found throughout this book of that natural beauty in the Bluegrass. The mill in Danville on page 30, the bird's-eye view of Frankfort on page 59, views around Wilmore on page 88, High Bridge on page 90, and Stanford with Crab Orchard views on page 96 are just a few. The natural beauty of Kentucky women were often shown with horses, found on page 12 and 13. The early historical roots of the Bluegrass run throughout this book, starting with two early institutions: the Kentucky State Penitentiary and the Institute for the Feebleminded in Frankfort. However, history in the Bluegrass started much earlier with Fort Boonesborough and Fort Harrod viewed on pages 104 and 112.

As people migrated into the Bluegrass area, roads were created and ferries were used for transport across the rivers and streams. Some of those ferries are still running, such as the one at Valley View on page 104, while two others still exist only on old postcards, one near Winchester on page 38 and one at High Bridge on page 92. Some bridges were added, such as the one at High Bridge and the Brooklyn Bridge. Both can be viewed in their respective counties, Jessamine and Mercer.

Many of the early roads can be observed in old postcards. Later into the 1940s, the Dixie Highway became a major road in some of the Bluegrass counties. Many of the main roads were surfaced with rock asphalt and oiled, as can be seen in this postcard published between 1907 and 1915. Notice the white fences.

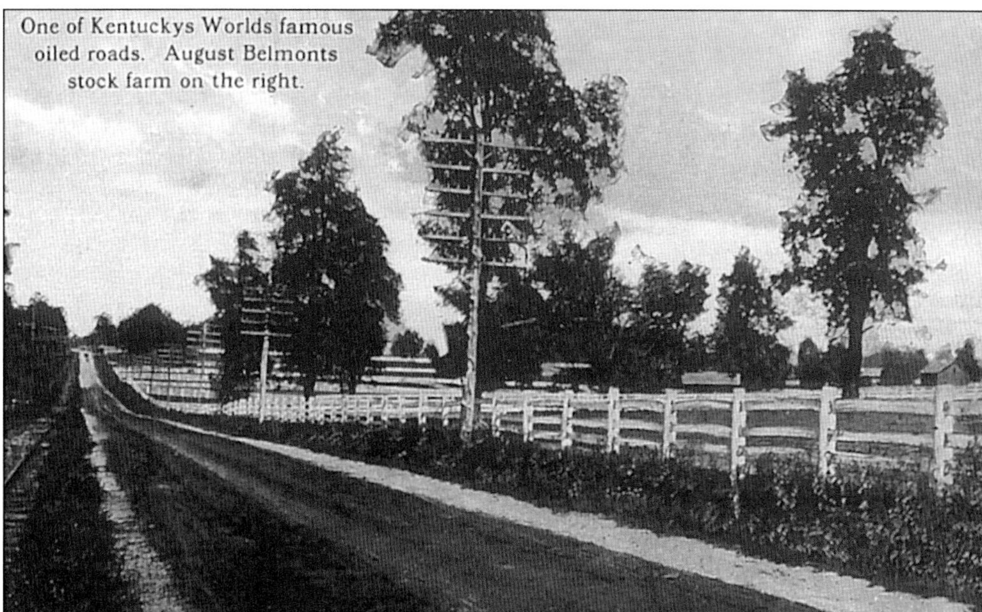

Other landmarks developed as people migrated to the Bluegrass area. One of the region's most scenic and practical landmarks was the stone fences, built between 1820 and the outbreak of the Civil War. Although myth attributes most of the stone wall in Fayette County to slave labor, some historians have conducted extensive research and found that most of these fences were constructed when there was a flood of Irish immigrants into the Bluegrass area to escape Ireland's severe potato famine. Although slaves may have built a number of the fences, it is now believed that they did so under the guidance of Irish stonemasons. Following the Civil War, those freed slaves remaining in the Bluegrass often peddled their masonry skills to horse farm and other landowners, building many of the stone fences constructed during the late 1800s. With an unlimited supply of limestone and the influx of skilled artisans, strong and durable fences were constructed.

Not surprisingly, a great number of stone fences may be found near streams or property boundaries. Many of the early roads developed along the old stone fences. As they became impractical, wood fences often replaced them or were built next to them. The postcard below, published between 1915 and 1930, shows an early stone fence.

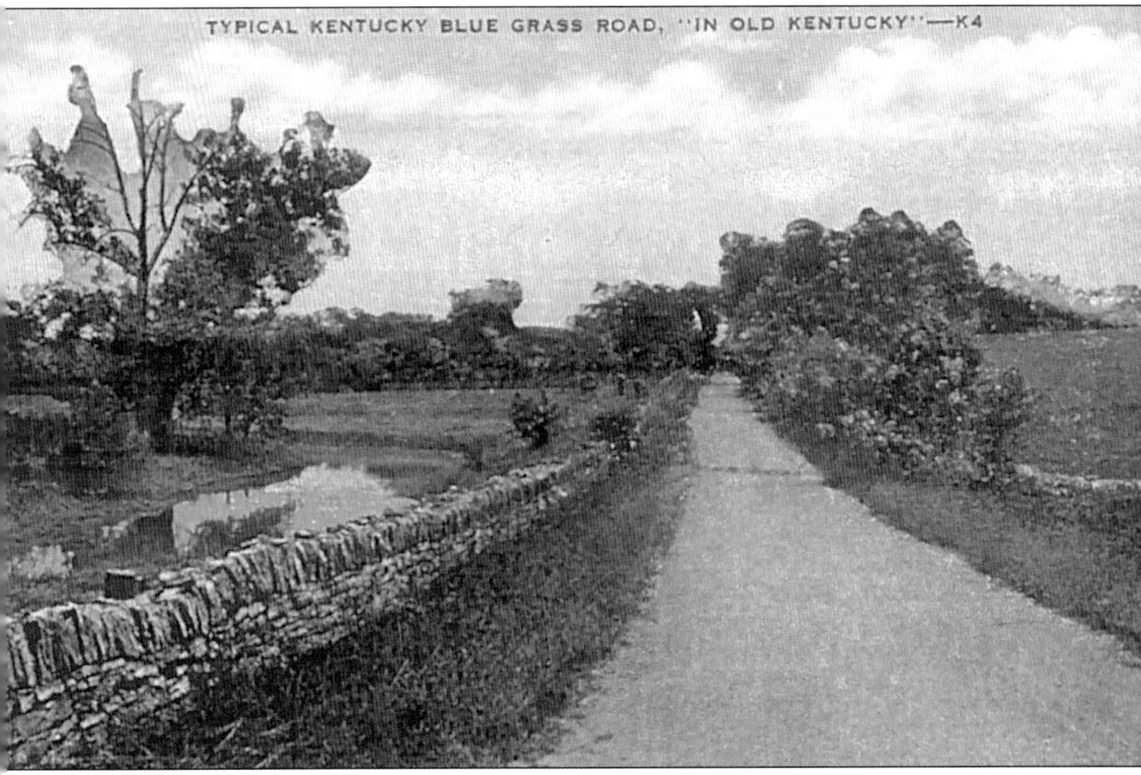

Kentucky is also known by its products, and hemp was one of those that the Inner Bluegrass was well adapted to raising. The first crop of Kentucky hemp was grown in 1775. In 1803, Hunt and Brand Company of Lexington produced the first hemp bagging made in the United States. From 1940 to 1860, Kentucky's production was the largest in the United States. Scores of factories made twine, rope, gunny sacks, and bags for cotton picking and marketing in the Deep South. Hemp was Kentucky's most important cash crop until 1915, when the market was lost to imported, tariff-free jute. It was grown again in Kentucky during World War II as a strategic war material. An early postcard below, published between 1907 and 1915, shows how a field of hemp looked then.

Now, the plant grows wild in the Bluegrass. Although smoking hemp has become illegal, and law enforcement officials continue to attempt to destroy it, individual plants can often be seen along unkempt roadsides or fences.

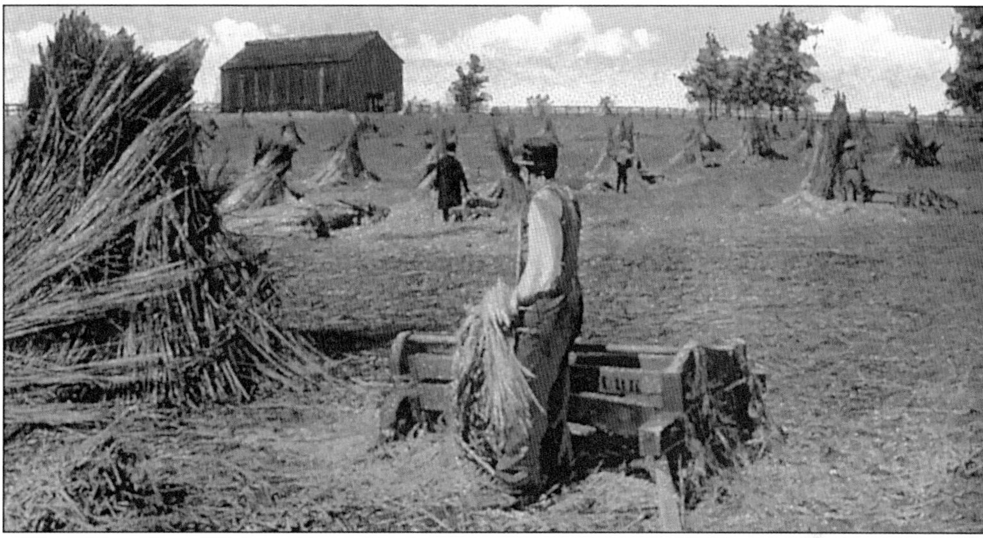

Lexington had a number of hemp factories, from 1880 through 1910, as the center of Kentucky's largest hemp-growing section.

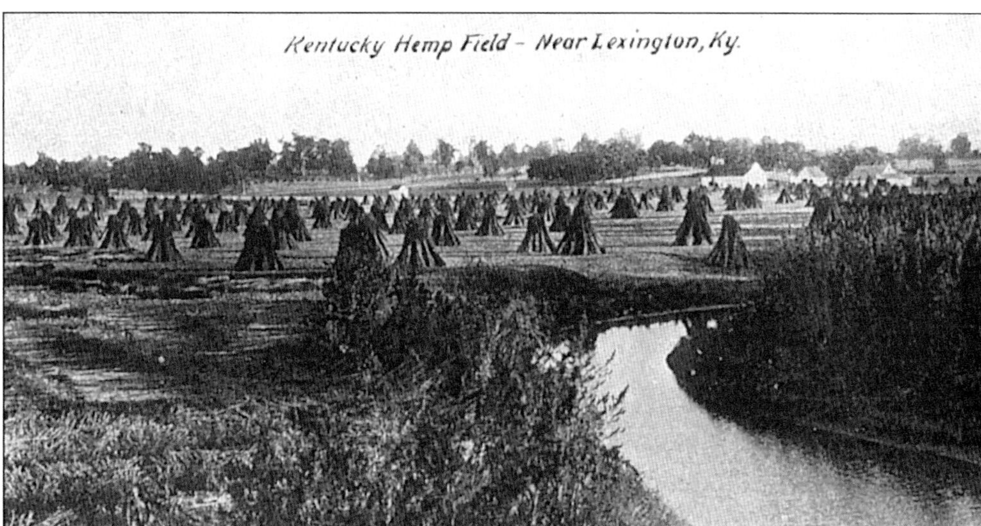

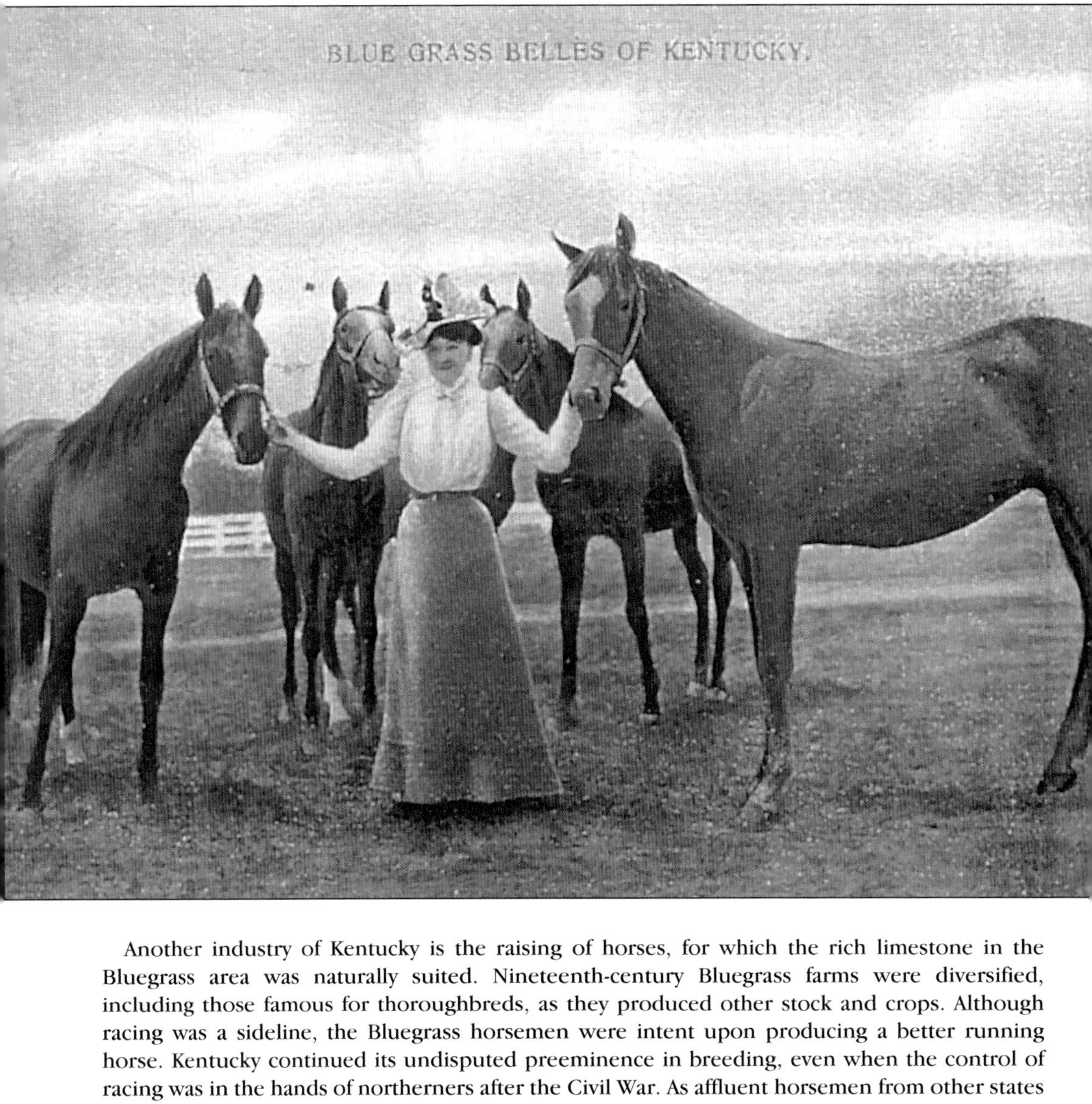

Another industry of Kentucky is the raising of horses, for which the rich limestone in the Bluegrass area was naturally suited. Nineteenth-century Bluegrass farms were diversified, including those famous for thoroughbreds, as they produced other stock and crops. Although racing was a sideline, the Bluegrass horsemen were intent upon producing a better running horse. Kentucky continued its undisputed preeminence in breeding, even when the control of racing was in the hands of northerners after the Civil War. As affluent horsemen from other states and nations bought Bluegrass farms to breed winners and strengthen their foals with the mineral rich soil, the demand for good Bluegrass farms increased. Many of those early Bluegrass farms can be seen in this book.

By the early 1900s, the Bluegrass area's association with horses was well established. The postcard above, dated 1908, shows the significance of horses in Kentucky. The caption, "Blue grass Bells of Kentucky," can have several interpretations, but it does emphasize the importance of horses to the Kentucky people.

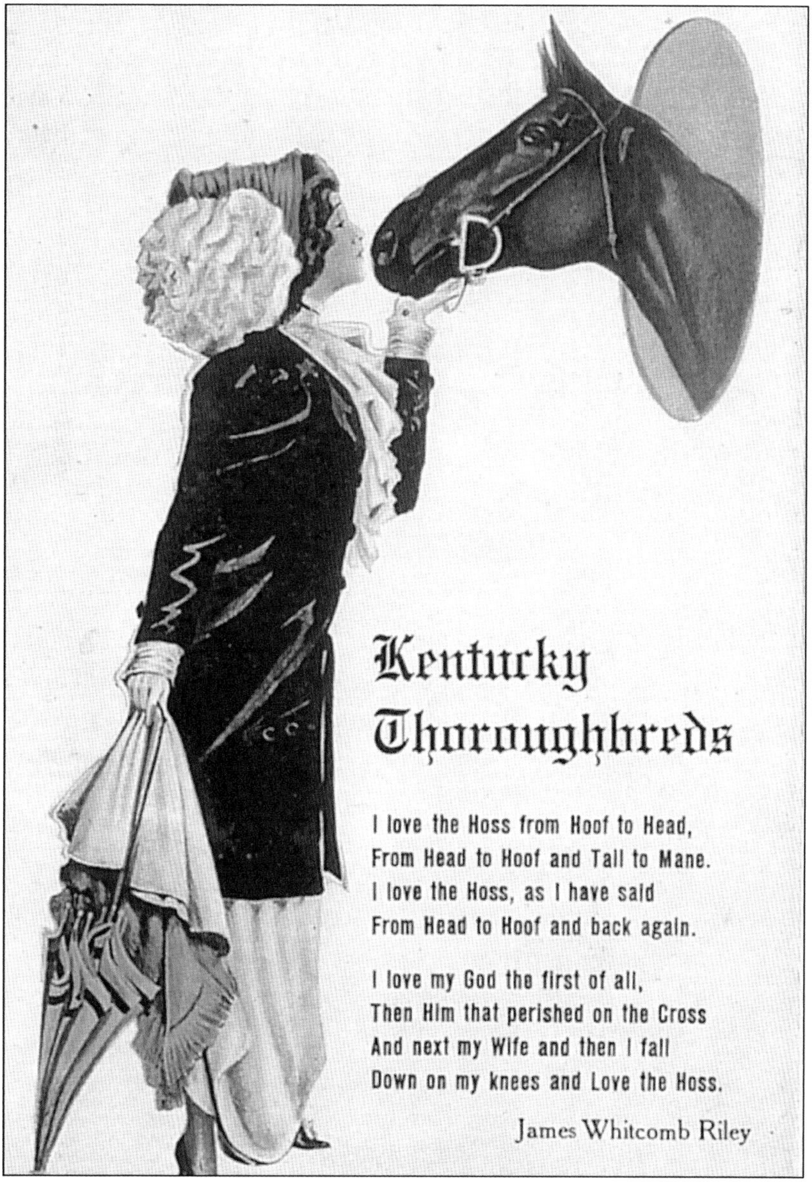

The Bluegrass was and is synonymous with horse racing. The Lexington Jockey Club often met at Ashland, home of Henry Clay. Lexington had two early race tracks that later became known as Red Mile Race Track and the Keeneland Track. Old postcards of those tracks are in the Lexington, Kentucky book previously written by this author. Although the Kentucky Derby Track is located in Louisville, horse racing was a very important part of the Bluegrass culture, as reflected in the early postcard and poem shown above.

Now, the horse is no longer a hobby for gentlemen farmers but is big business in the Bluegrass. Besides breeding, training, and racing, there are also sale companies, horse transportation companies, bloodstock research, computerized marketing services for breeding seasons, and numerous other services. The horse industry generates considerable tax revenue for Kentucky. As a major industry and employer, not to mention the many "ripple industries," the horse's contribution to the economic prosperity of the area is and has been enormous.

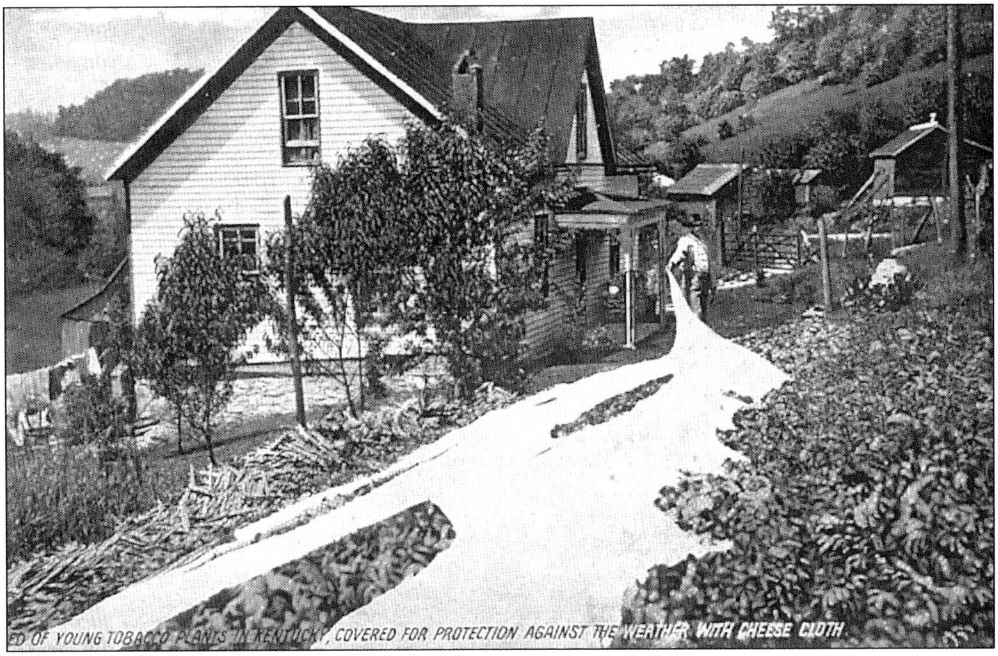

Another product of the Bluegrass region is burley tobacco, which follows a precise yearly calendar. In February and March, the seedbed is sterilized and fertilized until the seeds become tobacco plants. The postcard on the top of the page, dated between 1907 and 1915, shows a seedbed of young tobacco plants protected from the weather with cheese cloth. The seeds are too weak to compete with weeds in a field until they mature.

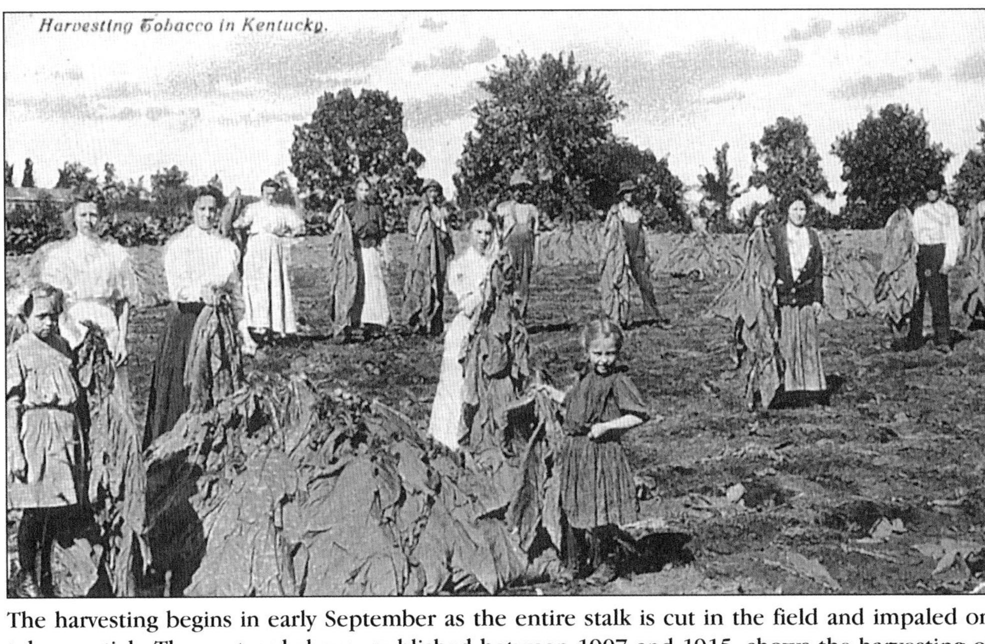

The harvesting begins in early September as the entire stalk is cut in the field and impaled on tobacco stick. The postcard above, published between 1907 and 1915, shows the harvesting of tobacco before machinery was available to help with the hard labor. Notice the children working in the field.

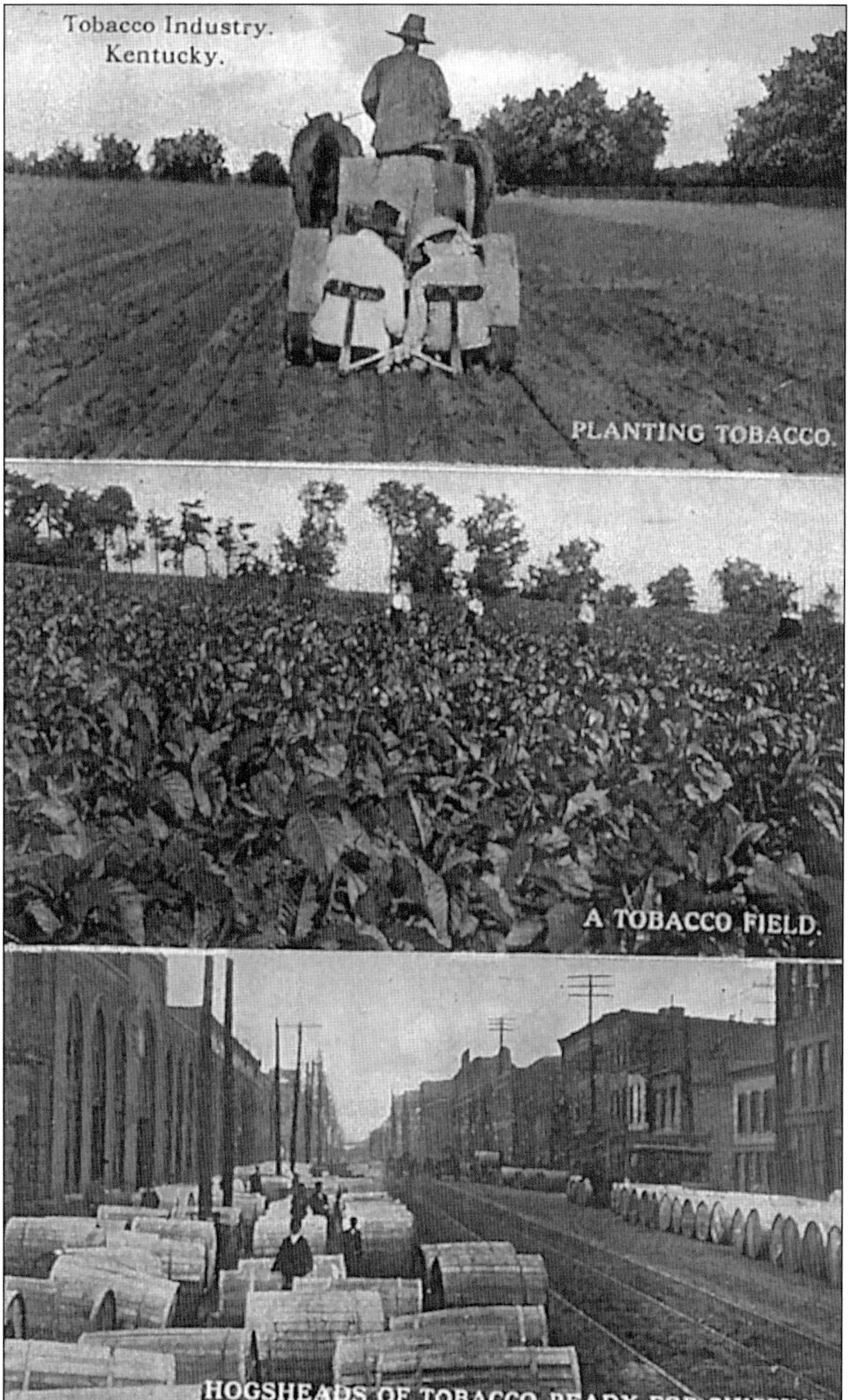

This postcard, dated 1915, was enlarged to show three of the stages in tobacco growing after the seeds are ready for planting. Notice the machinery used at the time.

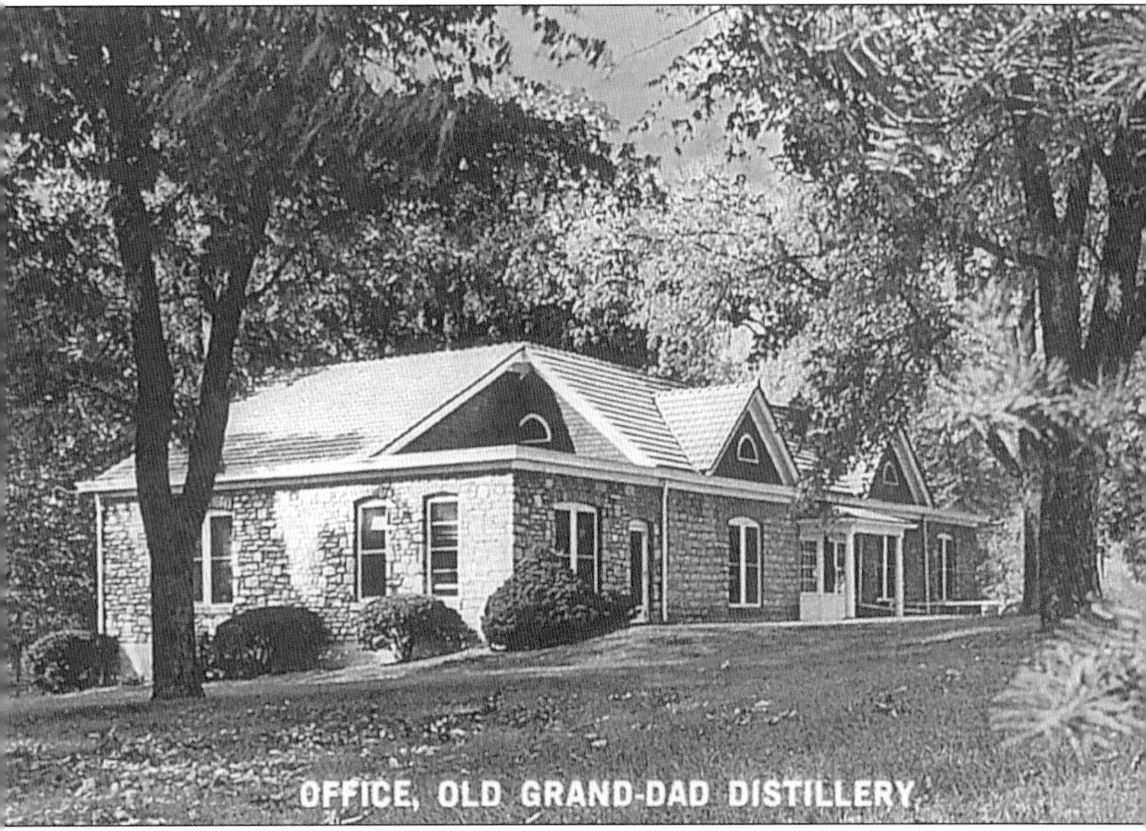

The third major product of Kentucky is liquor distilling, with bourbon whiskey as an original Bluegrass product. By 1811, there were over 2,000 farm distilleries in Kentucky, most of which were in the Bluegrass. This postcard shows the office of the Old Grand-dad Distillery, located on Elkhorn Creek near Frankfort, first established in 1882. Two other distilleries on the outskirts of Frankfort can be seen in the Franklin County chapter. Visitors from every land come to see these sources of whiskey.

These famous "things," previously discussed, have formalized a distinct characteristic tradition to the Bluegrass area as shown on old postcards. While I was limited in availability of old postcards, I did achieve some visual variety in most of the 17 counties. It may be interesting to note that the word Bluegrass was two words in the early days of postcard publishing. Postcards on page 9 had Blue Grass roads and page 12 had Blue Grass Bells, both reflecting the early 1900s. Collins, in his earlier History of Kentucky, used two words for the Bluegrass, suggesting that the concept and identification of the Bluegrass was more of an evolution in the early 1900s rather than a planned process.

That region is now under attack as urbanization has taken over. Kentucky horse farms have decreased as subdivisions have increased. Where horses and cattle formerly grazed, there are new homes or shopping centers. While everyone seems to be concerned about the changes occurring to the Bluegrass land, solutions have been few. Although these early farms, mansions, and buildings will be lost to future generations, they still exist in pictures and old postcards.

One

ANDERSON, BOURBON, AND BOYLE COUNTIES

This chapter will feature 31 old postcards of the first three counties in the Bluegrass area: Anderson, Bourbon, and Boyle. Anderson was organized in 1827, while Boyle was organized in 1842, both being taken from surrounding counties. Bourbon County was one of nine counties organized in 1789 by the Virginia legislature, before Kentucky was a state. The largest town and county seat of Anderson County is Lawrenceburg, which was established in 1820, while Bourbon County's largest town is Paris, having been established in 1789 by the Virginia legislature. Boyle County's largest town is Danville, also having been established in 1785 by the Virginia legislature.

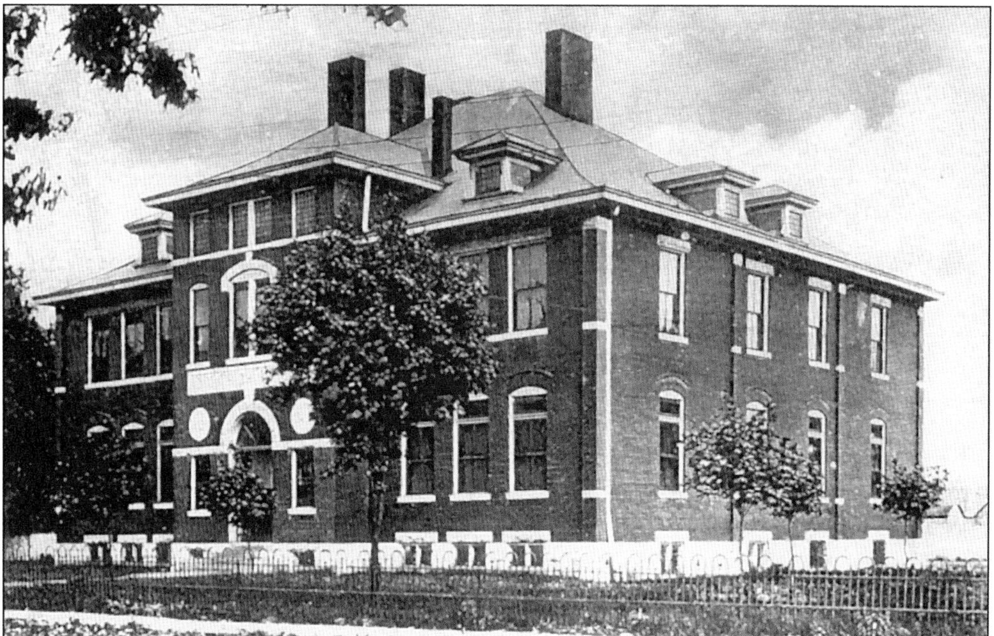

This is the earliest postcard that was found of Lawrenceburg, specifically the high school of Lawrenceburg, with a postmark of February 23, 1909. Postcards of Lawrenceburg during this time period are now very scarce.

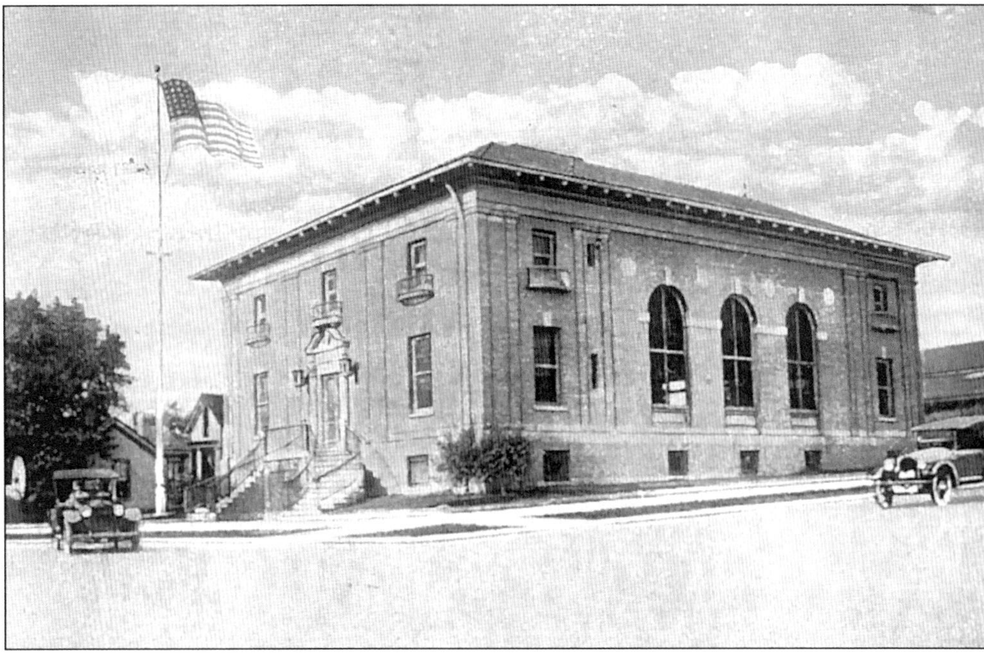

This is a view of the post office at Lawrenceburg, Kentucky, postmarked 1941. Views during this time period are more common. Several distilleries were part of the history of this county, one of which was the Wild Turkey Distillery on US 62.

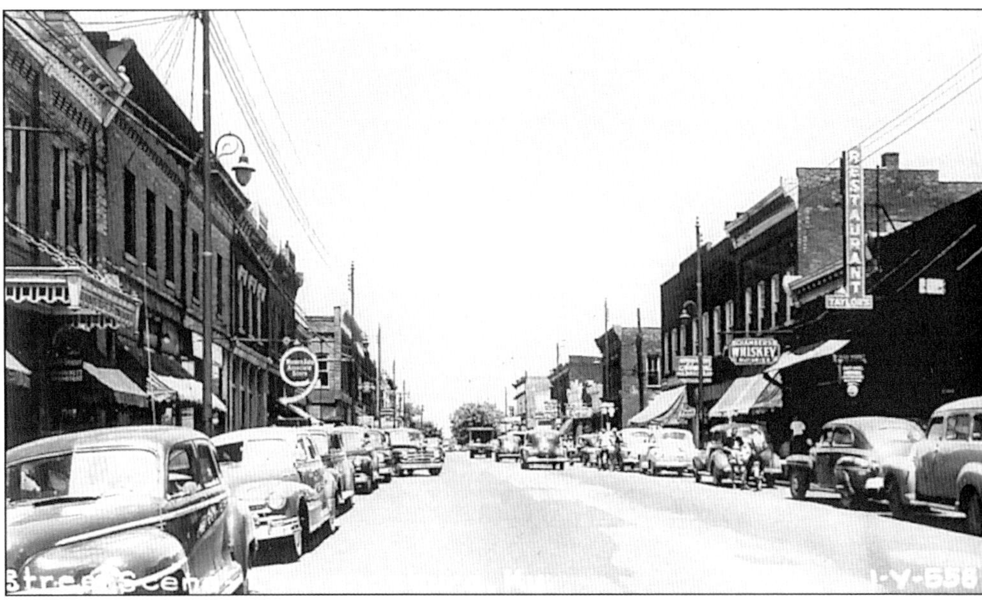

This is a street scene of Lawrenceburg, *c.* 1940s. Stores identified on the right were Taylor's Restaurant, Chambers Whiskey Sundries, and a Paint sign. On the left is the sign of the Western Auto Associate Store. About 3 miles from Lawrenceburg was a distillery called Tyrone, which a town built around in 1869. Later in 1888, the Southern Railroad built the Tyrone Bridge over the Kentucky River near the town of Tyrone. Prohibition closed the distillery, and the town never rebounded.

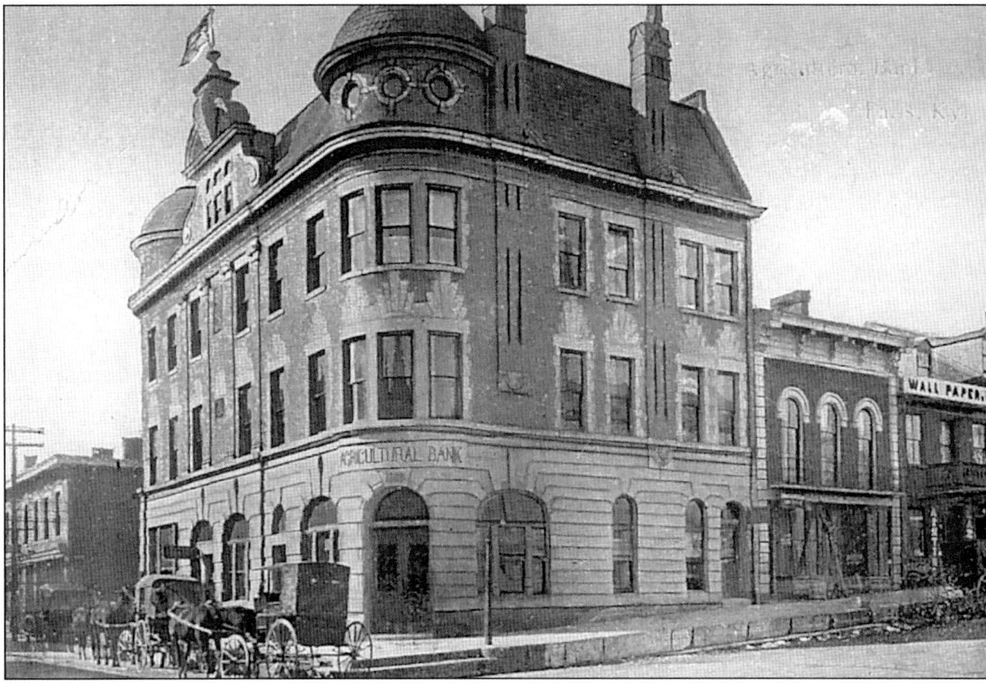

The next five postcards are related to downtown views of Paris, Kentucky. This picture of the Agricultural Bank was published in 1917. Notice the sign advertising wall paper on the third building and the horses with carriages in front.

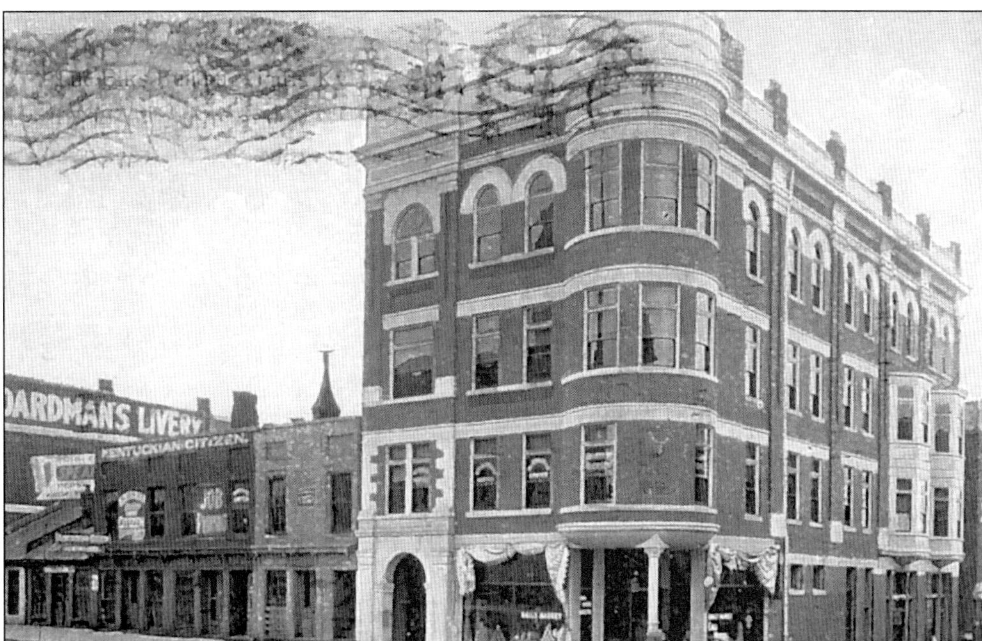

This view of the Elks Building was published in 1915. The third building can be identified by a sign, "The Kentuckian Citizen," and a job printing advertisement in the window. The other windows had names of lawyers identified on them. The corner store was called a daily market.

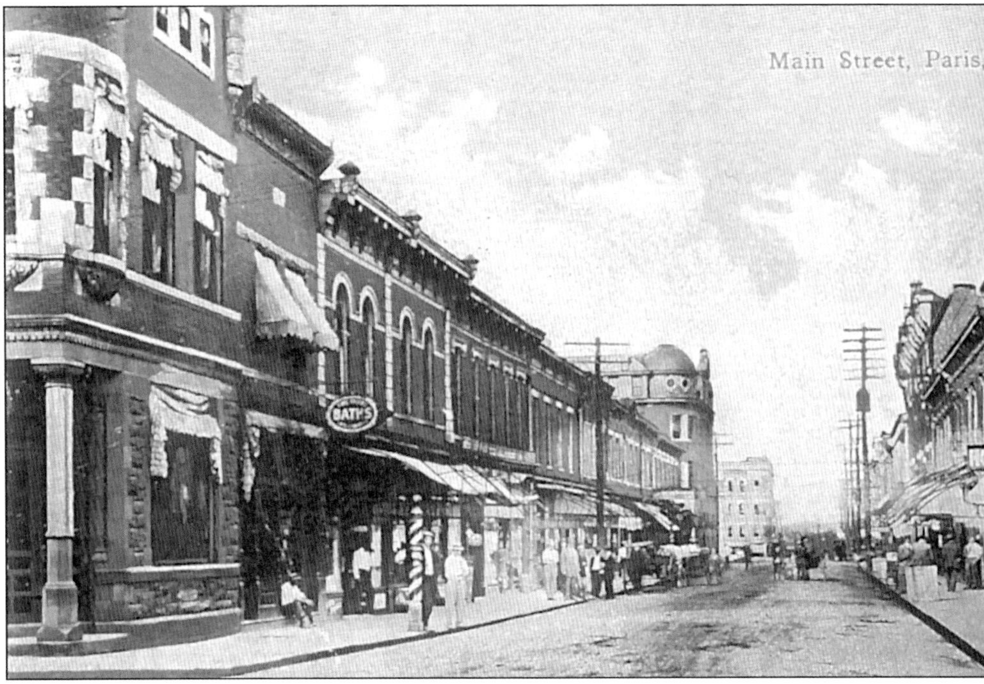

This view, published between 1907 and 1915, shows a view of a building on the left corner and Agricultural Bank on the far right of the same street. The only identifiable sign was "Baths," but notice the barber shop pole with two men next to it.

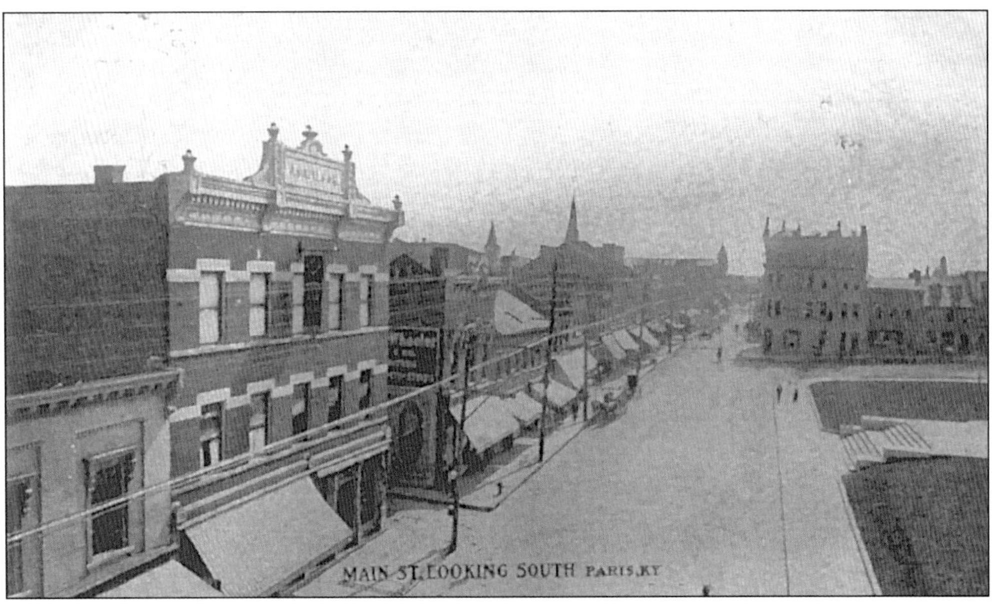

This view, postmarked in 1907, shows main street looking south in Paris, Kentucky. The name, Wheeler, can be identified on the side of the third building. Notice the right sidewalk that is across from the courthouse and part of the next picture. Paris is near the center of the county on Stoner Creek fork located on the Licking River.

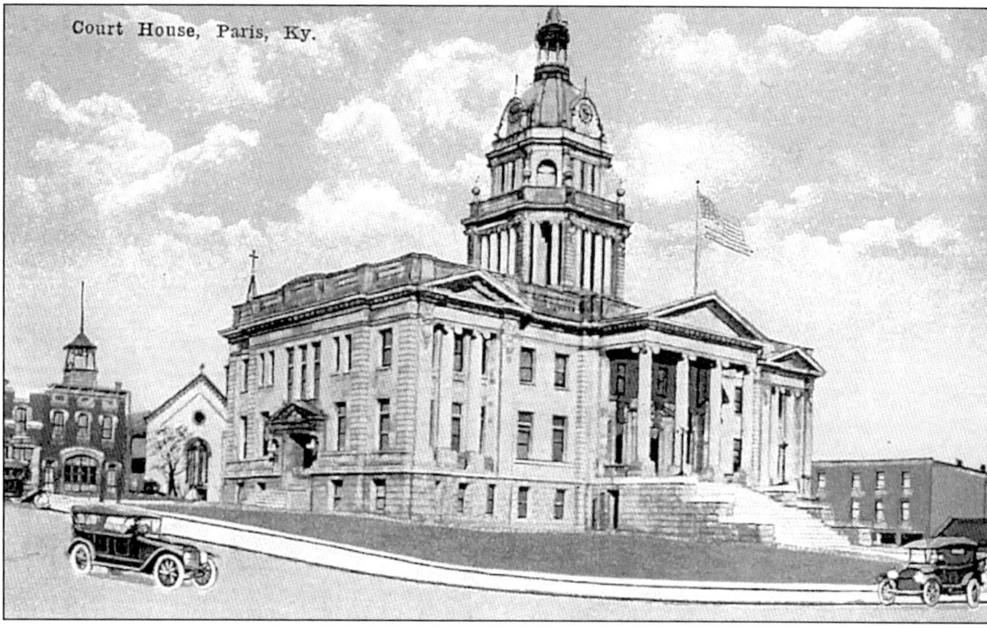

This is a view of the courthouse in Paris. This is the fourth Bourbon County Courthouse built from 1902 to 1905. The second and third courthouses were destroyed by fire in 1872 and in 1901, respectively.

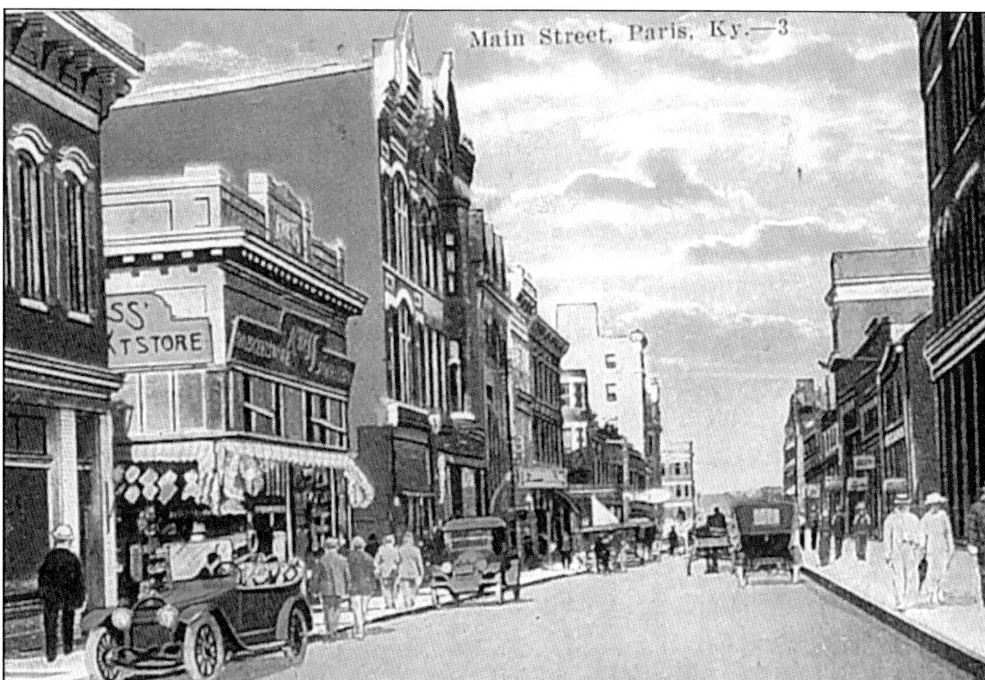

This is a 1920s view of main street in Paris. On the left is "Kress' 5 10 25 cent Store"; other signs are not distinguishable. A handwritten message on the back stated, "Had supper here—a funny little place." Paris was first named Hopewell in 1789, and it was changed to Paris the next year.

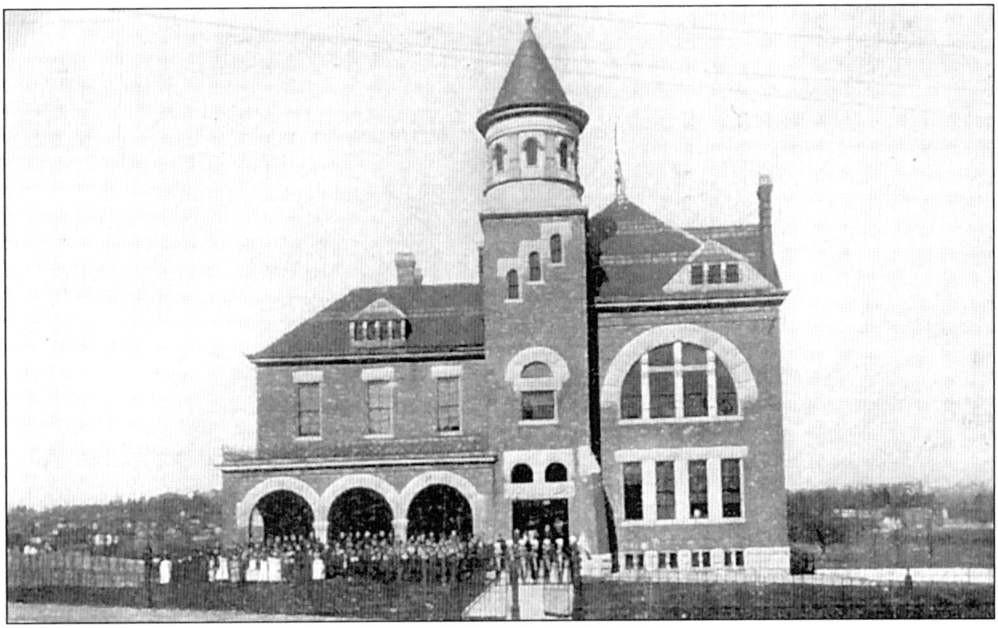

This view of the city school in Paris was published between 1901 and 1907. Notice the people posed with a dirt road and hitching post in front of the school.

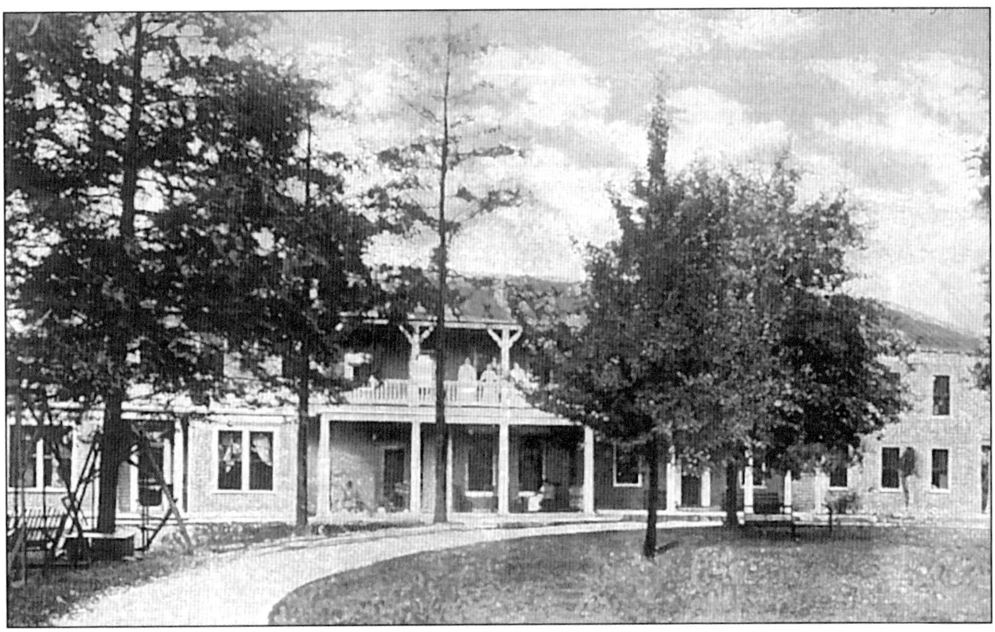

This view shows the Bourbon College of Paris with a postmark of September 13, 1912. Notice the swing sets and people posed on the porch. This college is not currently part of Paris, and information about it was not found.

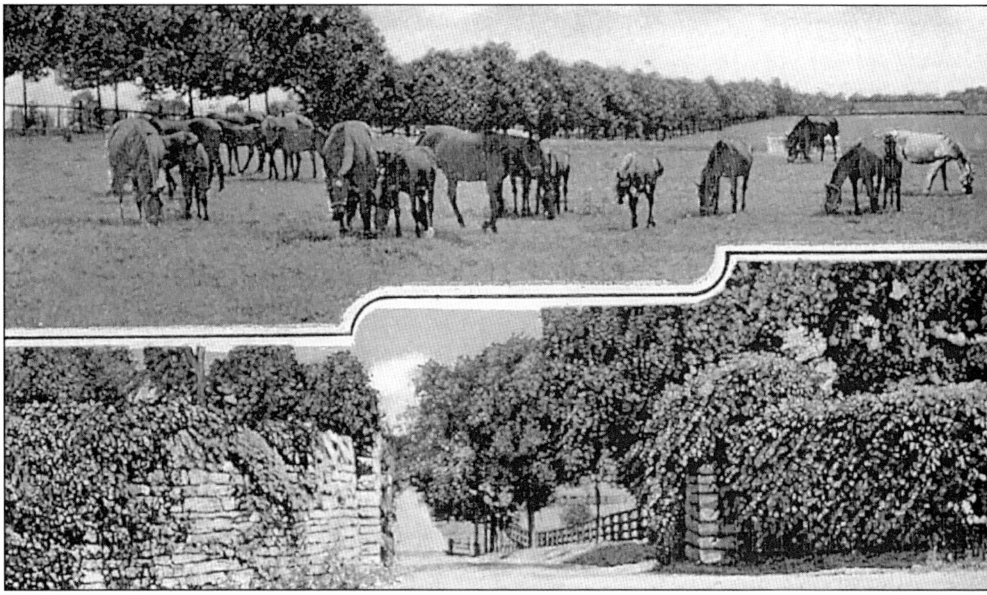

This is a view of the Claiborne Farm in Bourbon County, on Winchester Road near Lexington. It was, at one time, considered among the outstanding thoroughbred horse farms in the area. This picture of the stone entrance was taken between 1930 and 1945 and refers to the area of "old Kentucky."

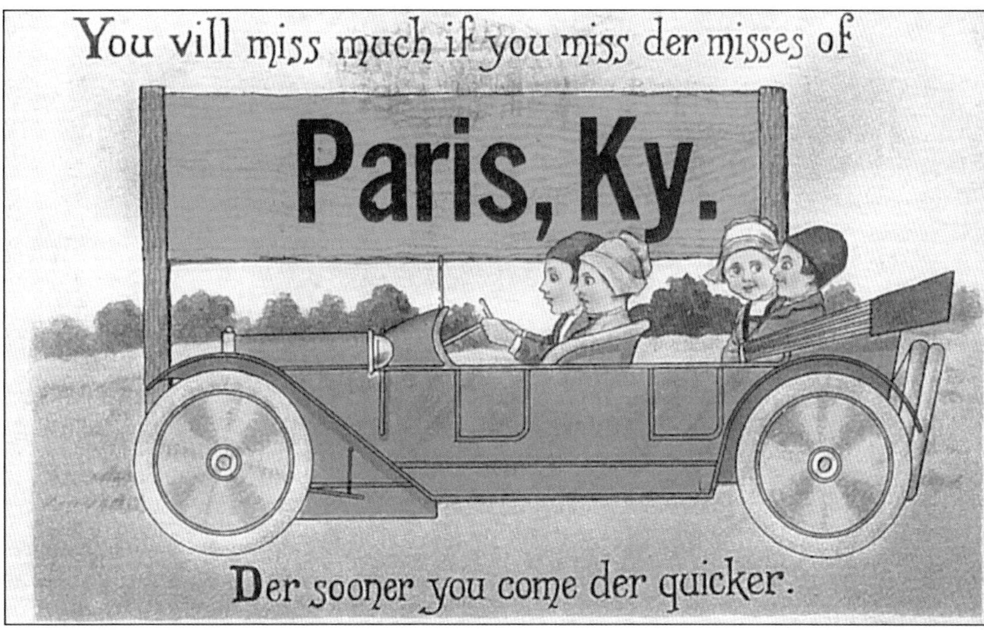

This postcard, mailed in 1914, is a cute postcard with Paris, Kentucky, on the front. It shows an early car with two couples going to Paris, typical of generic postcards advertising specific towns during this time period.

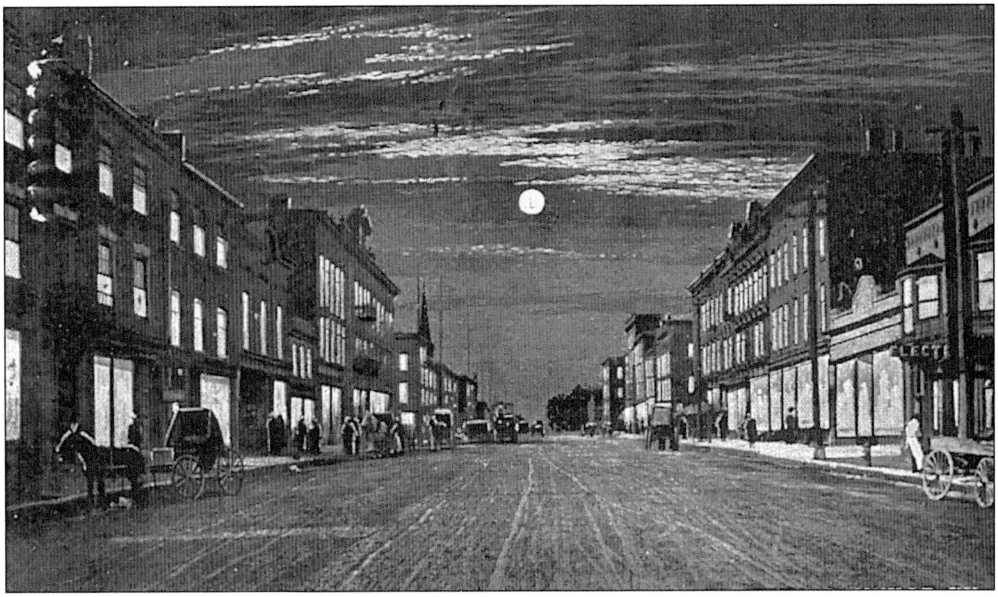

The next two postcards will show downtown Danville, Kentucky, in Boyle County. This view of main street at night was postmarked July 30, 1913. Notice the lighted stores, dirt street, and carriages.

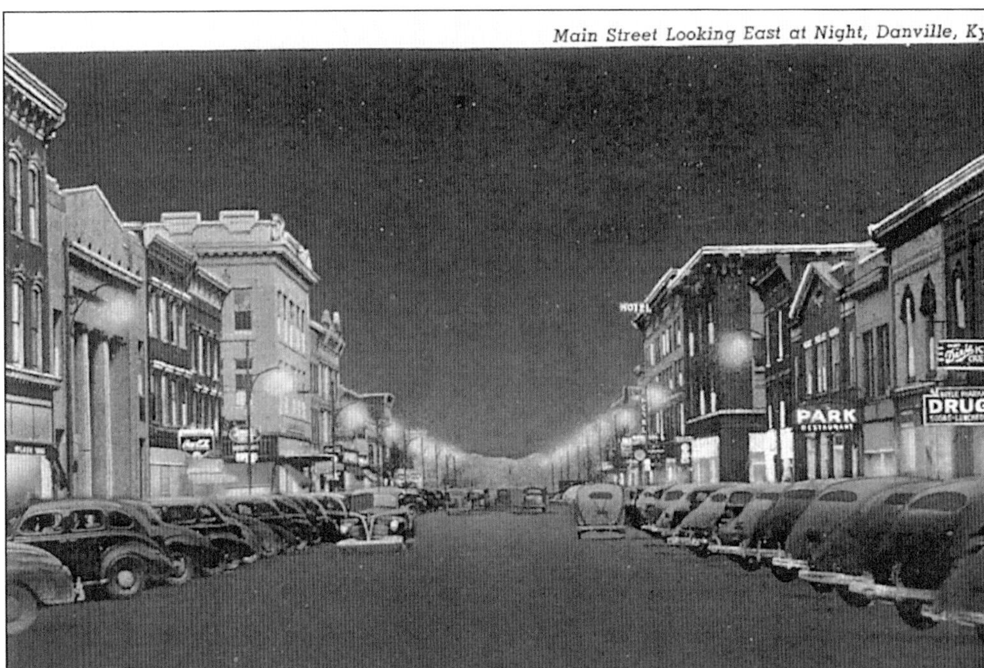

This east view of downtown Danville shows main street at a later time period between 1930 and 1945. One sign on the right shows the Boyle Pharmacy with Drugs, Sodas, and Luncheonette, and another sign above it reads Dixie Ice Cream. Other signs included the Park Restaurant and a hotel.

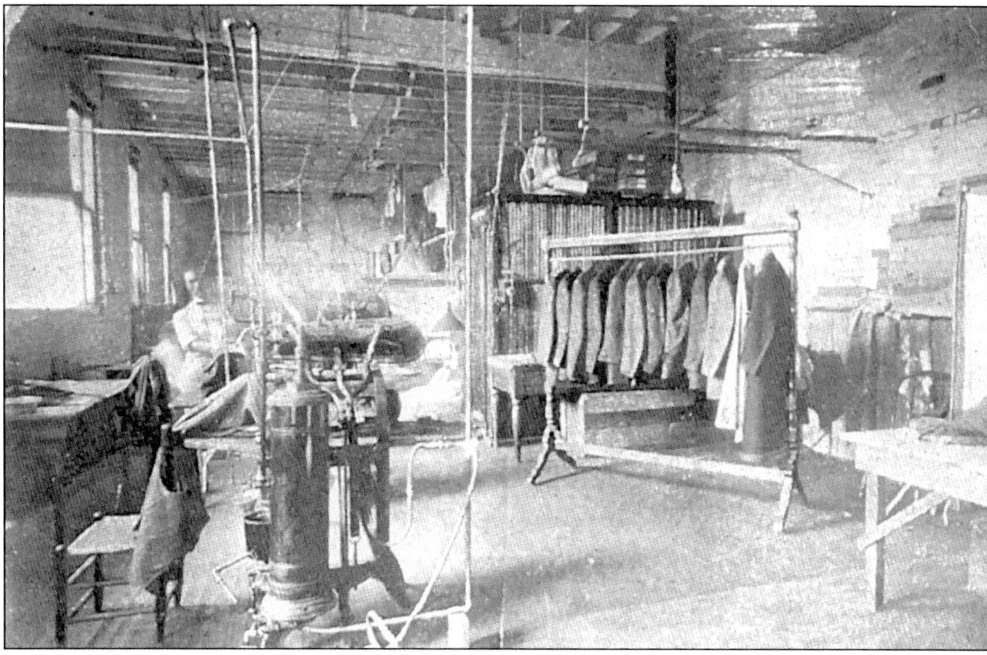

The next three postcards were used for advertising in Danville. This card, published between 1907 and 1915, shows the inside of the Danville Laundry and Dry Cleaning Company. On the back was written, "Dear Friend, Are you one of our many satisfied customers? If not, why not? A trial of our sanitary cleaning and pressing of ladies and gentlemen's suits will make you one of our permanent customers."

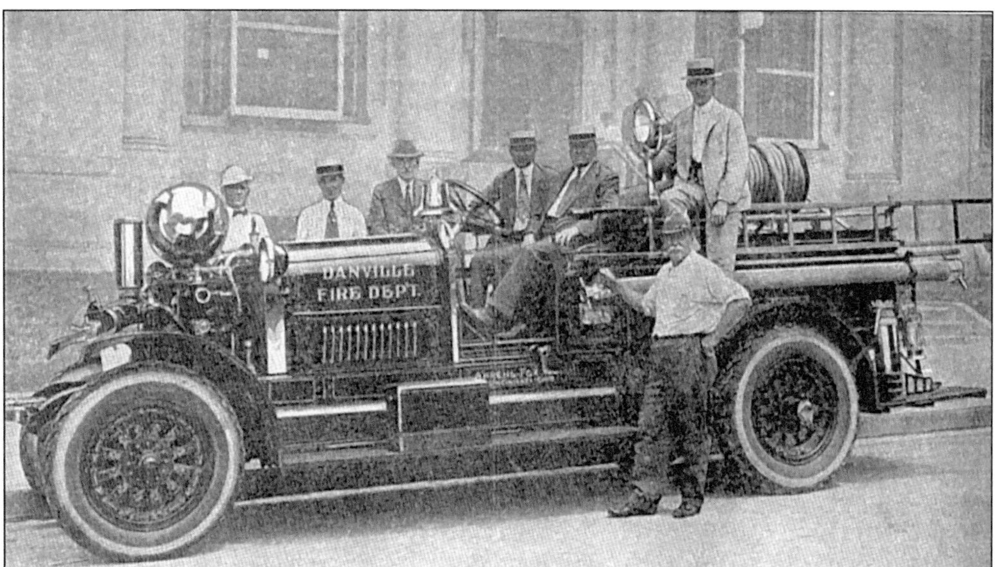

This is a picture of the Danville Fire Department, with the advertising, "Ahrens-Fox, model K-4, Delivered to Danville, Kentucky August 6, 1920, made in Cincinnati."

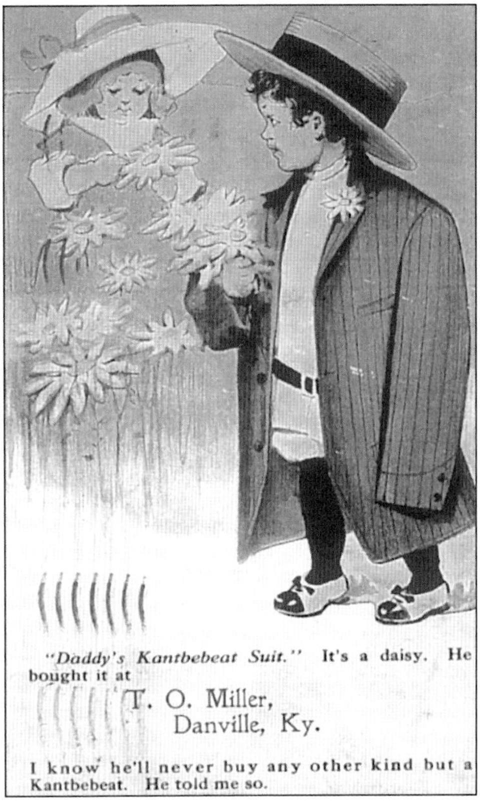

This cute postcard is advertising T.O. Miller Clothing in Danville. The children were called the Kantbebeat Kids, and the Kantbebeat Company had tailor-made clothing manufactured by Goldman, Beckman & Company in Cincinnati, Ohio. This was #6 of a series that were sent out by the company.

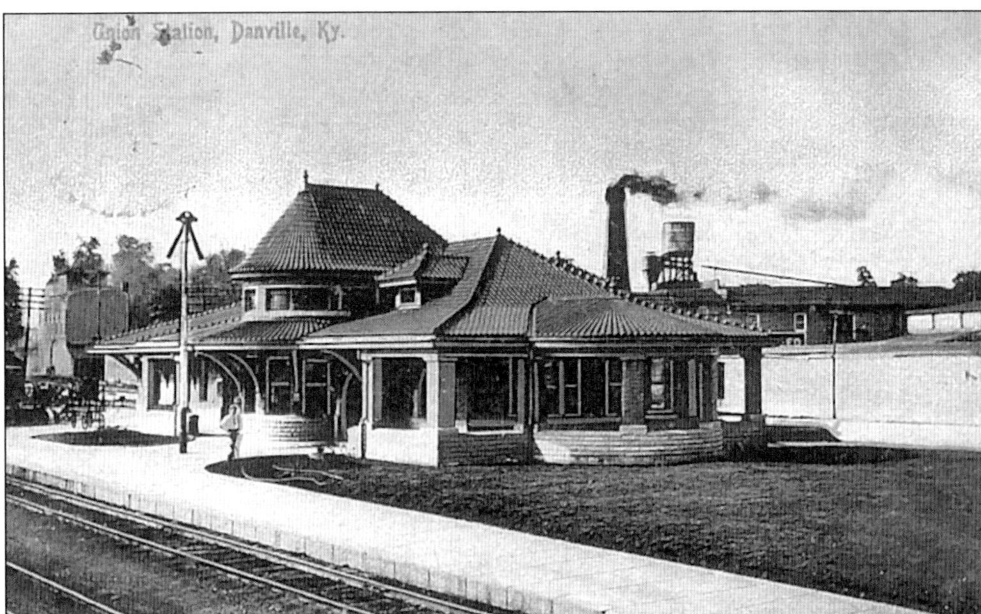

This is a 1909 postmarked view of the Union Station in Danville. Later in the century, the Southern Railroad went through Danville. Danville is known for many beginnings, such as the first U.S. Post Office and the first college in the west.

This is a view of the current county courthouse in Danville. It was built from 1860 to 1862, used as a hospital by Union troops during the Civil War, and renovated in 1873. Alterations have been made during this century.
This was the second courthouse in Boyle County, the first having burned in 1860.

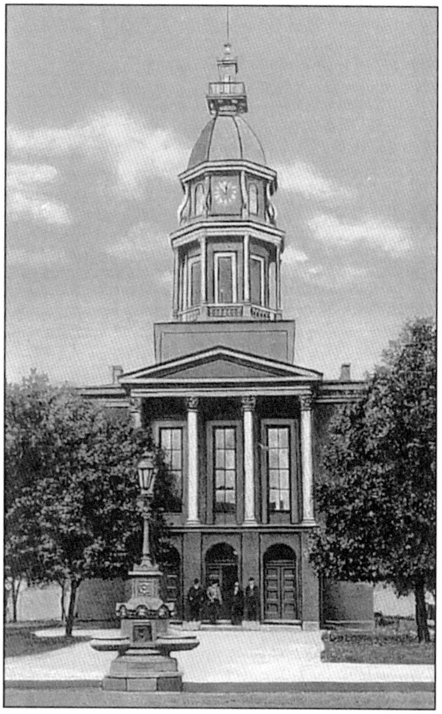

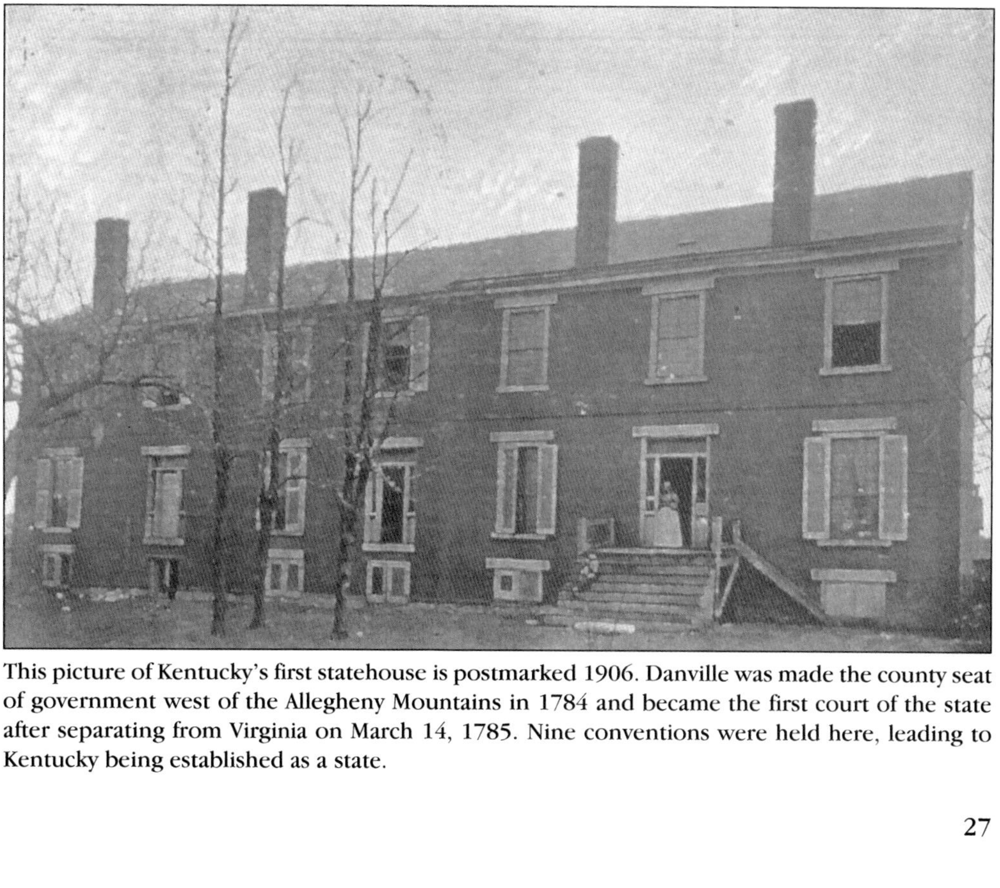

This picture of Kentucky's first statehouse is postmarked 1906. Danville was made the county seat of government west of the Allegheny Mountains in 1784 and became the first court of the state after separating from Virginia on March 14, 1785. Nine conventions were held here, leading to Kentucky being established as a state.

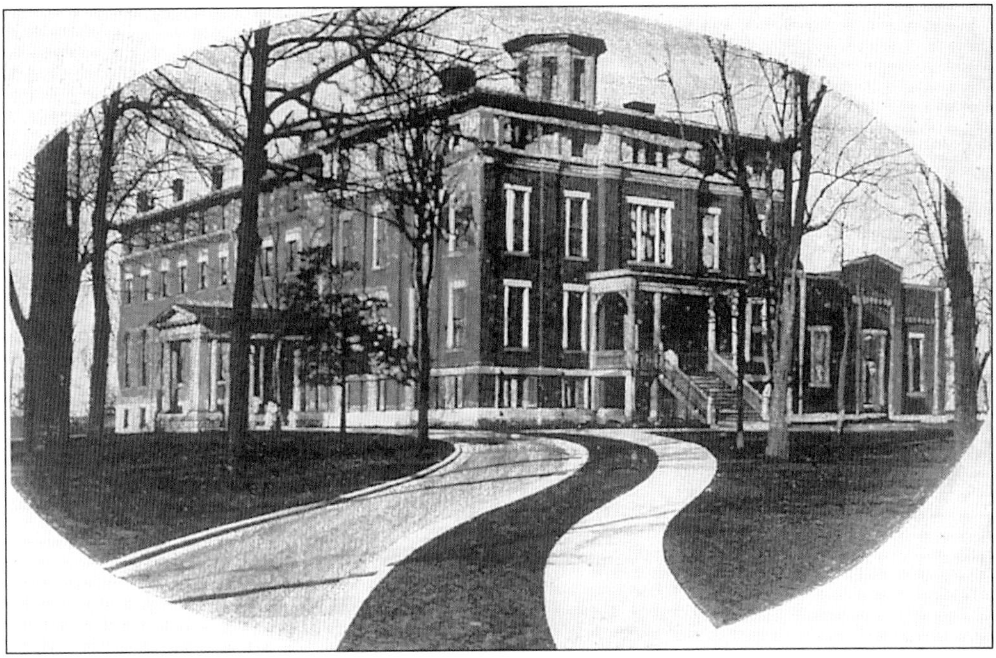

The next two postcards will show views of Centre College in Danville, with this one being postmarked 1909. Centre College was founded in 1819 and became one of the best-known schools in the South.

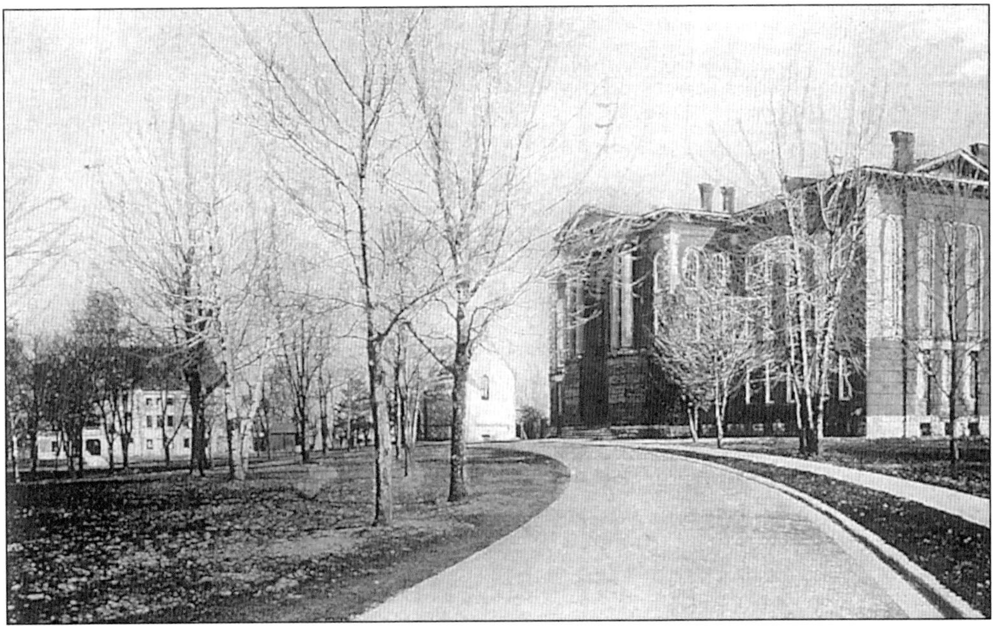

This view of Centre College is postmarked 1908. The main building is an excellent example of the Greek-Revival style of architecture.

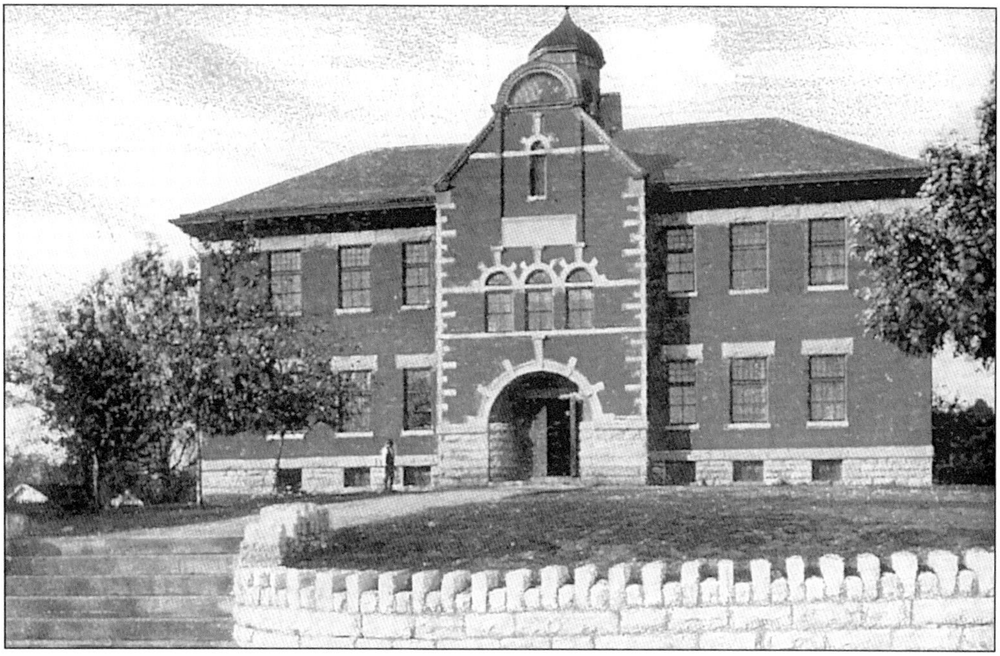

This postcard, published between 1907 and 1915, shows the public school of Danville. Notice the Kentucky limestone that was used in the building and in the fence.

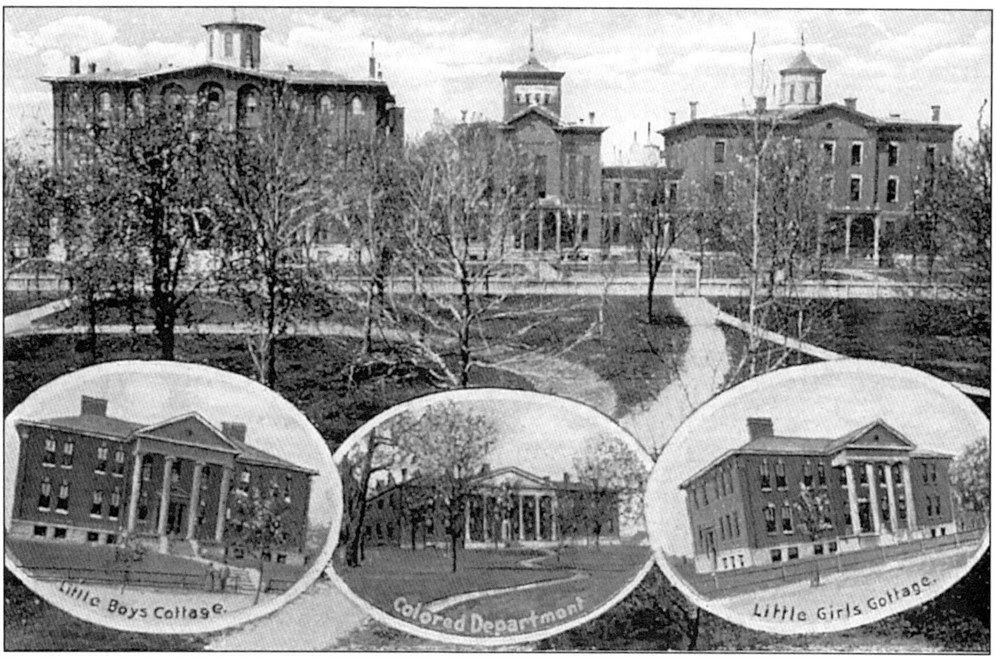

This postcard, published during the same time period, shows the Kentucky School for the Deaf. It was opened in 1823 and was the first state School for the Deaf in the United States. The school has continued to give the deaf and sightless an education, outlook, and a place of usefulness in the world for years.

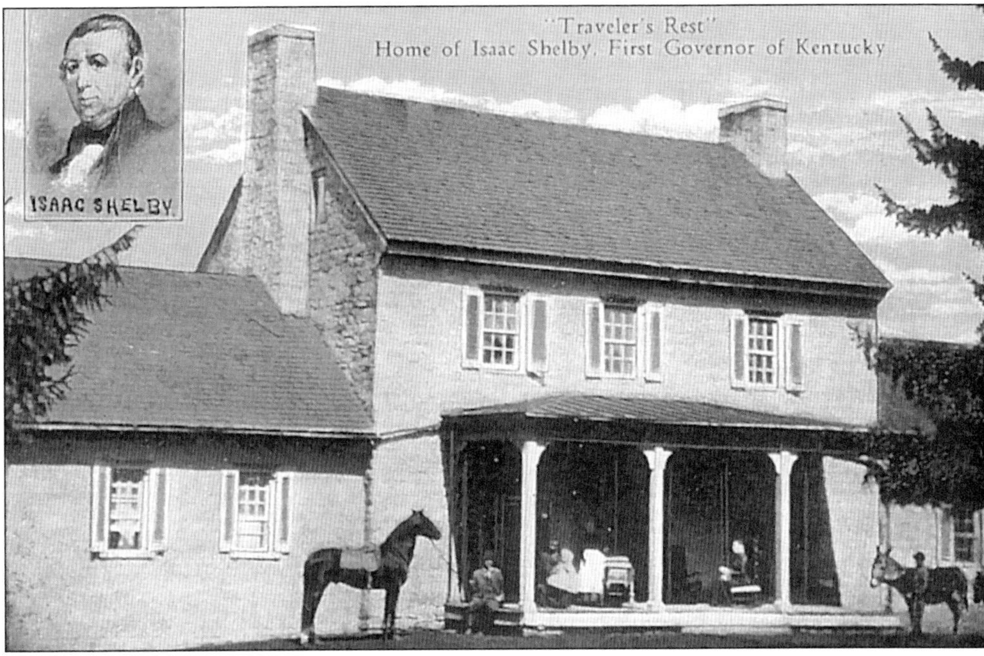

This postcard shows the home of Isaac Shelby, the first governor of Kentucky, near Danville. He became a leader in Kentucky politics before statehood during war time with the British and participated in the conventions leading to statehood. When Kentucky became a state in 1792, he was elected for four years and returned for another term from 1812 to 1816. This home was the finest around when built and burned in 1905.

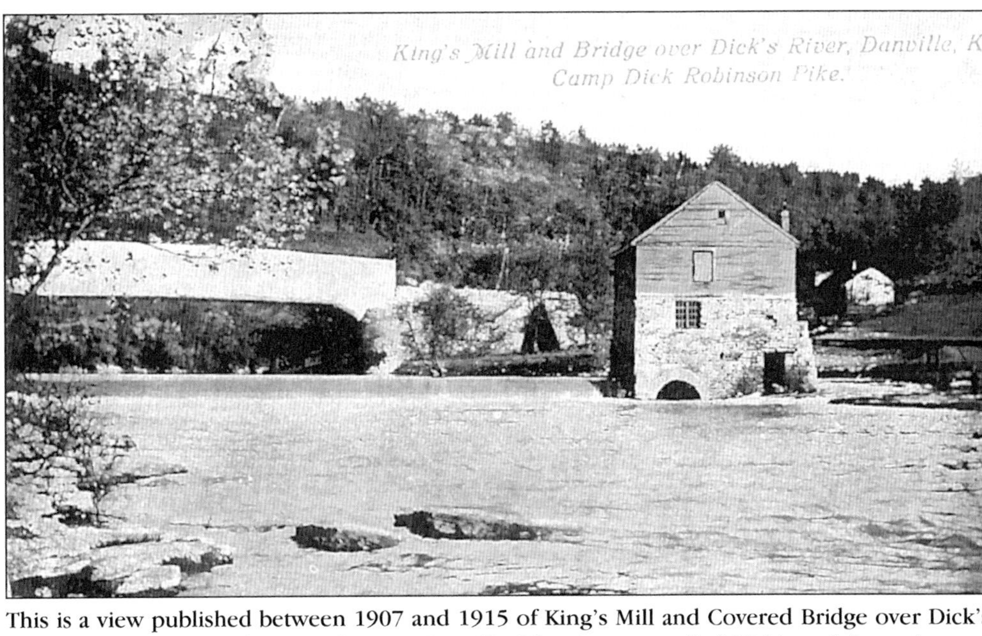

This is a view published between 1907 and 1915 of King's Mill and Covered Bridge over Dick's River on Camp Dick Robinson Pike near Danville. The river was called Dick's and, later changed to Dix River. Mills were very common in the early days of Kentucky, and this is a good example of a covered bridge and mill made from limestone available at that time.

Two

Clark and Estill Counties

This chapter will feature old postcards in two counties of the Bluegrass, Clark and Estill. Clark County was established in 1792 as the 14th county in the state and is surrounded by various bodies of water: the Kentucky River as a boundary line with Madison County, the Red River as a boundary line with Estill County, Boone's Creek as the boundary line with Fayette County, and Lulbegrud Creek as a boundary line with Powell County, all counties of the Bluegrass. Winchester is the county seat of Clark County and was incorporated in 1793.

Estill County was formed in 1808 as the 50th county in the state. The Kentucky River enters Estill County at its southeast corner. It flows through centrally and out at the northwest corner, creating a beautiful area of nature that is now the Daniel Boone National Forest.

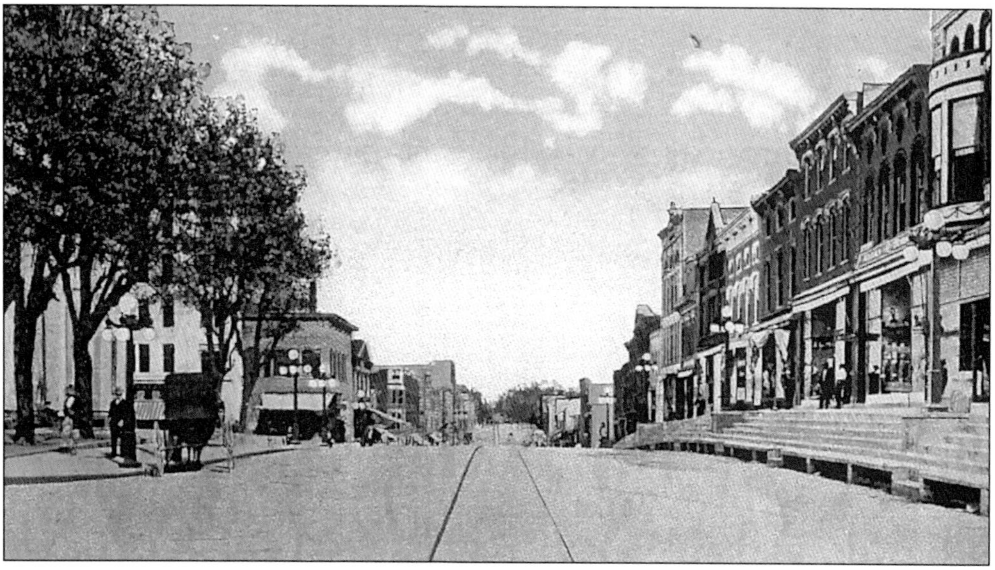

The first 15 old postcards will feature buildings of Winchester in Clark County. This northern view of main street in downtown Winchester was published between 1907 and 1915.

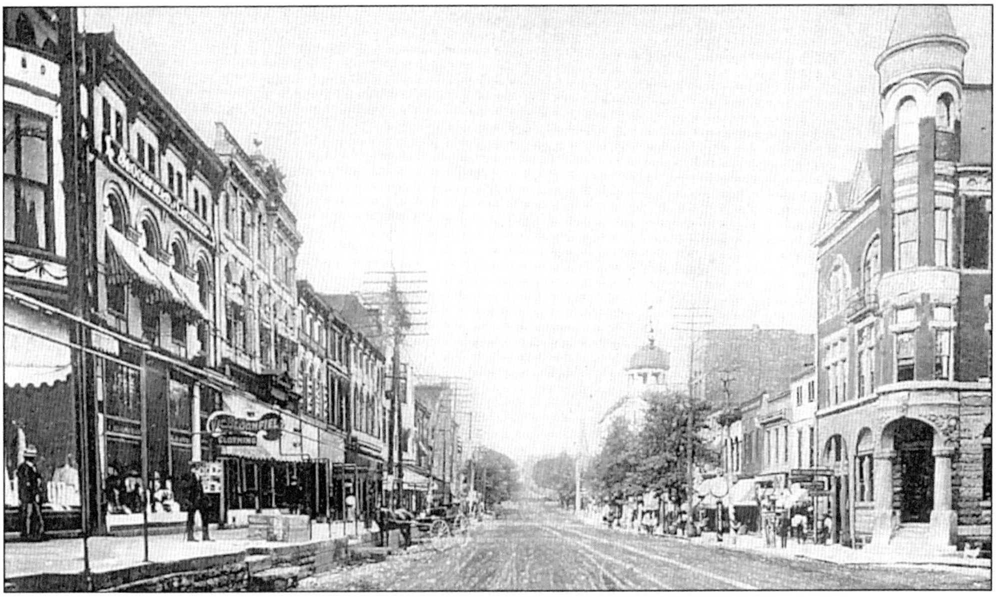

This view of South main street in Winchester was postmarked July 15, 1908. On the left is one identifiable sign that reads, Vic. Bloomfield, Clothing.

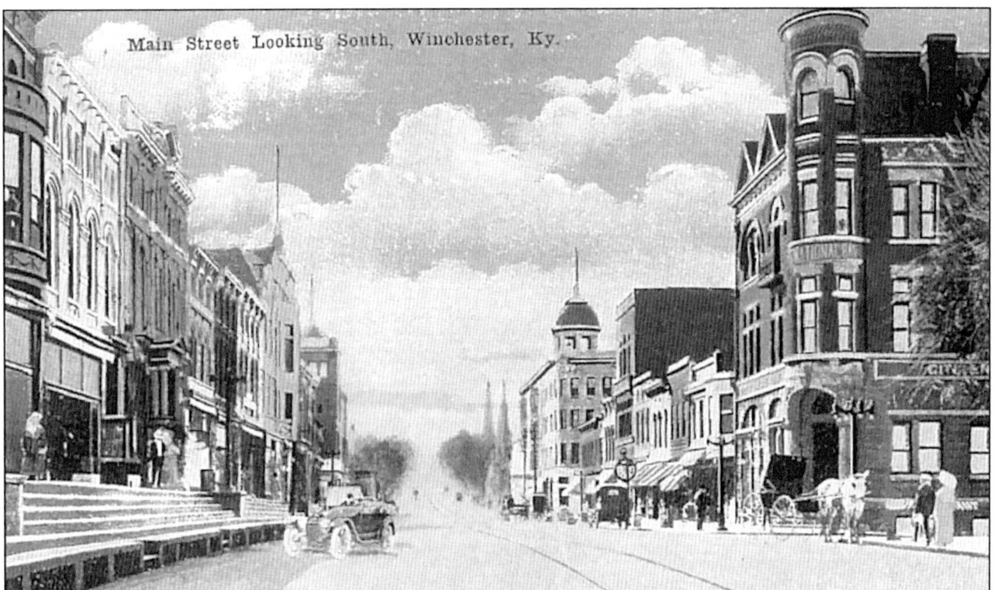

This view of south main street is similar to the previous view but was published later, between 1916 and 1930. Citizens Bank is now identified as the right corner building and the clothing sign is not visible.

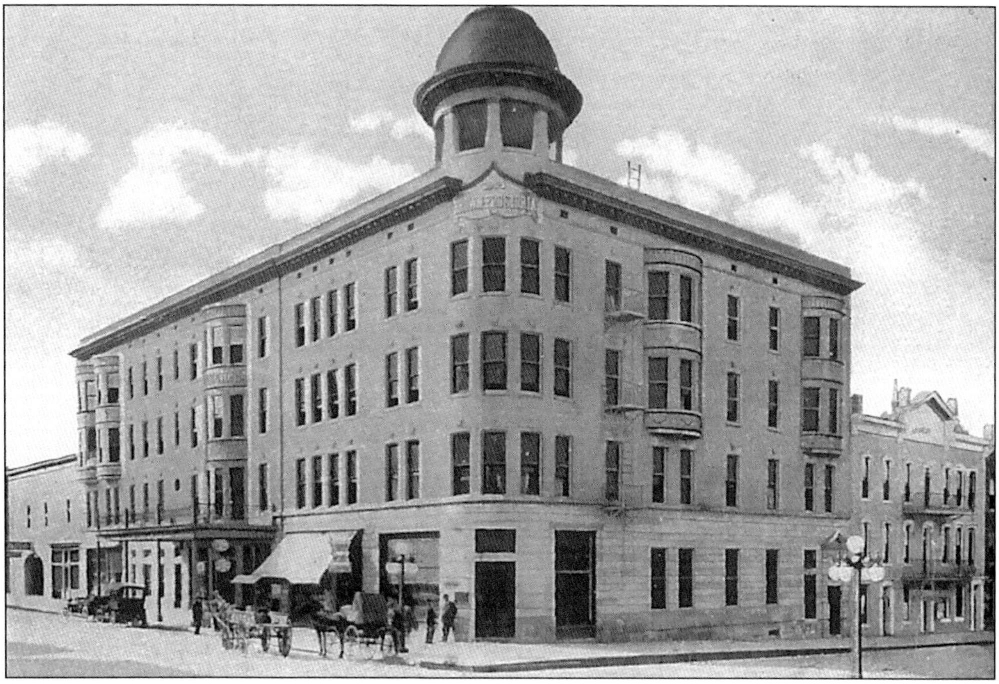

This postcard shows the Brown-Proctor Hotel between 1907 and 1915 in Winchester.

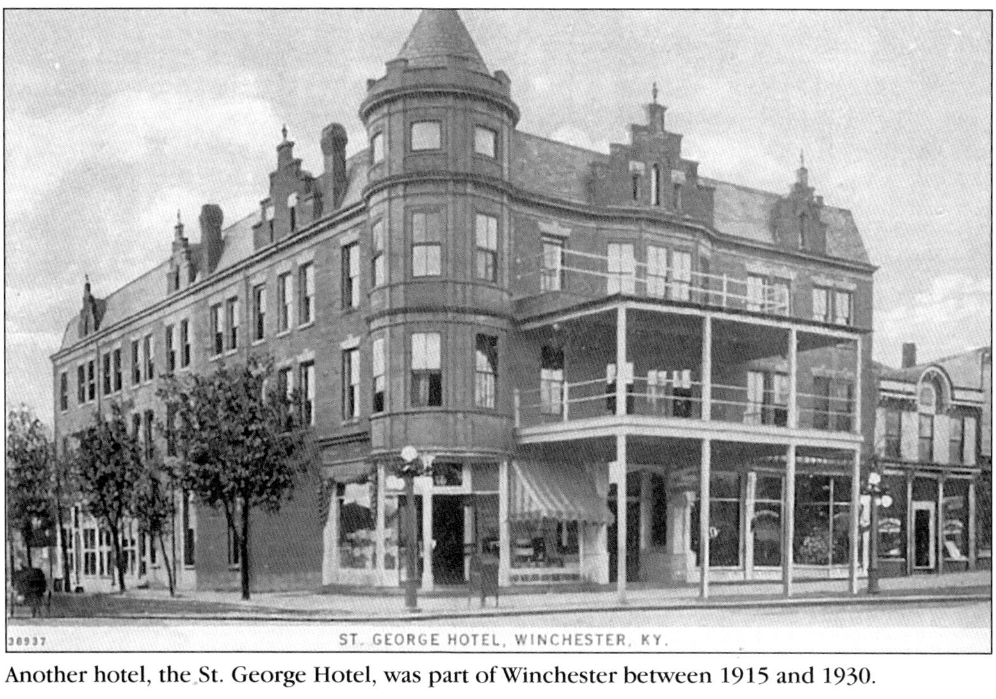

Another hotel, the St. George Hotel, was part of Winchester between 1915 and 1930.

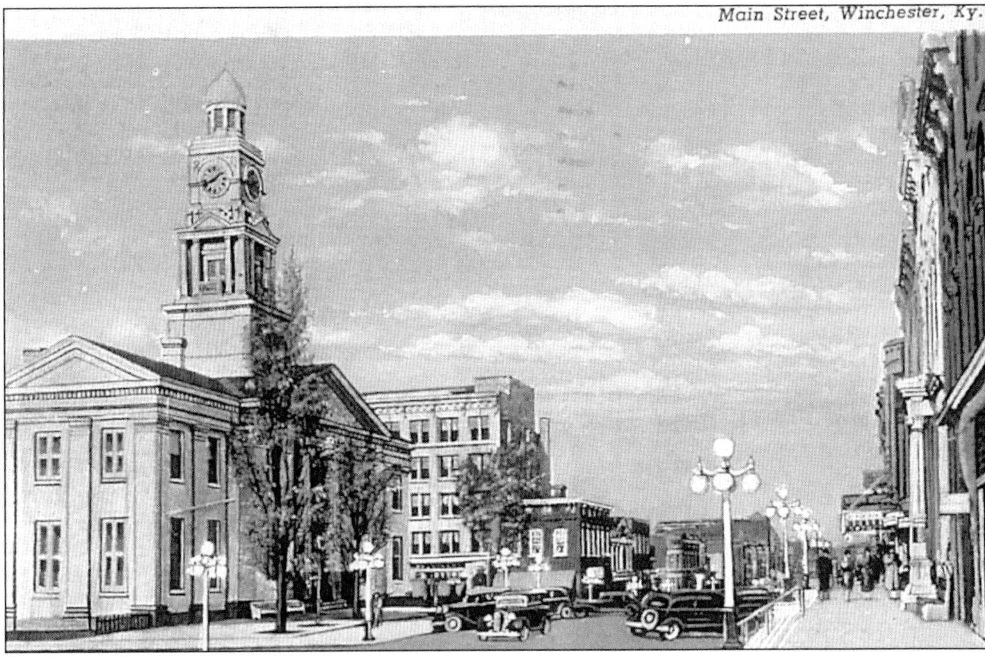

This view shows the county courthouse in Winchester on main street. This is the fourth courthouse, having been built from 1852 to 1855. The postcard was sent in 1952.

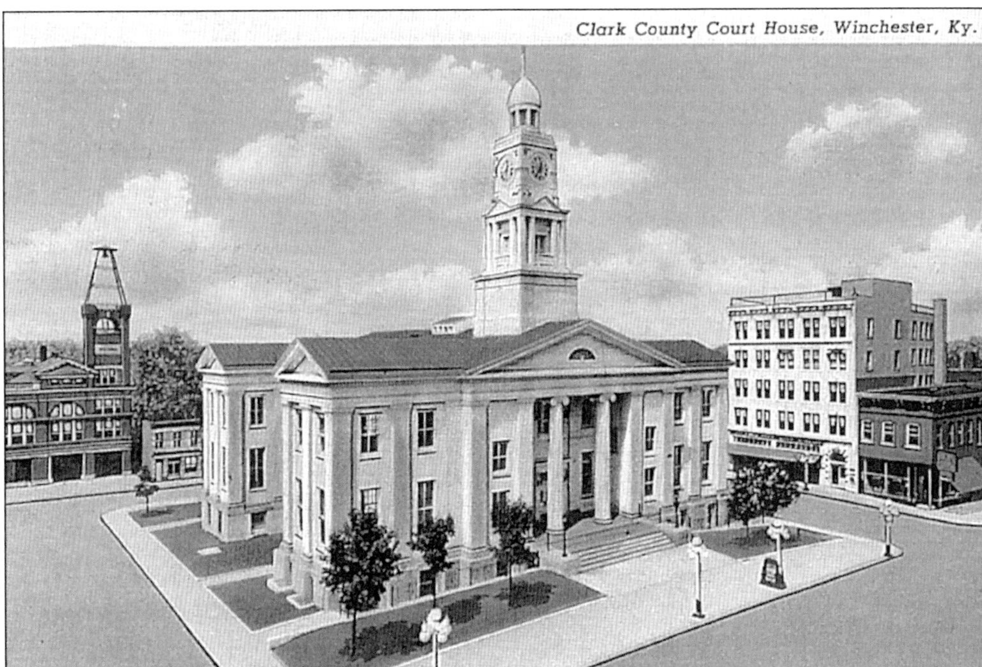

Another view of the county courthouse shows the fire department behind the courthouse. The courthouse has been renovated several times and was listed on the National Register of Historic Places in 1974.

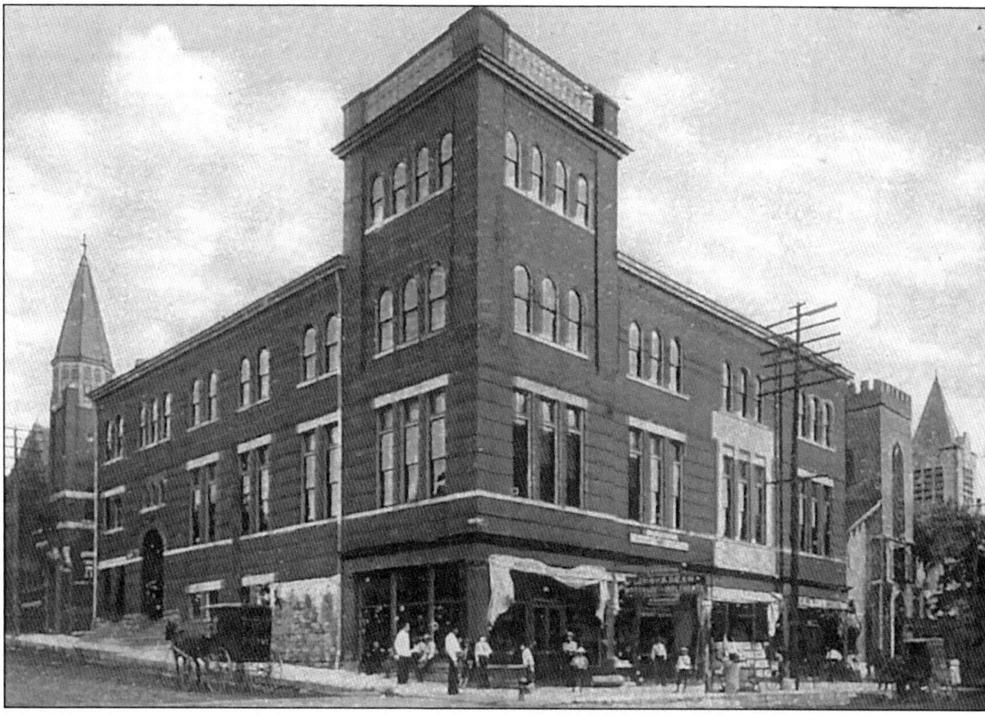

This postcard, with a postmark of 1911, shows the opera house in Winchester.

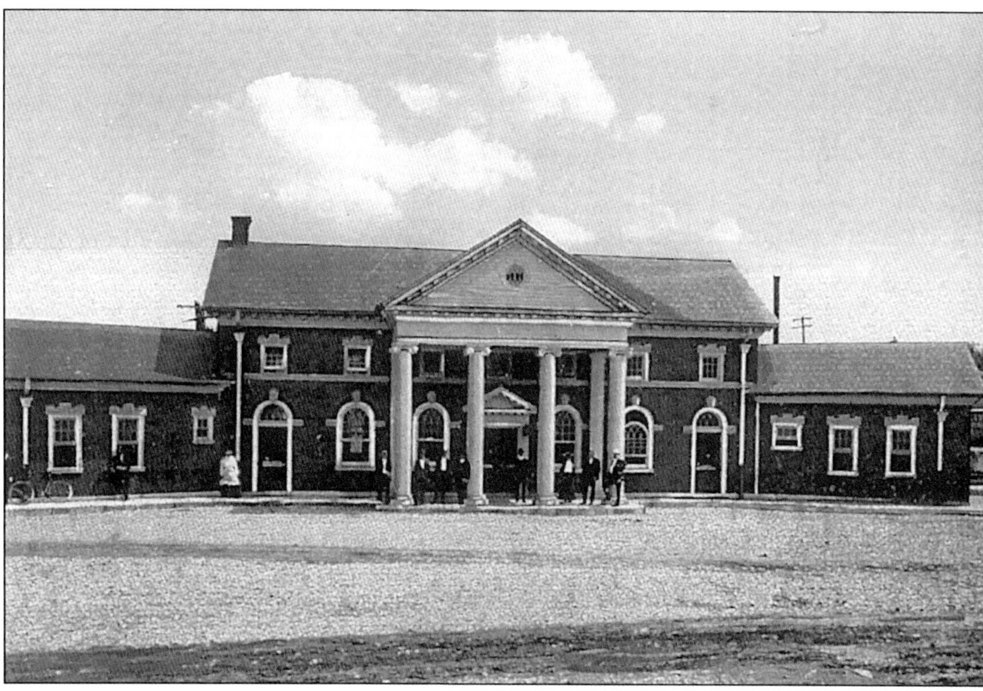

This postcard, published between 1907 and 1916, shows the Union Depot in Winchester.

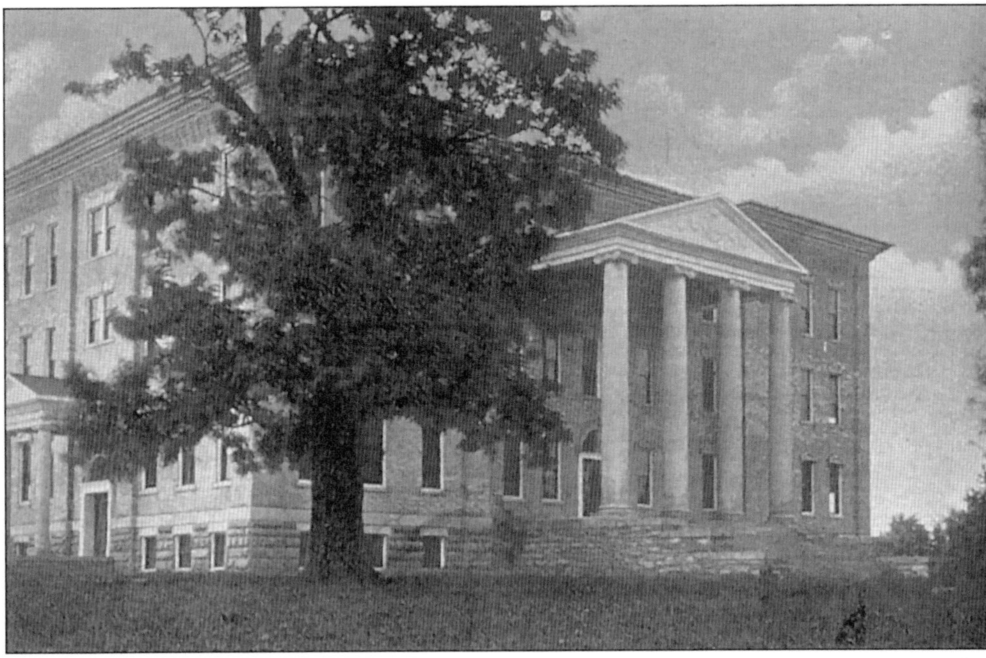

This postcard shows the Kentucky Wesleyan College between 1907 and 1915. It was founded in 1858 and accredited in 1948.

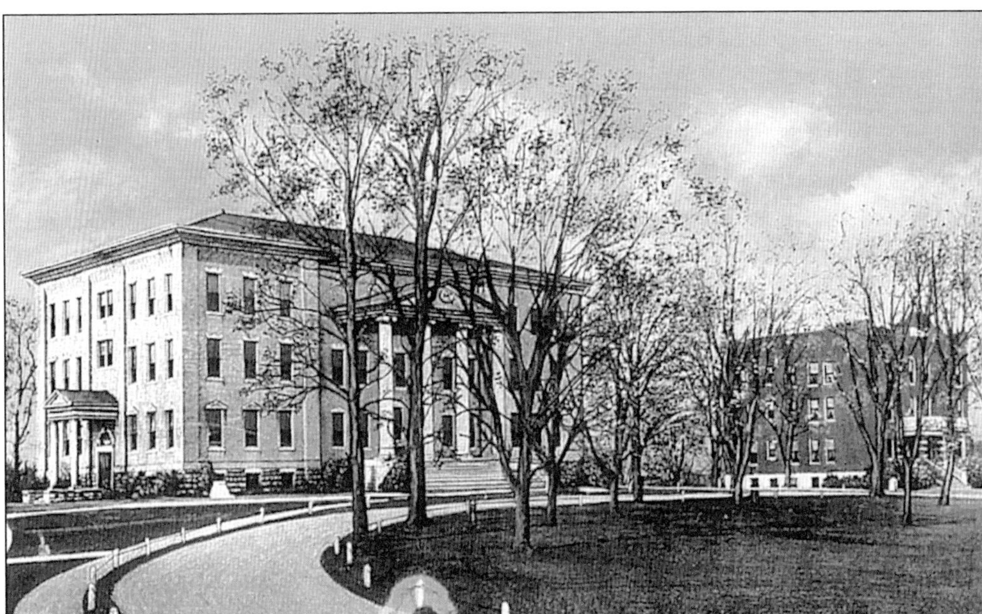

This view of Kentucky Wesleyan College is from the 1930s. The college is now in Owensboro, Kentucky.

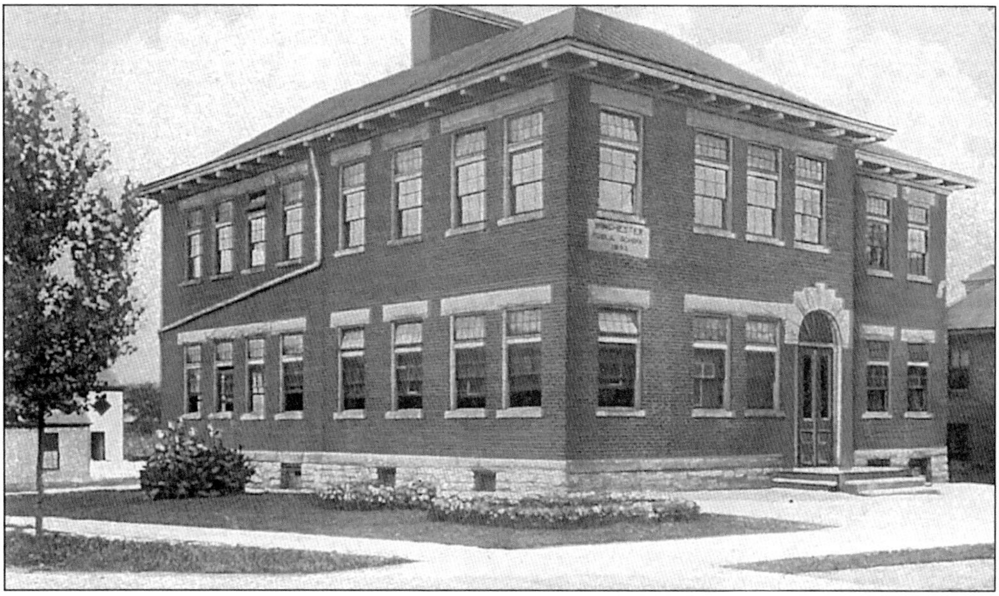

This view shows the Washington Street School around 1909.

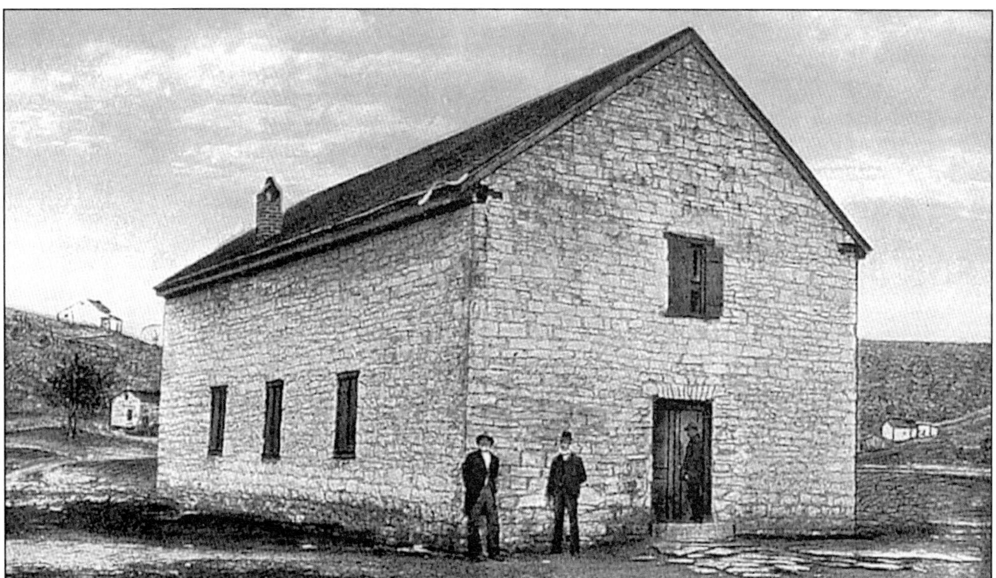

This is a picture of the old Stone Meeting House in Clark County. It was built before 1796 by a colony of Baptists who came from Virginia.

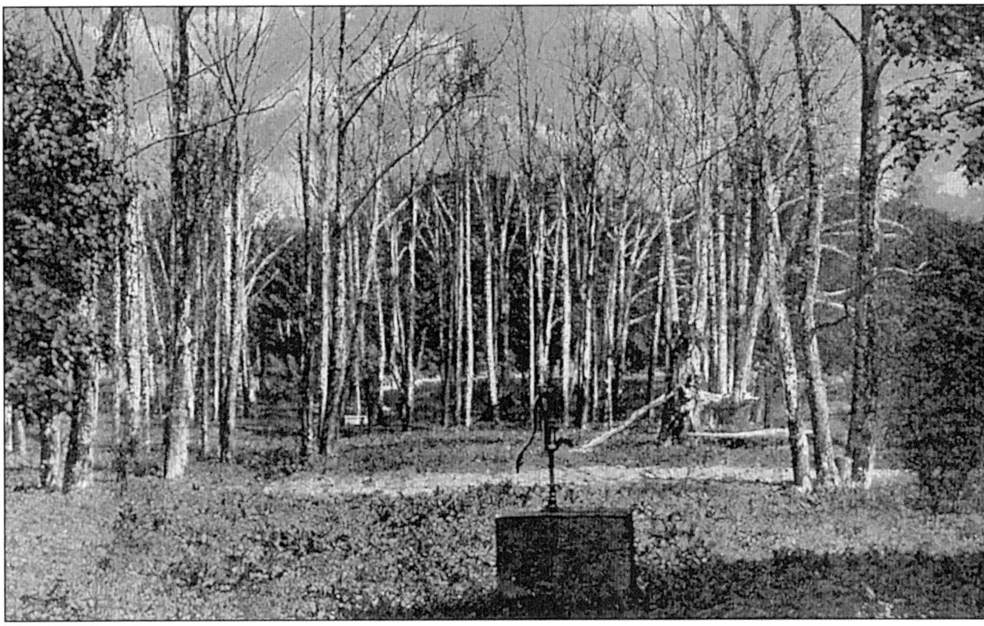

This postcard is titled, "the most historic spot in Kentucky, the fort near Winchester." Clark County, being separated from Boonesborough in Madison County only by the Kentucky River, had several settlements that pushed across the river into Clark County. Strode's Station, which is about 2 miles from Winchester, was settled in 1779 and could have been one of the early stations referred to in this postcard, while Boonesborough was the first permanent fort in this county. A postcard can be viewed of it in Madison County.

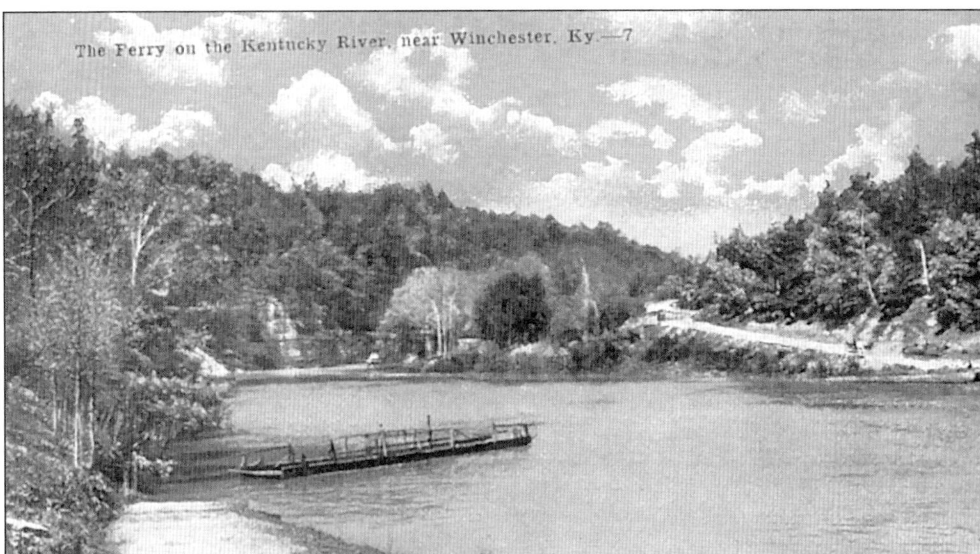

This view shows the ferry on the Kentucky River near Winchester around 1907. Ferries were commonly employed as a means of crossing the Kentucky River in earlier days, and they varied in capacity, depending upon the traffic that the road carried. Many of them yielded considerable revenues to their operators. This ferry at Boonesborough was one of the best equipped of the Kentucky River ferries.

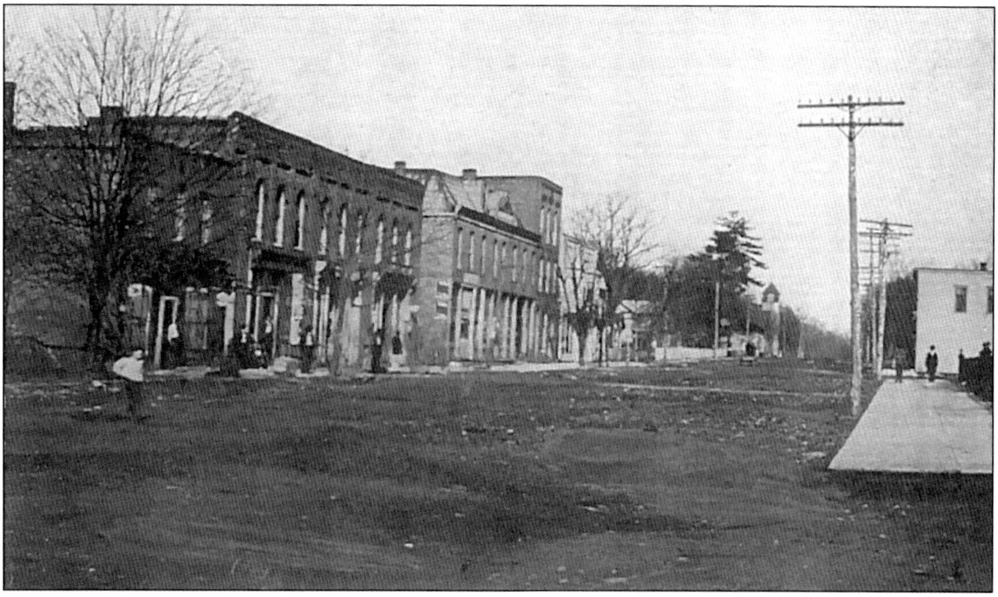

The following old postcards will show areas of Estill County. This county is known for its natural beauty and is situated between the old Bluegrass and mountains of Kentucky. This postcard shows the main street of Irvine with a postmark of 1911. Irvine was located on the Kentucky River at the intersection of Ky. Highways 52 and 89.

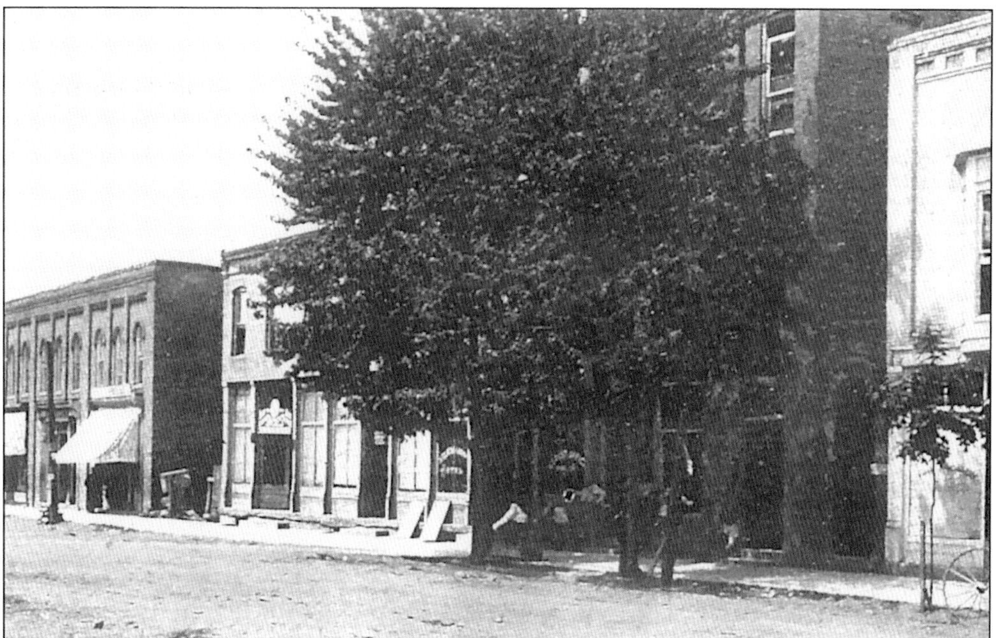

This view shows the east side of main street in Irvine. The city is the county seat and was established in 1812 on the northern bank of the Kentucky River. The railroad station in Irvine was established in 1902.

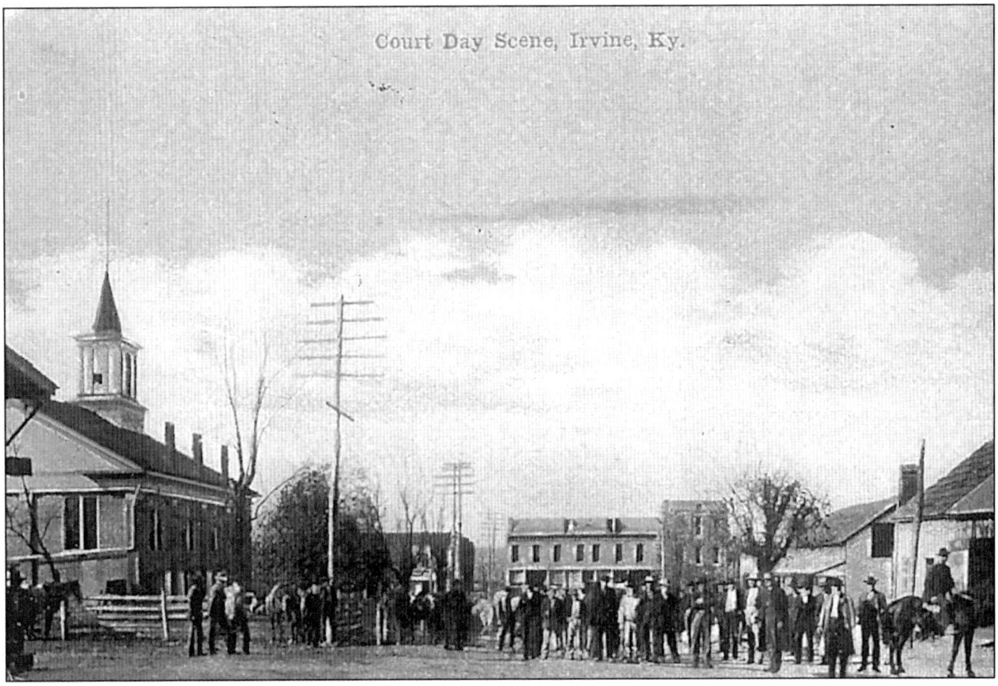

This view shows Court Day in Irvine, and main street can be identified in the background. This picture was published between 1901 and 1907.

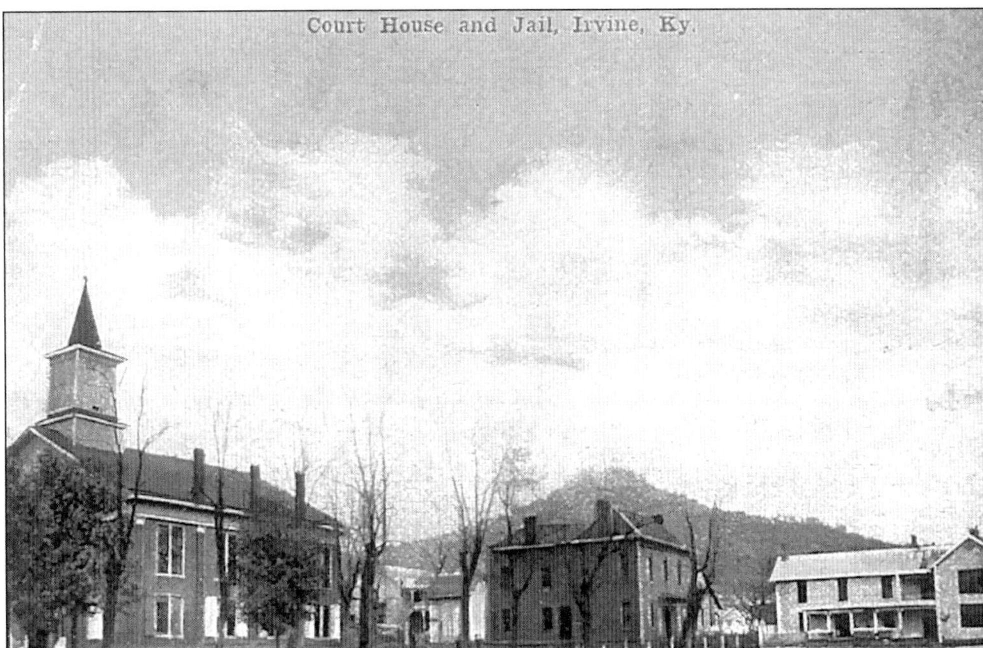

This view, opposite from the previous one, shows the courthouse and jail in Irvine. This courthouse was the second courthouse from 1867 to 1941. It was dismantled for the third and current one.

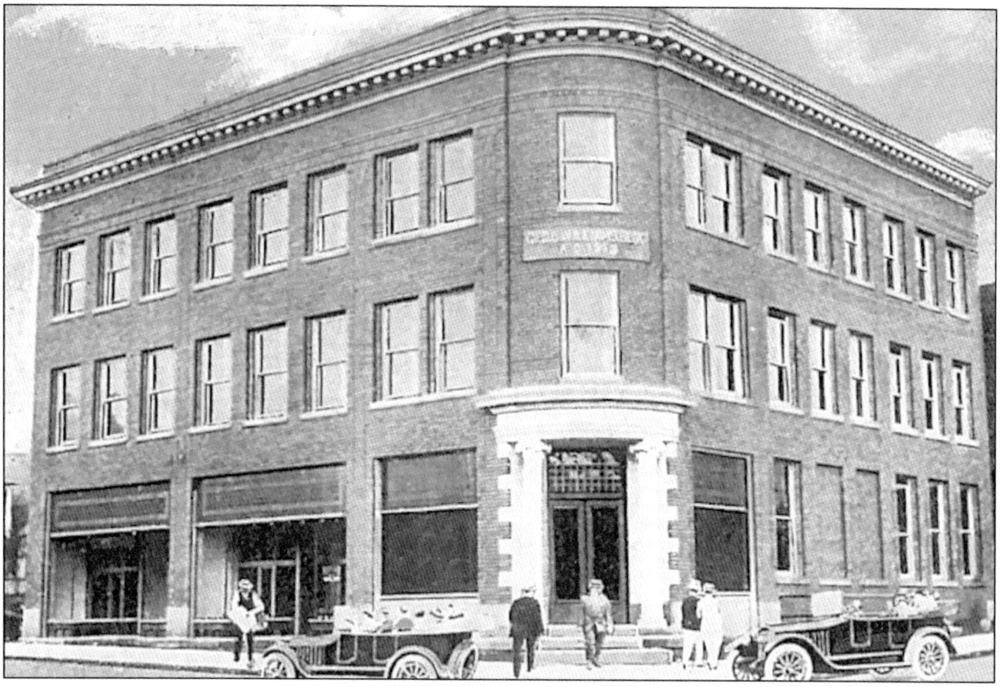

This postcard was mailed to J.Frazier and Son in Pilot, Kentucky, by the Williams Bank with W.T.B. Williams & Sons, Bankers of Irvine. It was postmarked 1923 with a notice from the W.T.B. Williams & Son Bank: "Sir-Your's for the 6 inst. received and we have credited your account with $438.82 the amount enclosed. Thanking you very much." This bank was merged with the Ravenna State Bank in 1929 to form the Union Bank and Trust Company of Irvine. It was still present in 1954 but not in the same building.

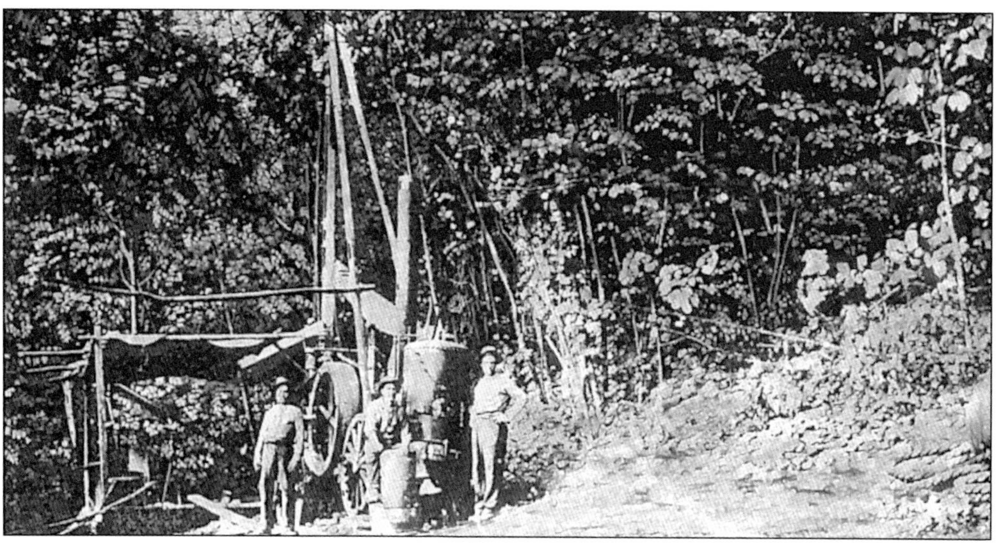

This postcard, published between 1907 and 1915, shows oil drilling in the Irvine Fields. Notice the equipment being used. These postcards were part of Peggy Brown's family collection. Her grandfather was in the oil business in Irvine, and he was the father of Lennie Alcorn, who attended Berea College. She can be seen on two old postcards at Berea College.

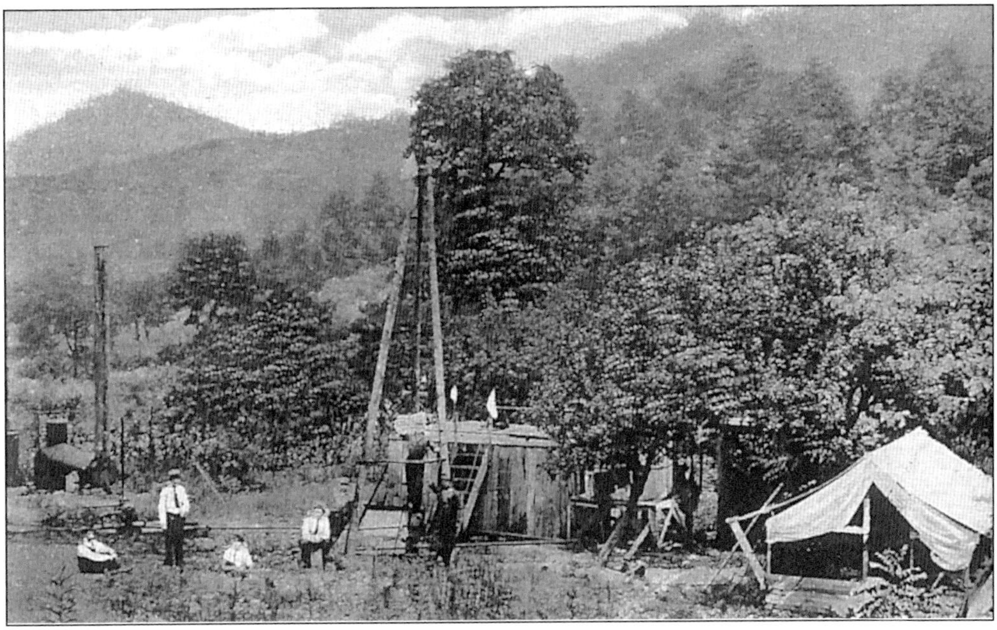

This postcard, published between 1907 and 1915, shows the Sweet Lick Oil Field near Irvine, and proprietors are listed as Gibson and Willard. This county was rich in minerals.

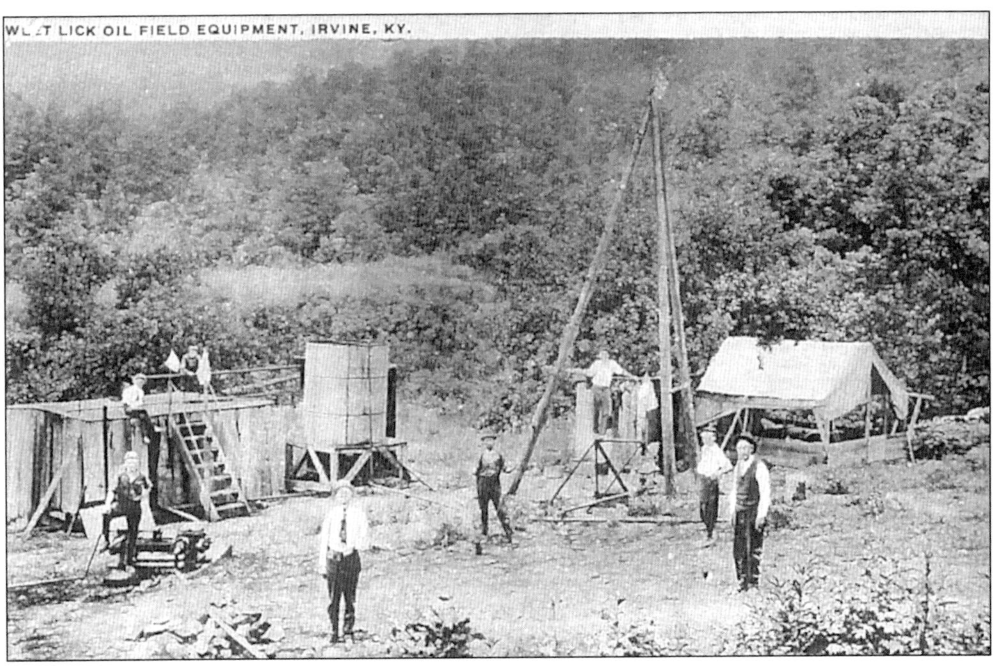

This postcard, published during the same time period by the Irvine Drug Store, shows the Sweet Lick Oil Field equipment near Irvine.

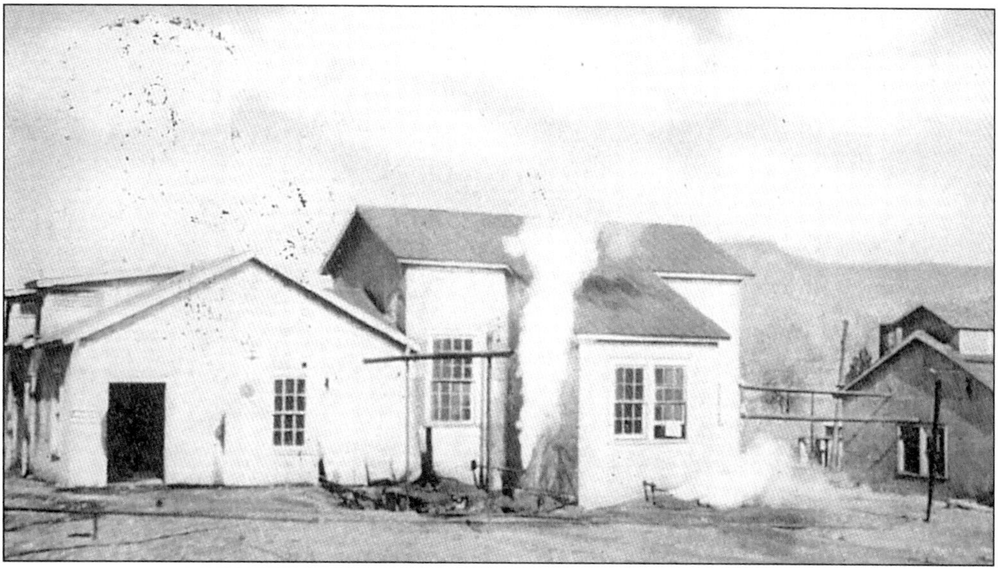

Ravenna was 2 miles from Irvine, and strangers have difficulty distinguishing Irvine from Ravenna. This postcard has Estell County Oil Fields printed at the top. Estill County was misspelled on the postcard, indicating that postcards can have incorrect information. It had a postmark of 1923. The economic picture of the county was diversified by the opening of oil and gas wells.

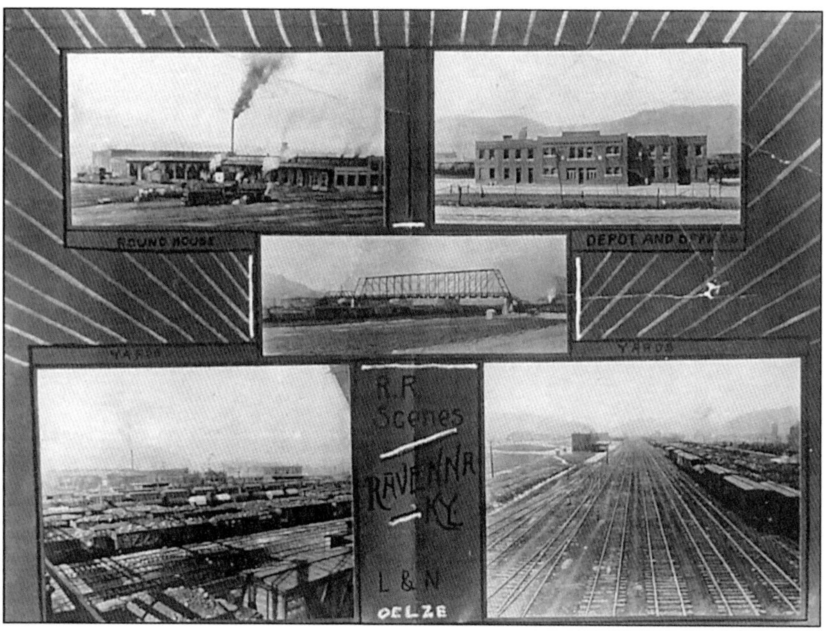

This photo postcard shows railroad scenes of the L & N Railroad in Ravenna. The five views include the round house, the depot, offices, the bridge, and two different yards. Ravenna became the L & N Railroad shops and yards around 1900, and land was sold for ownership around 1915. By 1921, Ravenna was incorporated as a sixth class city, and in 1950, the population was 979. In the 1930s and 1940s, the L & N Railroad was the major railroad in the eastern part of the Bluegrass, while the Southern Railroad was major in the western part of the Bluegrass.

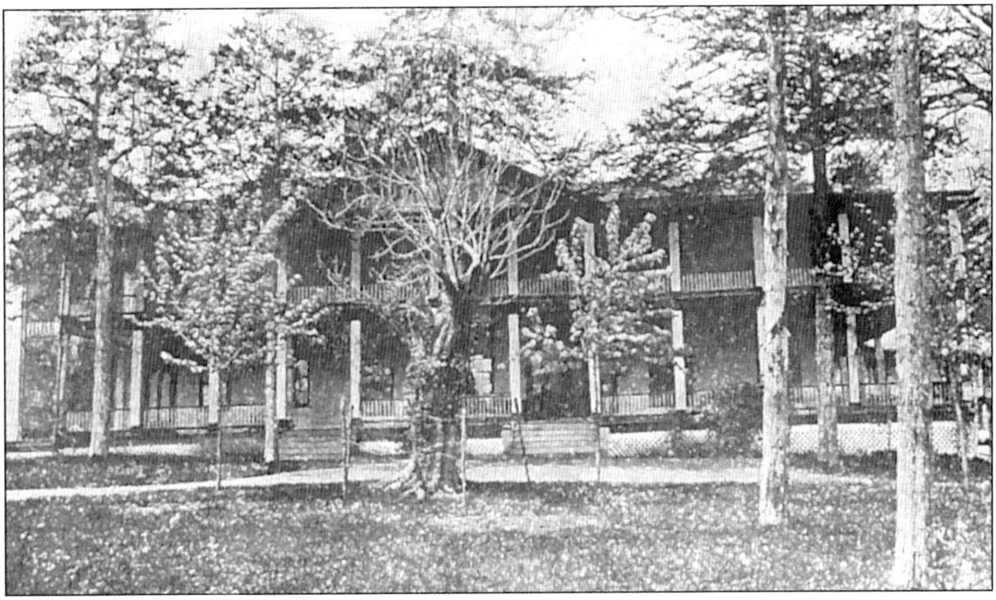

This is a view of Estill Springs, Kentucky's grand old summer home half a mile from Irvine. It has a postmark of 1906 and a handwritten note saying, "This picture gives only a small portion of the building." When prosperity came to the area, this hotel was built with 112 rooms, galleries, and a ballroom. Entertainment was provided for all tastes, such as horseback riding, bowling, tennis, and dancing. Music was provided by a string orchestra.

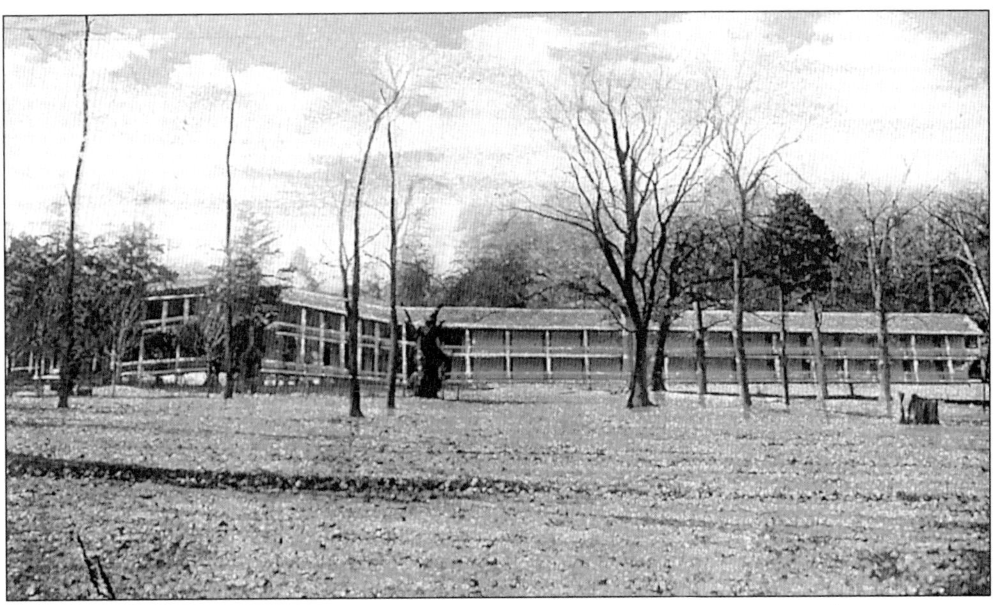

Another view of the Estill Springs Hotel was postmarked August 22, 1912. Estill Springs was a celebrated watering place for many years, with at least five different medicinal waters. The hotel burned in 1924 and was never rebuilt.

Three

FAYETTE COUNTY

Fayette County has an interesting history that will be displayed in 27 old postcards covering this whole chapter. The county was formed in 1780 by the state of Virginia as one of the original three counties that comprised the whole district of Kentucky. Lexington is the largest city in the county and has many architectural treasures as the major town of the "old" Bluegrass. The following postcard of downtown Lexington will be the only one of that city in this book, since this author published a book on Lexington in 1998 and showed it in more detail with over 200 old postcards.

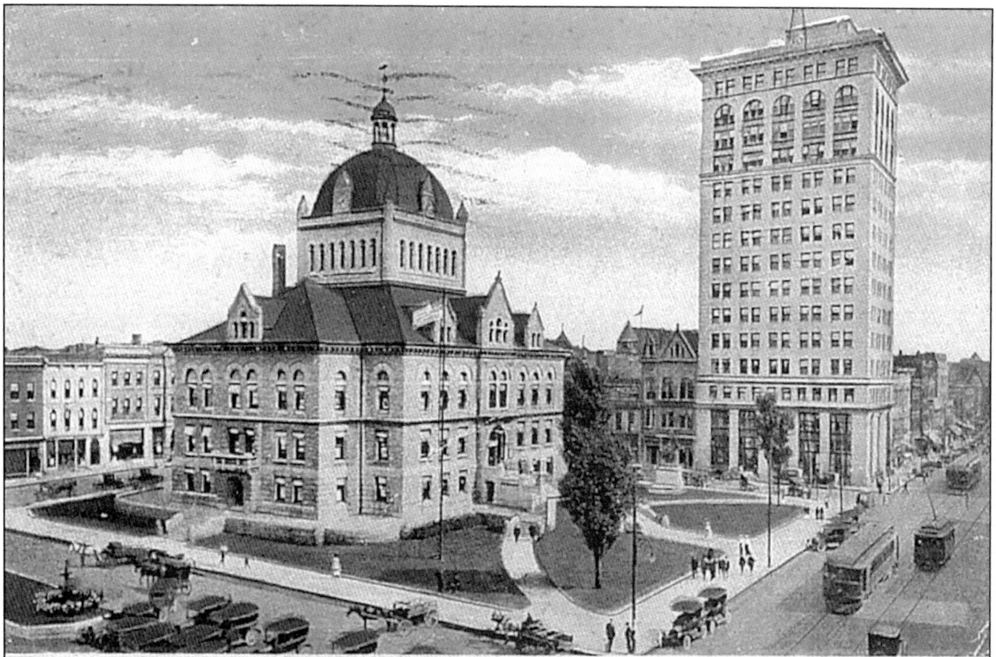

FAYETTE COUNTY COURT HOUSE AND FAYETTE NATIONAL BANK BLDG., LEXINGTON, KY. 77058

This 1930s postcard shows the present and fifth Fayette County Courthouse, which was completed in 1900. Lexington was established as the county seat in May 1782. Notice the surrounding buildings, the Fayette National Bank Building, the trolleys, and downtown traffic.

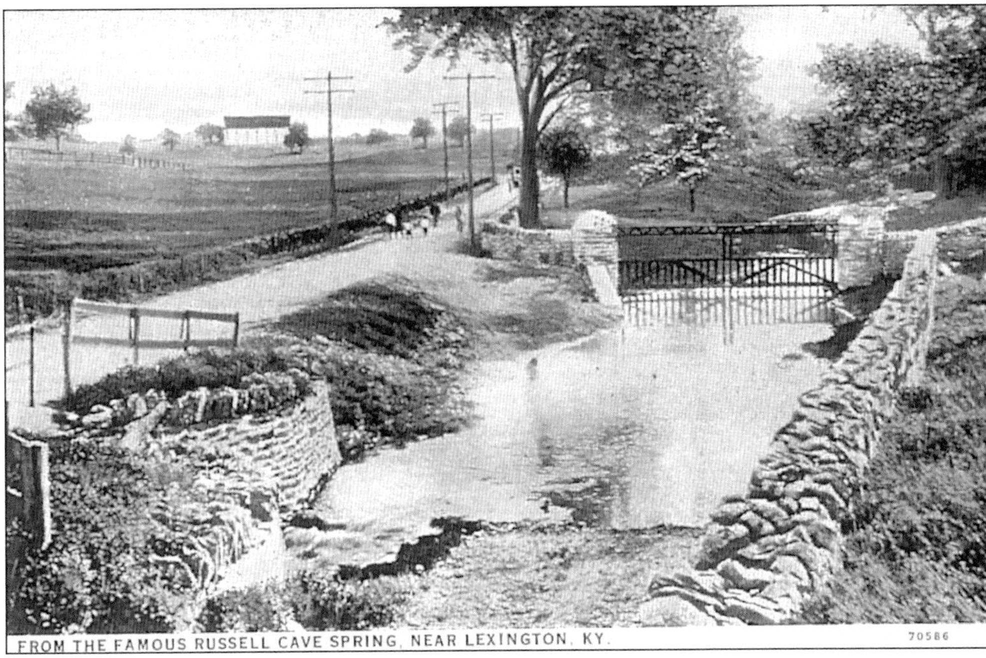

This postcard, published between 1907 and 1915, shows the Russell Cave Spring, near Lexington. Notice the stone fences. Russell Cave is one of the great winding caverns of Kentucky, being traced back under the Bluegrass for miles. The water was so prized by Ben Ali Haggin, a millionaire of mining fame, that pipes were laid to carry its water into his distant palatial home.

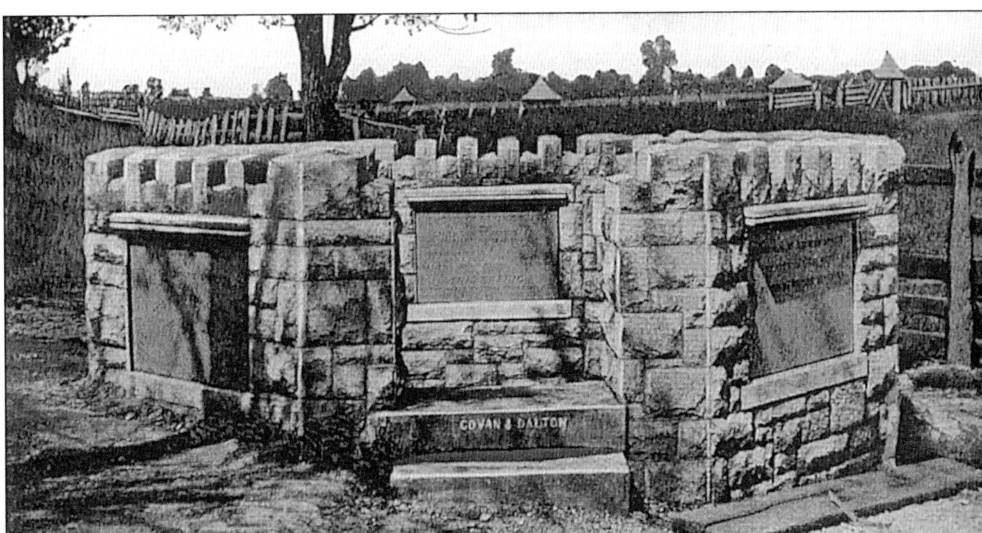

This postcard, published around 1950, shows the Bryan Station Spring near Lexington. The octagonal 4-foot stone wall was built around the spring that supplied water to the early pioneers of the station when defending Lexington against American Indians. This defense of Bryan Station halted other Indian invasions into Kentucky and kept Lexington free from any serious attacks. The part played by the pioneer women in the defense of Bryan Station was immortalized by the inscription of their names on the walls of this memorial.

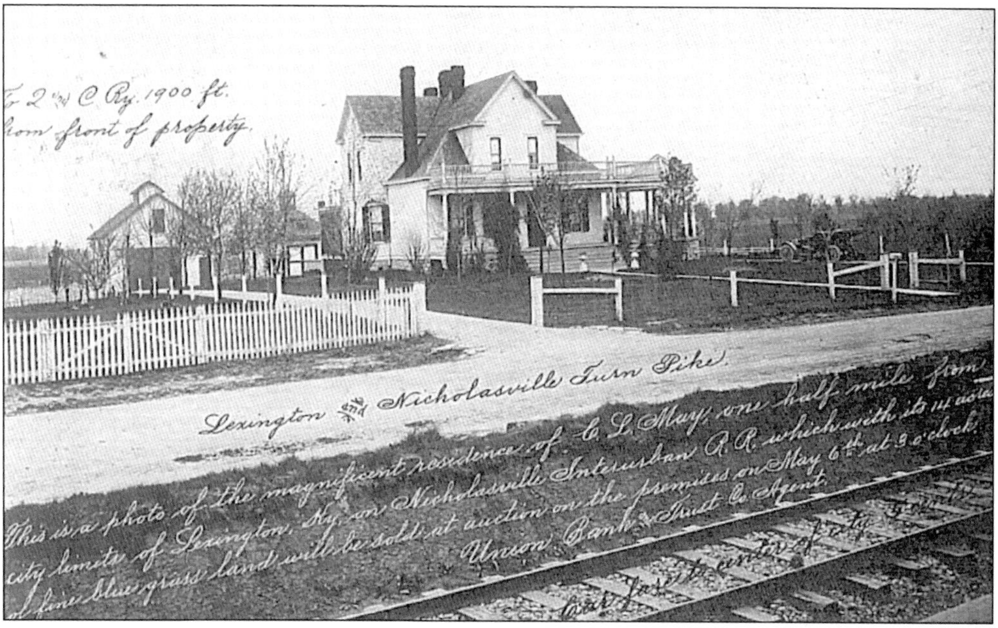

This is a photo postcard sent on May 5, 1911, for the sale of this home and property south of Lexington. This was the residence of C.L. May, 1/2 mile from the city limits of Lexington on the Nicholasville Interurban Rail Road. The property had 14 acres of Bluegrass land and was to be sold at auction on May 6th. According to the May 7th *Lexington Leader* newspaper, the property sold for $11,000 to a Mr. J.N Vaughn. Advertisement for this auction was printed on this postcard by the Union Bank and Trust Company of Lexington and sent to many potential buyers.

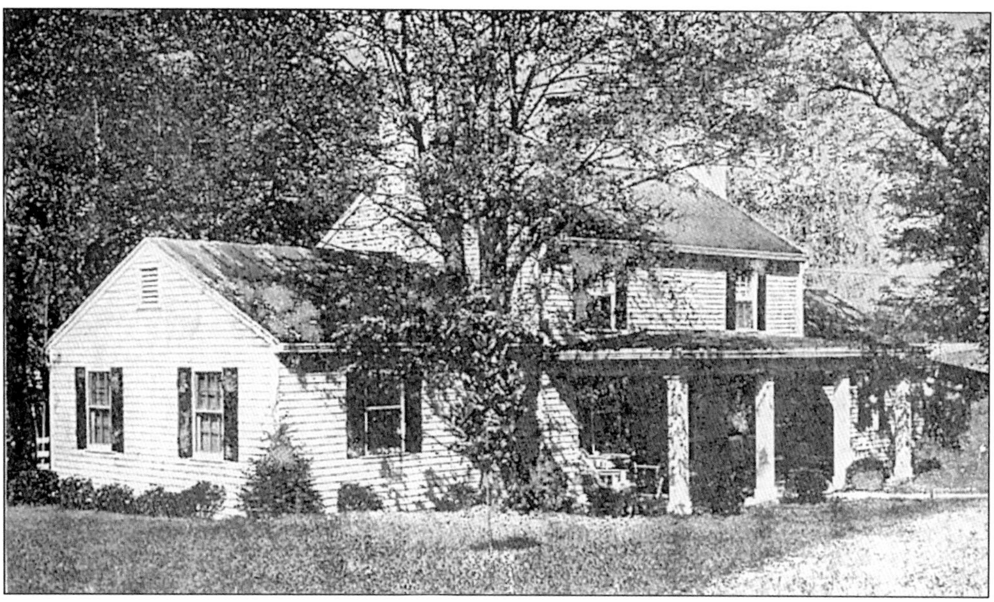

This postcard shows property 6 miles from Lexington off of Paris Pike, called Hillandale. The house was built by Samuel Bryan in 1784. Postcards were printed such as this one, to advertise the open house of this old home on May 12–13, 1950, for the purposes of selling it.

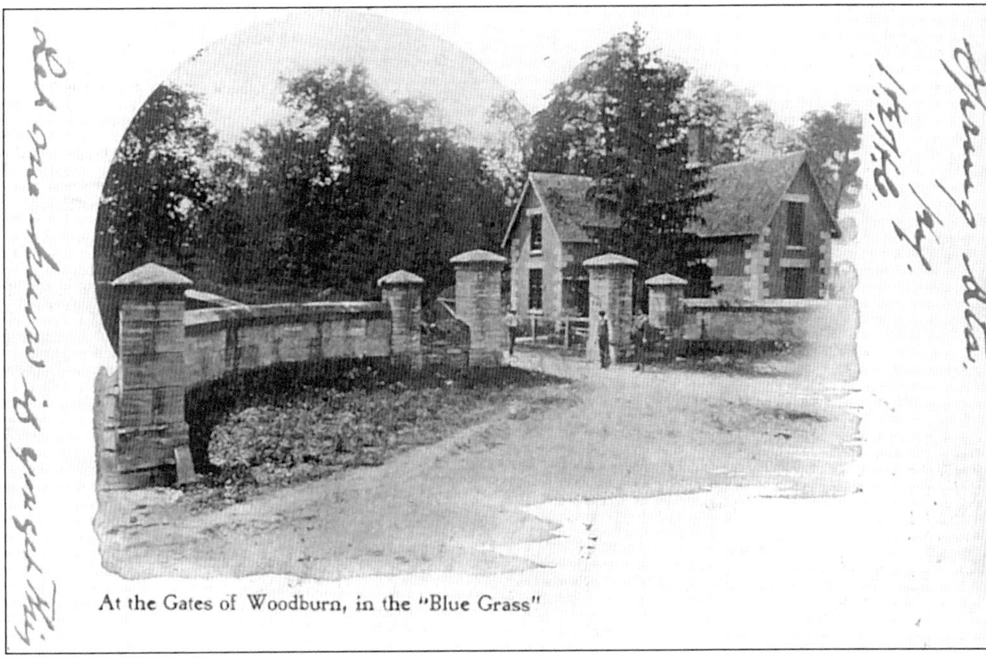

This postcard, sent in 1905, shows the gates of Woodburn, one of the many fine farms in the Bluegrass. Notice "Blue Grass" is two words.

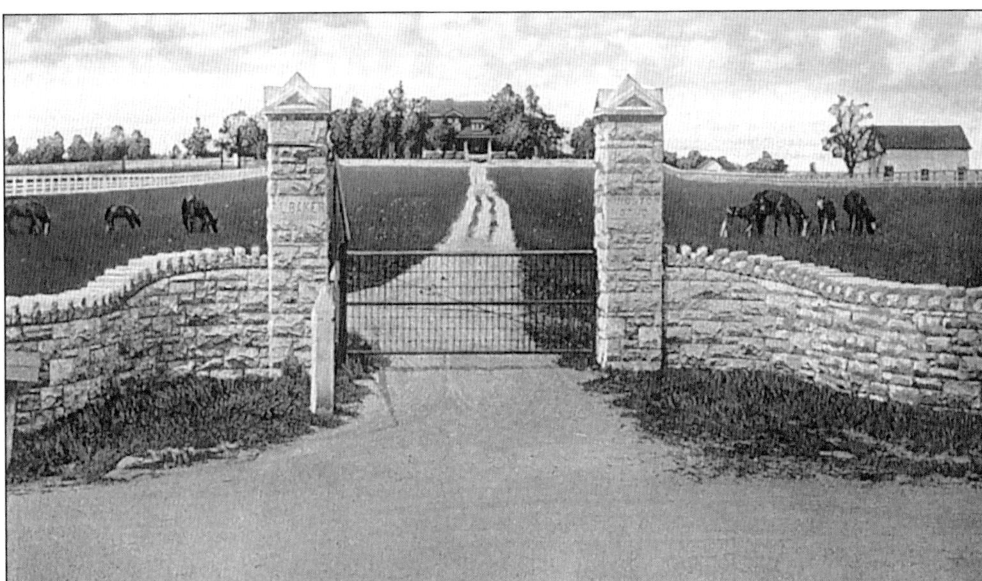

This postcard shows the entrance to another Bluegrass farm, Kingston Stud, a stock farm near Lexington. Notice the stone fence and additional white fences encompassing horses and the home.

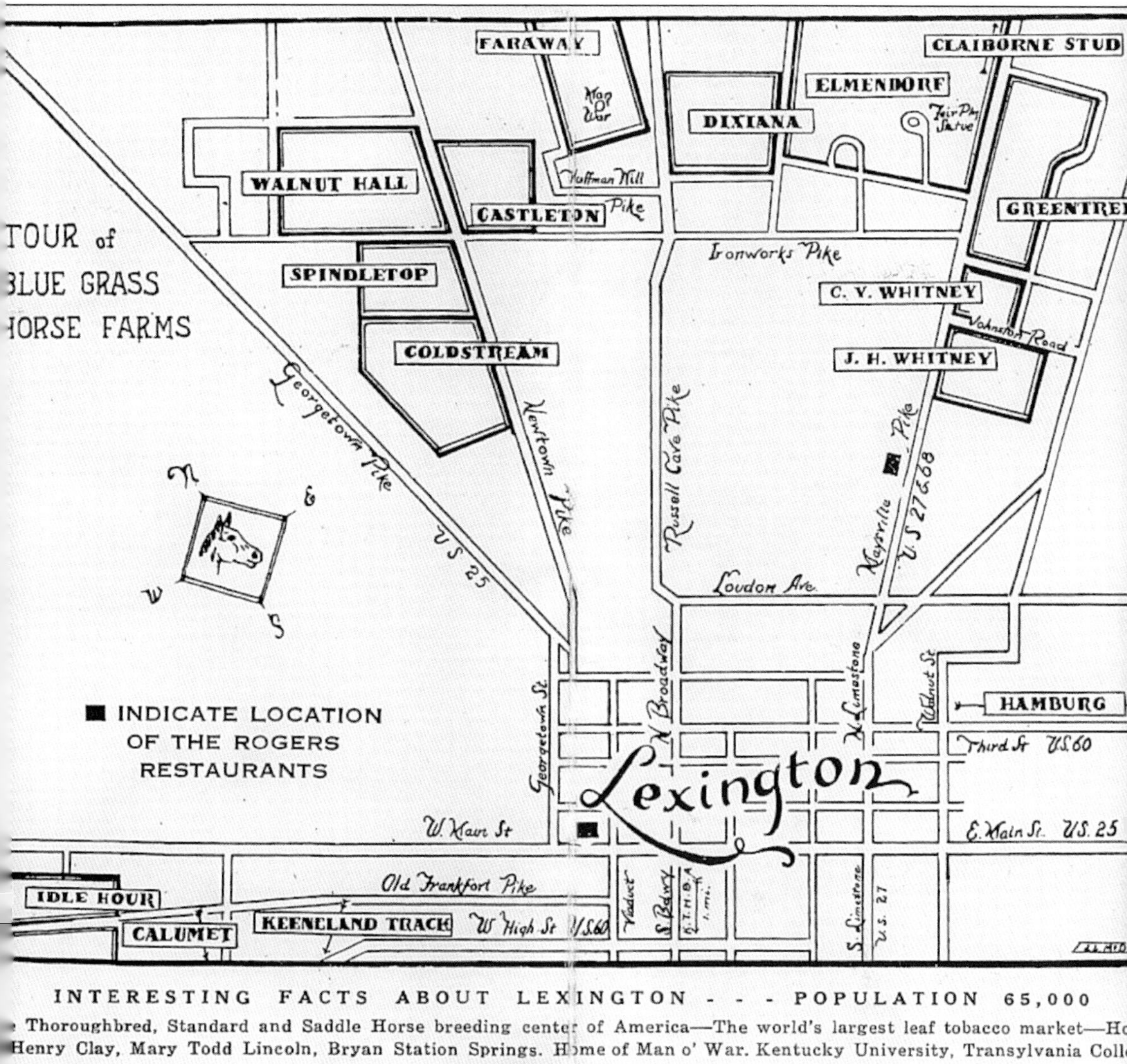

This postcard, an unusual fold-out, has a map of the local Bluegrass horse farms and interesting facts about Lexington. The fold-out was printed around the 1940s for patrons of Rogers' Restaurants in Lexington. Several horse farms are shown on this map, and seven of those will be featured using old postcards, starting on the left with the Idle Hour Farm, the Hamburg Farm, and on the lower right, the Greentree, Dixiana, Elmendorf, Walnut Hall, and Spindletop Farms. The Calumet Farm and Keeneland Race Track were shown in the 1998 *Lexington, Kentucky* book by this author and publisher.

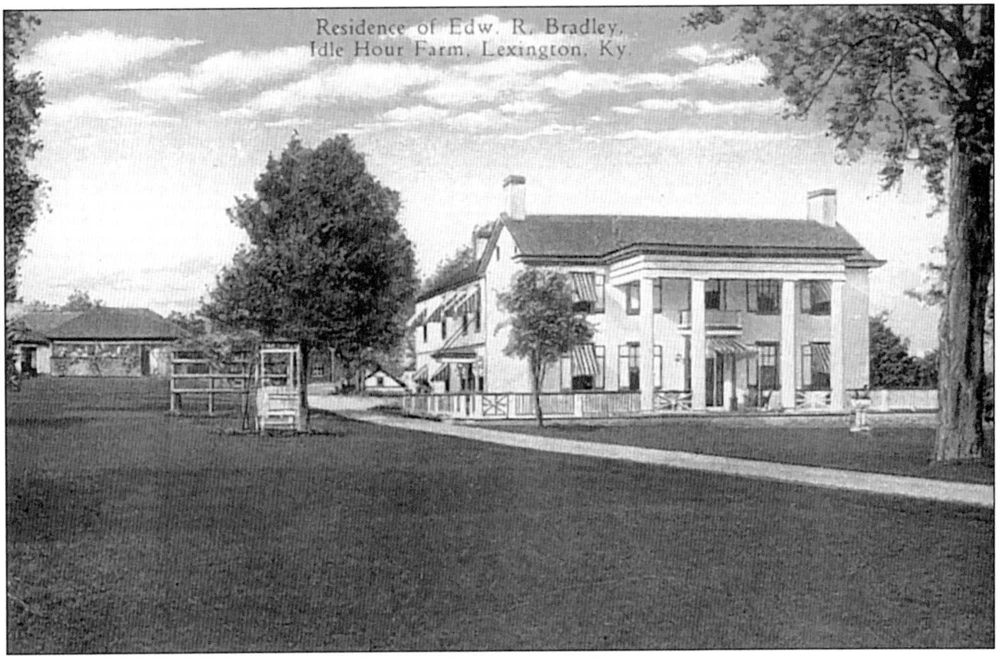

This is a view of the Idle Hour Farm and the 1,300-acre estate of Edward R. Bradley. The postcard was published around 1915. In 1930, Colonel Bradley hosted his annual charity race meet serving Burgoo, a speciality of this area. A two-year-old colt was named "Burgoo King" in honor of Mr. Looney, the "Burgoo King." See the last postcard of this chapter for more about Burgoo.

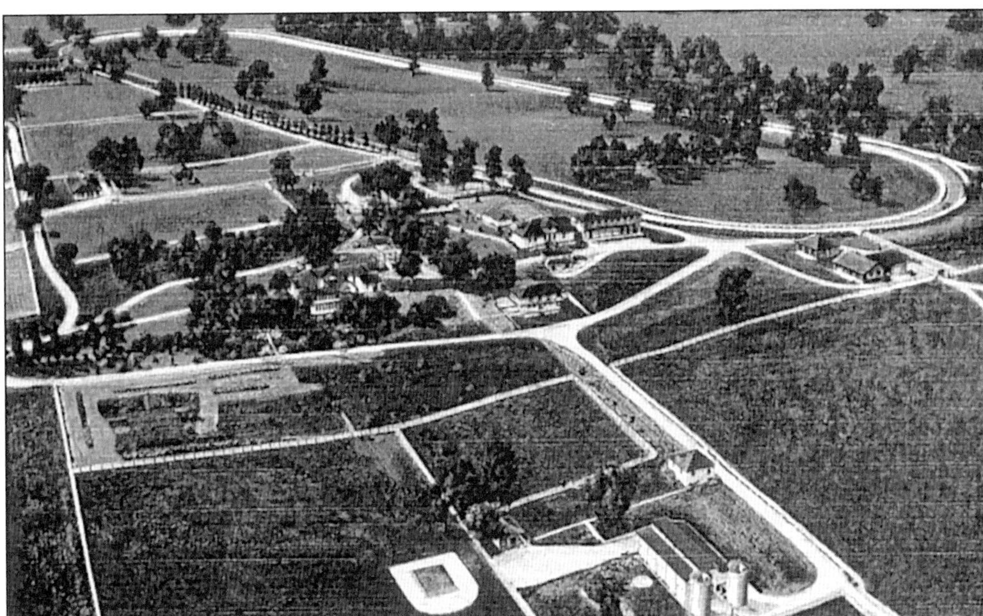

Here is an aerial view of the Idle Hour Farm, published around the 1930s. At one time, there were miles of fencing painted white and green, the racing colors of Colonel Bradley. Notice the oblong race track at the top.

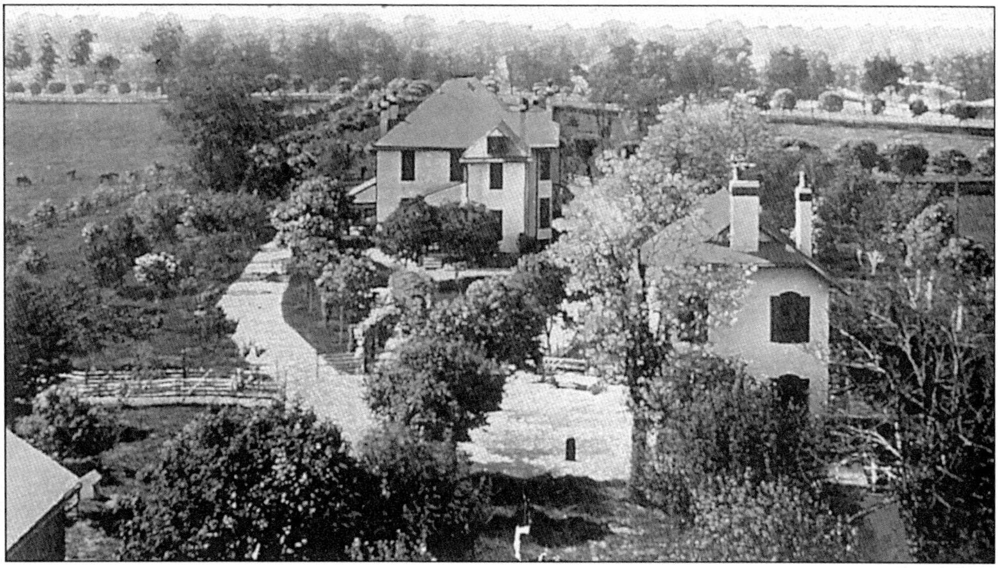

This is an aerial view of Hamburg Place around 1915 with the caption, "One of Kentucky's Celebrated Blue Grass Thoroughbred Farms." The farm was purchased in 1898 by John E. Madden, who paid $30,000 for 235 acres.

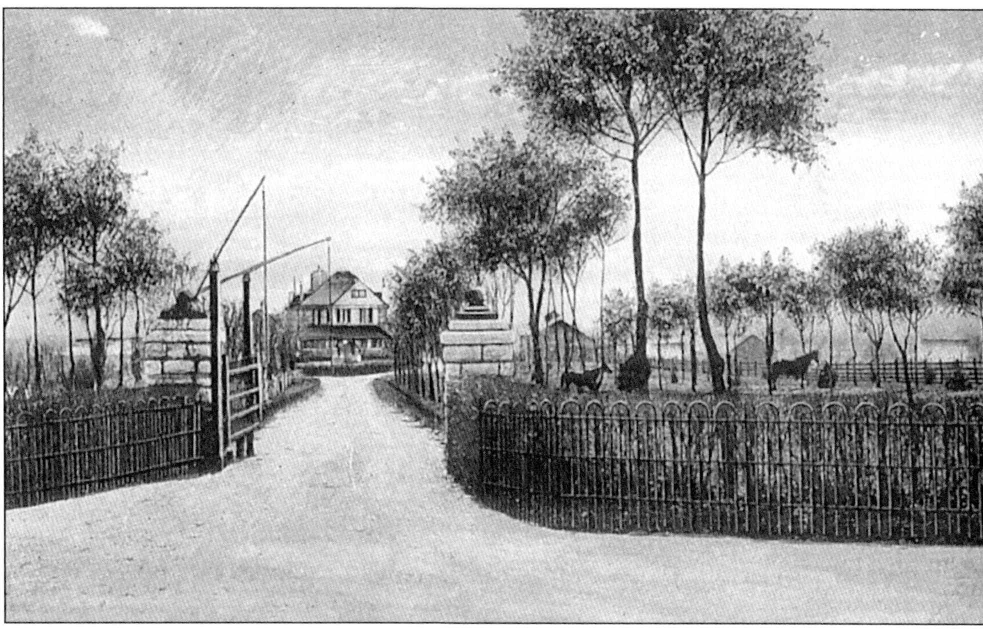

This image shows the main entrance to Hamburg Place and J.E. Madden's famous Stock Farm. It was the birthplace of five Kentucky Derby winners and the burial place of Nancy Hanks, one of the greatest of all trotting horses. During her racing career of five seasons, Nancy Hanks never lost a race.

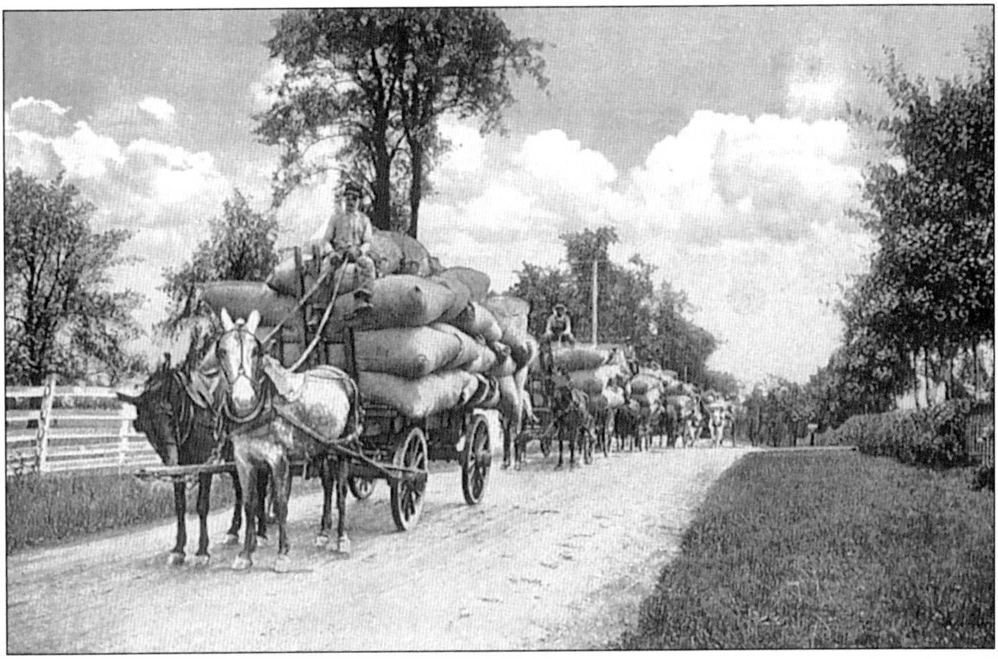

This is a 1930s view of Hamburg Place being delivered Bluegrass seed. Beef cattle and acres of tobacco have been raised on the farm, but the majority of the horses were bred for sale as yearlings.

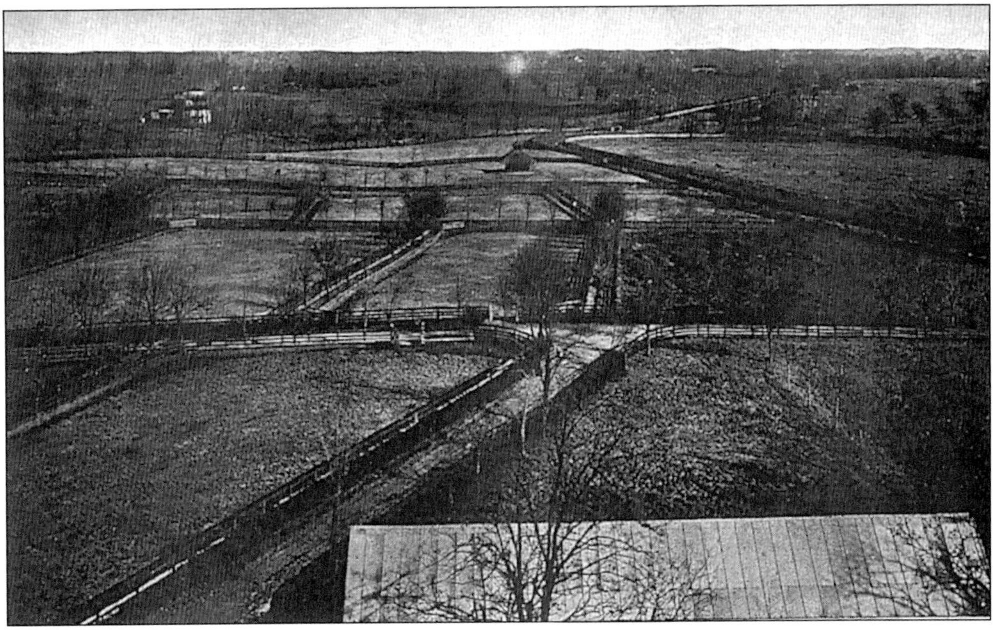

This is a bird's-eye view of Hamburg Place around the 1930s. Like many farm owners close to Lexington, the Maddens have sold parts of their acreage for surrounding subdivisions in later years.

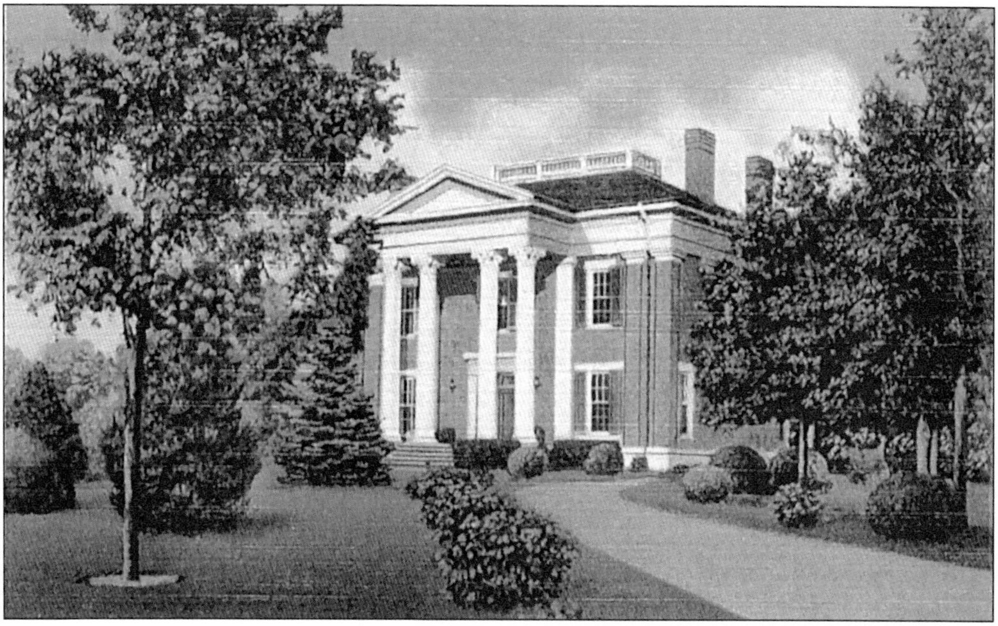

This postcard shows a 1930s view of Greentree Farm. This 750-acre farm was owned by Mrs. Payne Whitney, who was devoted to the breeding and racing of thoroughbreds. It produced two Kentucky Derby winners for 1931 and 1936.

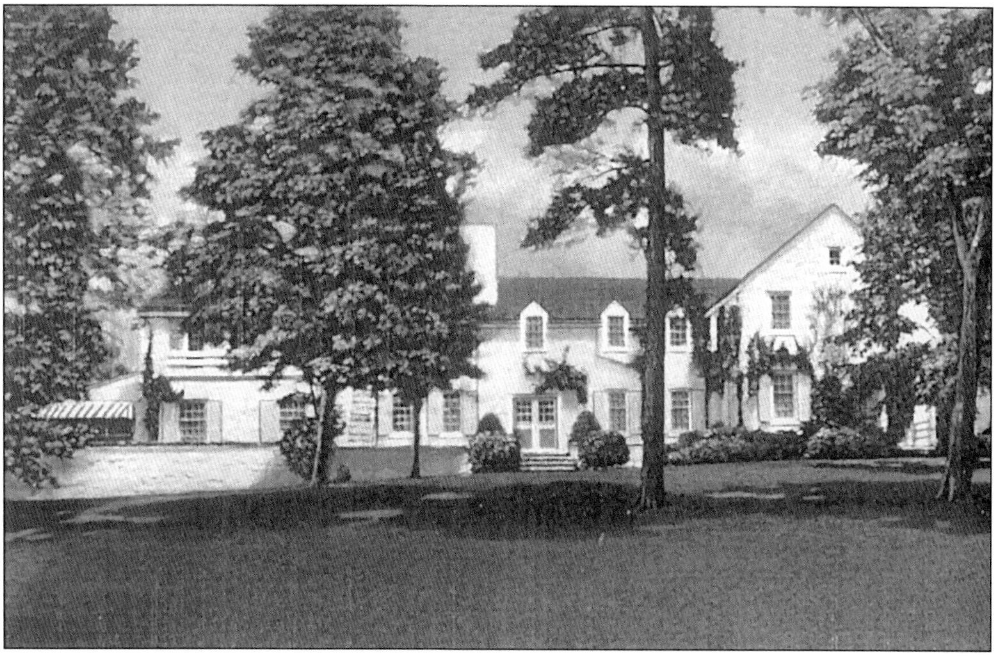

This postcard shows a 1930s view of Dixiana Farm. This 900-acre thoroughbred and American saddle horse farm was owned by Charles T. Fisher, a detroit sportsman. The main entrance to Dixiana is also the main entrance to Domino Stud, sharing the expense of the road. Dixiana is a farm of spectacular beauty, with its rolling hills, tree-lined drive, and rugged stone fences.

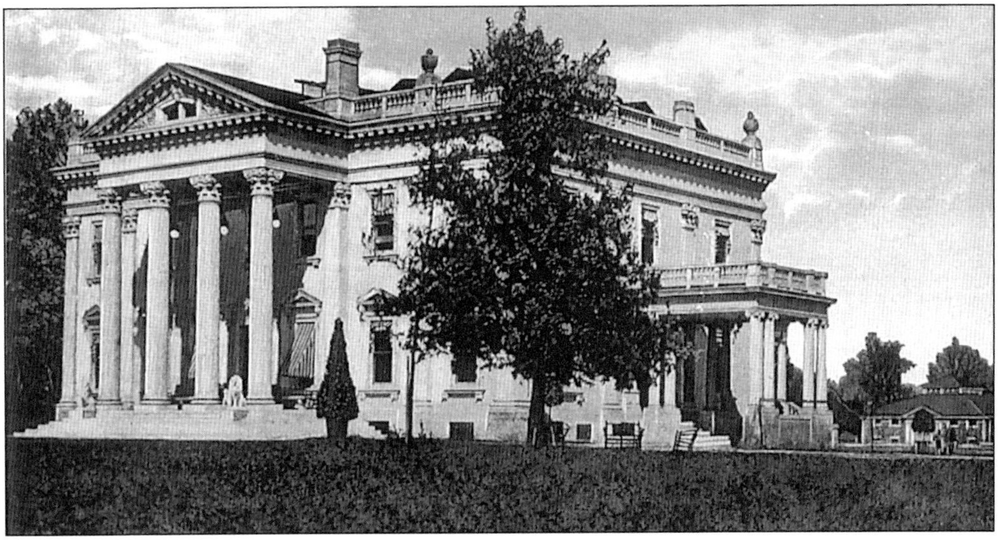

This *c.* 1910 view shows Green Hills, the home of J.B. Higgins, owner of Elmendorf Farm. James Ben Ali Haggin built this mansion in 1887 for $300,000, and it was razed in 1929 by Joe Weidner, subsequent owner, because taxes on the then unoccupied home were excessive. The marble columns were left standing in what is now a horse pasture, a memento of the lifestyle of one of Kentucky's most colorful horsemen.

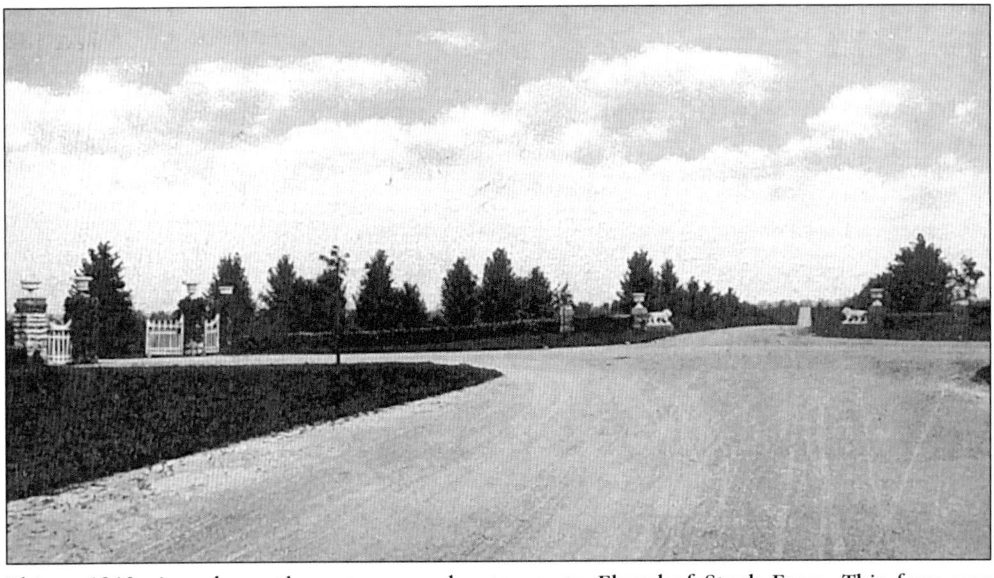

This *c.* 1910 view shows the gateway and entrance to Elemdorf Stock Farm. This farm was purchased by the mining entrepreneur, James Ben Ali Haggin, the same year that he built the mansion. He gradually consolidated neighboring properties until he had increased the farm size to 10,000 acres, becoming the largest horse breeder in the country at that time.

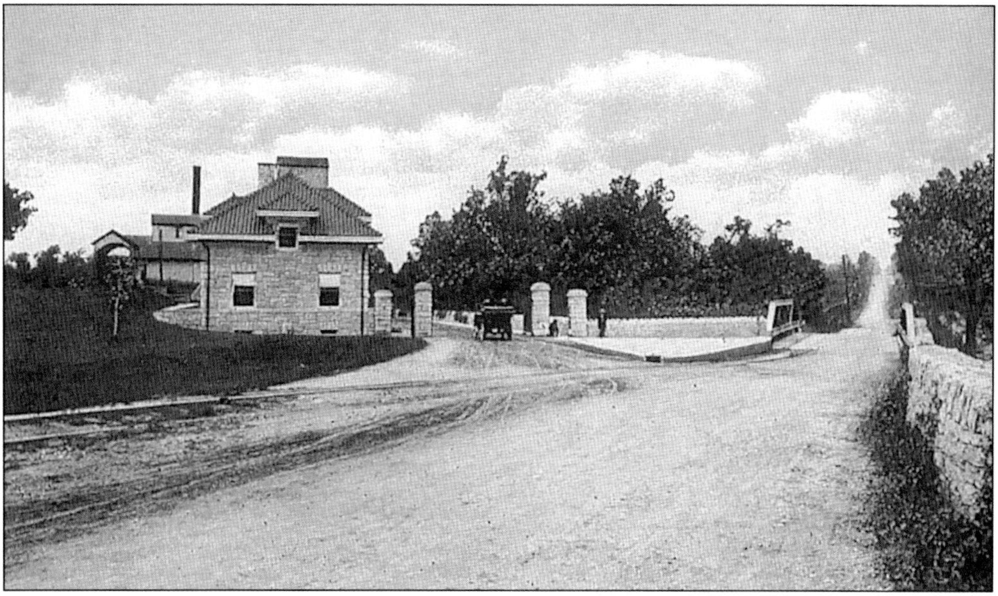

This view of similar vintage shows the office and power plant of Elmendorf Stock Farm. James Ben Ali Haggin employed over 1,000 people on the farm, many commuting daily from Lexington, to produce corn, wheat, fodder, tobacco, and hemp, as well as horses.

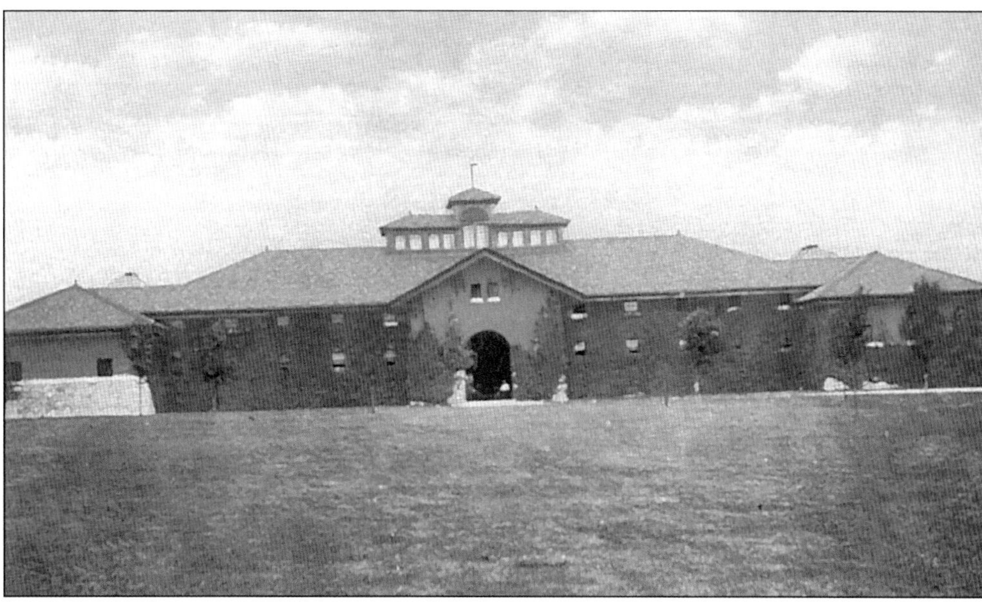

This view shows the horses' home at Elmendorf Stock Farm. This farm was, at one time, the longest farm in the process of producing thoroughbred horses in Kentucky and probably the nation.

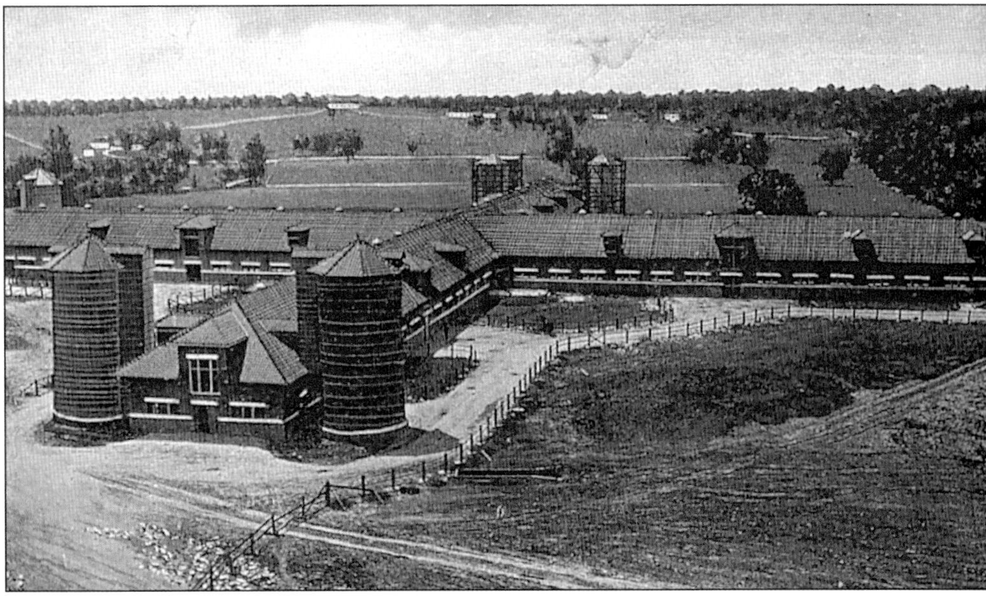

This view of similar vintage shows the milk stables at Elmendorf Farm. Mr. Haggin developed a model dairy on the farm and built some of the most famous barns in the country.

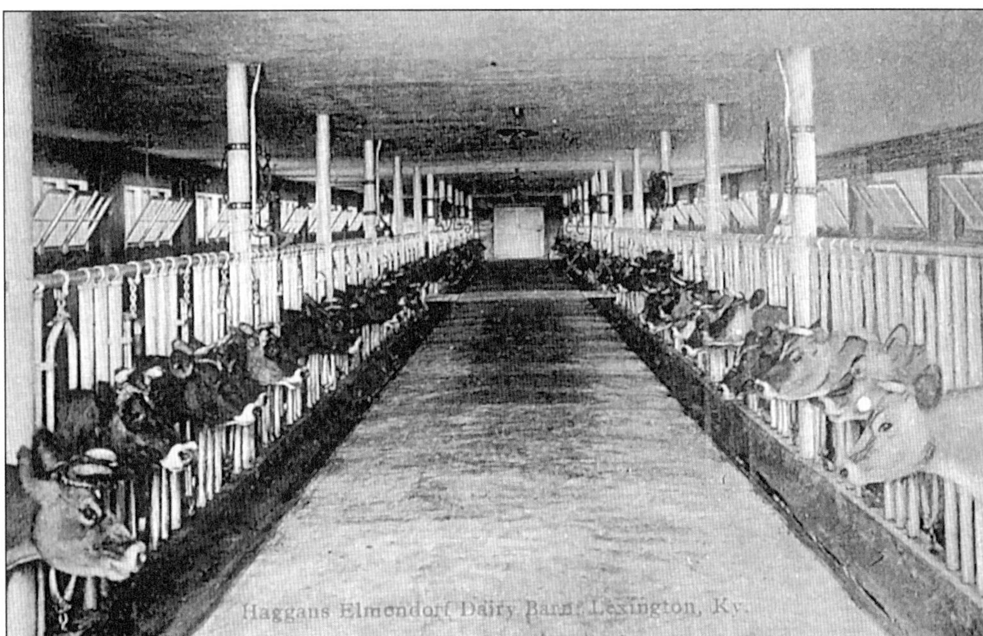

This postcard shows a view of the dairy farm at Elmendorf Farm. Mr. Haggin died at the age of 92 and had an estate worth millions. Elmendorf was subsequently divided into several farms, each of which became outstanding horse farms.

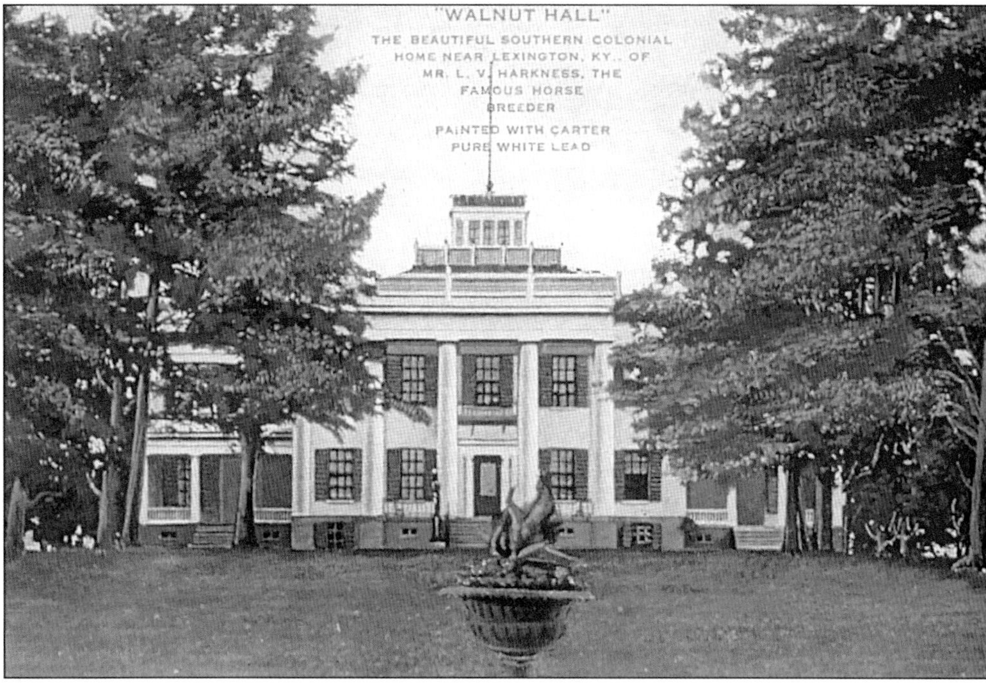

This is an advertising postcard for Carter pure white lead paint, showing the famous Walnut Hill. It was published between 1907 and 1915.

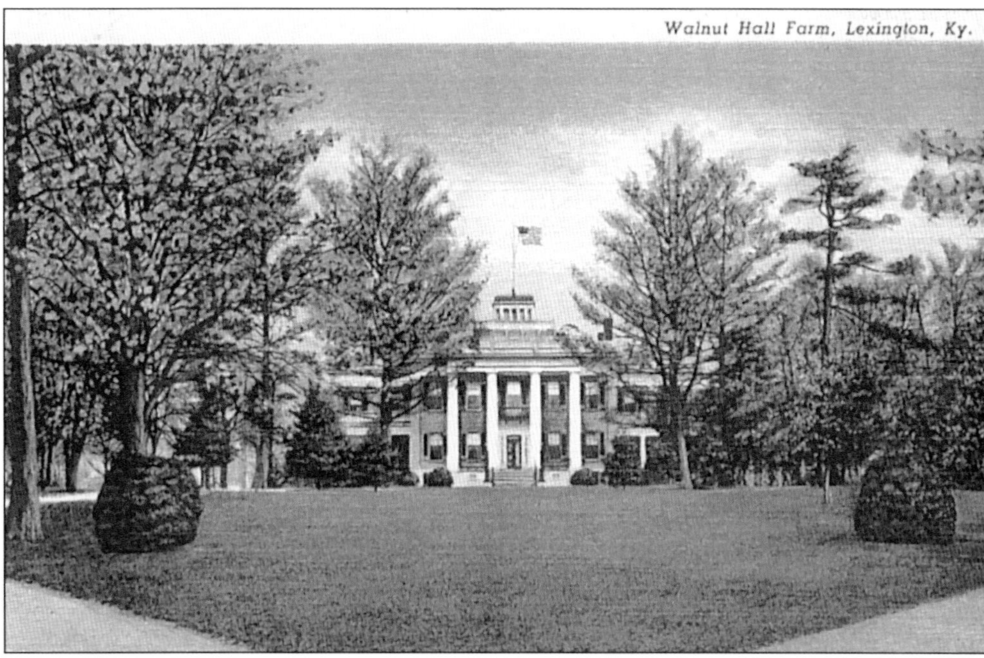

This is another view of Walnut Hill Farm *c.* the 1930s. The farm was established in 1829 by Mr. Harkness, and it was, at one time, the oldest trotting horse farm in continuous operation. There were 11 miles of road, 42 miles of fencing, 15 tenant houses, and 15 barns on the farm.

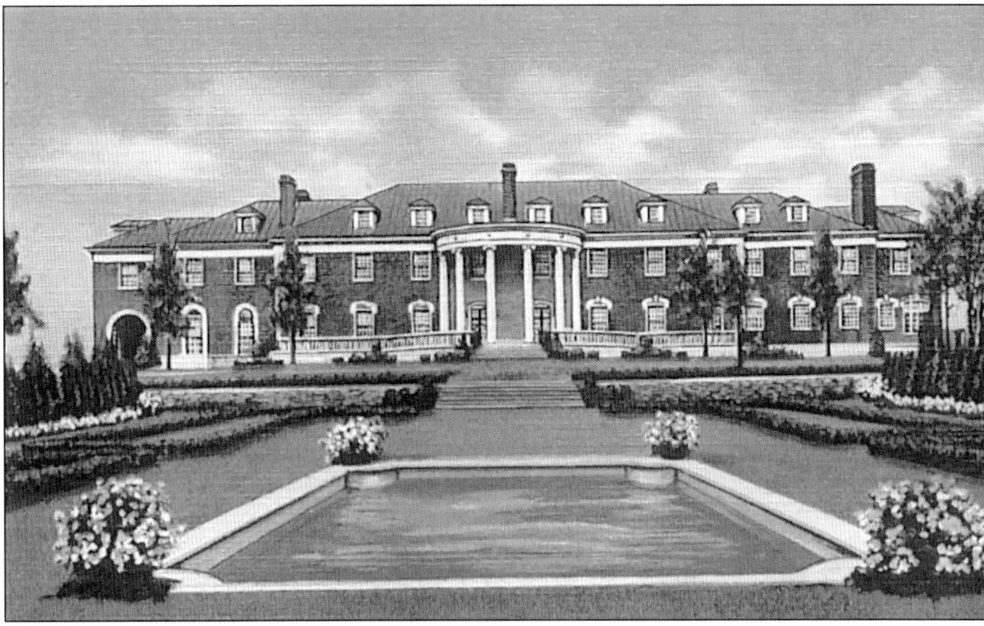

This is a view of the Spindletop Stock Farm. The 800-acre farm was purchased by Mrs. Yount in 1935 as an outstanding saddlebred horse farm. The mansion, Spindletop Hall, was built at a cost of $1 million. The horses won shows all over the county. Mrs. Yount later sold Spindletop to the University of Kentucky.

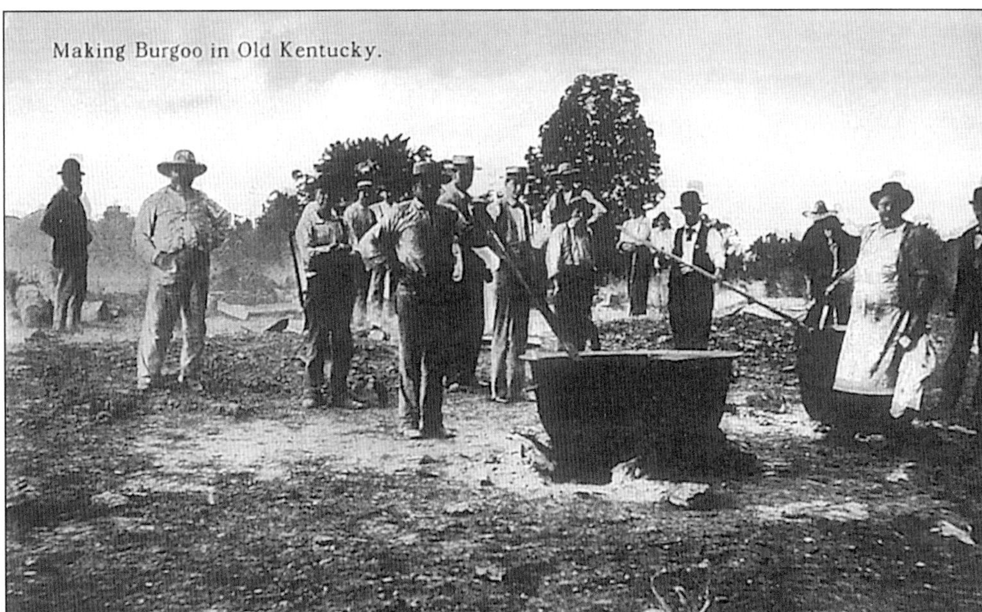

This is a rare postcard of making Burgoo. Burgoo, a concoction of meat, vegetables, seasoning, and sherry wine, has a history of being served to Morgan's men during the Civil War by Gus Jambert, a French cook. The taste continued to be popular in this area. Colonel James T. Looney, born in Lexington in 1879, became known as the "Burgoo King" by serving this Kentucky dish at horse sales, races, and political meetings.

Four

Franklin, Garrard, and Harrison Counties

This chapter will feature old postcards from three Bluegrass counties: Franklin, Garrard, and Harrison. Franklin County, 18th in formation, was established in 1794. A majority of the county flows into the Kentucky River, with tall cliffs and smaller streams such as the Elkhorn, Big and Little Benson, and Flat Creeks affording good sites for gristmills and sawmills. The town of Frankfort, capital of the state, is situated on both sides of the Kentucky River.

Garrard County is the 25th county in order of formation. It was established in 1796 and is situated in the middle of the state on the east side of Dick's (Dix) River, bounded by the Kentucky River and other counties. The county seat, Lancaster, is situated 2 1/2 miles from Dick's (Dix) River.

Harrison County was the 17th county in order of formation. It was established in 1793, and it lies on both sides of the South Licking River. The county seat, Cynthiana, was incorporated in 1802 and is situated on the right bank of the South Linking.

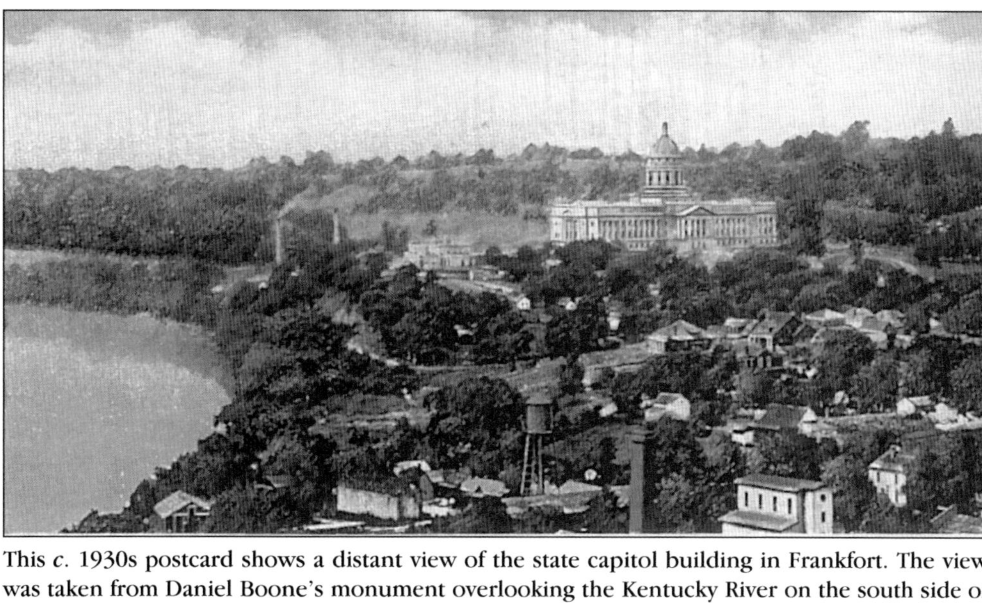

This *c.* 1930s postcard shows a distant view of the state capitol building in Frankfort. The view was taken from Daniel Boone's monument overlooking the Kentucky River on the south side of the downtown district. Frankfort is the seat of Franklin County and Kentucky State Government.

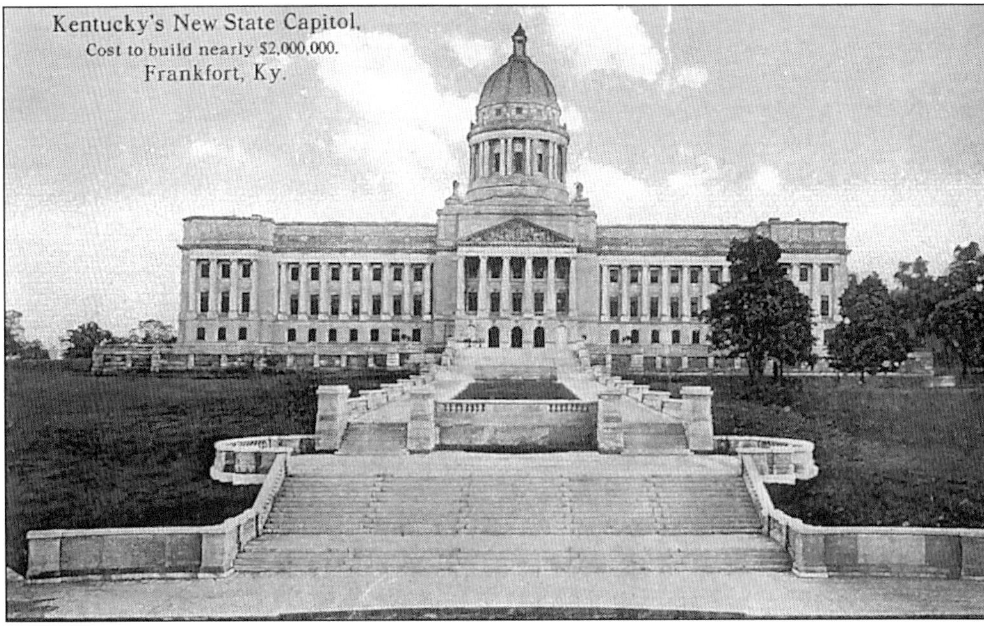

This postcard shows a closer view of the same capitol, completed in 1909. The 1910 session of the general assembly was the first to hold a session there. The cost was nearly $2 million as printed on the postcard.

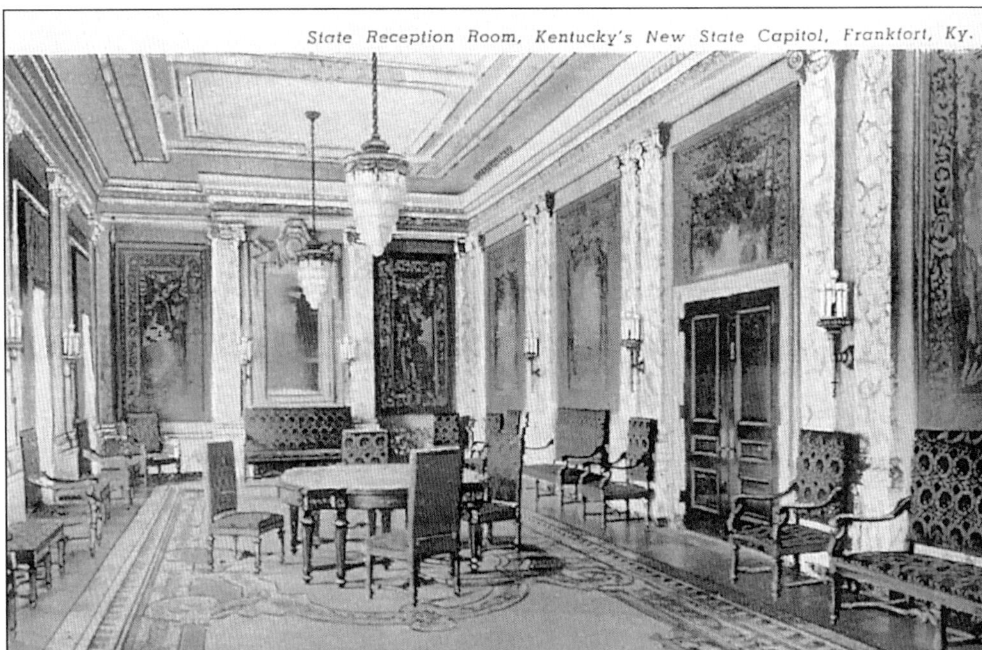

This postcard shows the inside view, published between 1930 and 1945, of the State Reception Room in the Kentucky State Capitol. It was considered the most beautiful room in the building, adjoining the governor's office. The design is originally of Louis XVI, to resemble the reception room of Queen Marie Antionette in the Palace of the Grand Trianon at Versailles, France.

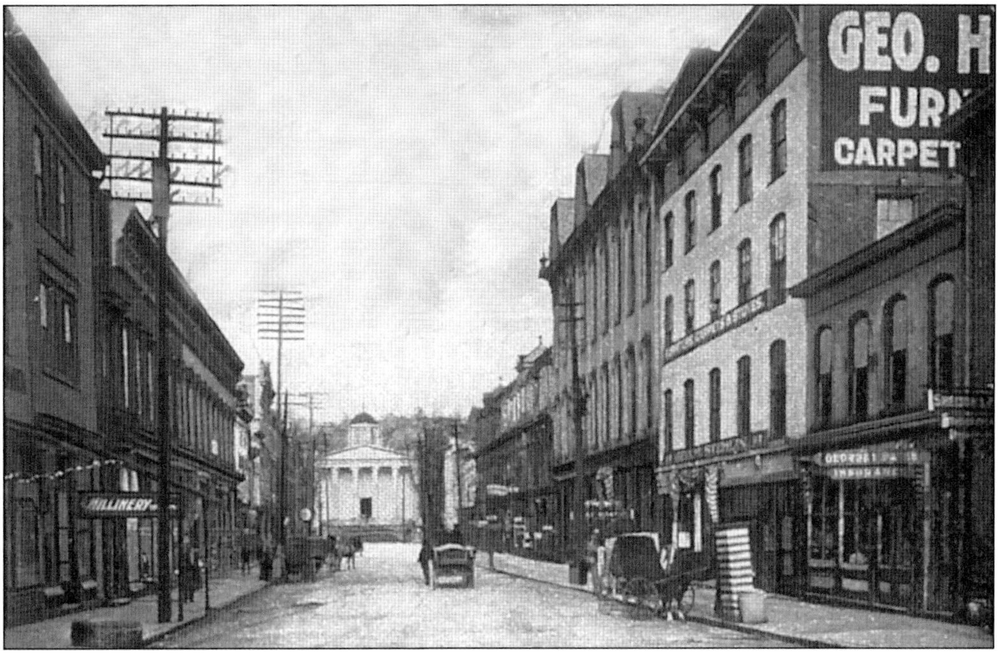

This view shows St. Clair Street between 1907 and 1915 in Frankfort, Kentucky, with the old capitol at the end of St. Clair Street. This was the third permanent capitol of Kentucky, first occupied in December 1829 and continued until the new capitol was built in 1909. It now houses the State Historical Society and other state offices.

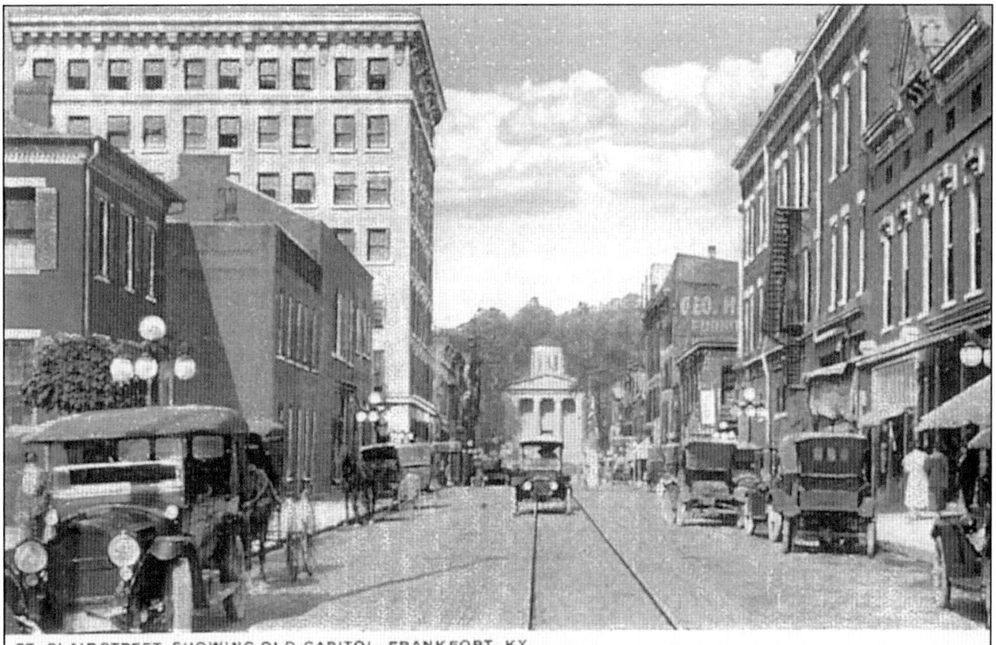

This postcard shows the same view of St. Clair Street between 1915 and 1930. Notice the presence of cars rather than carriages in the street during this time period.

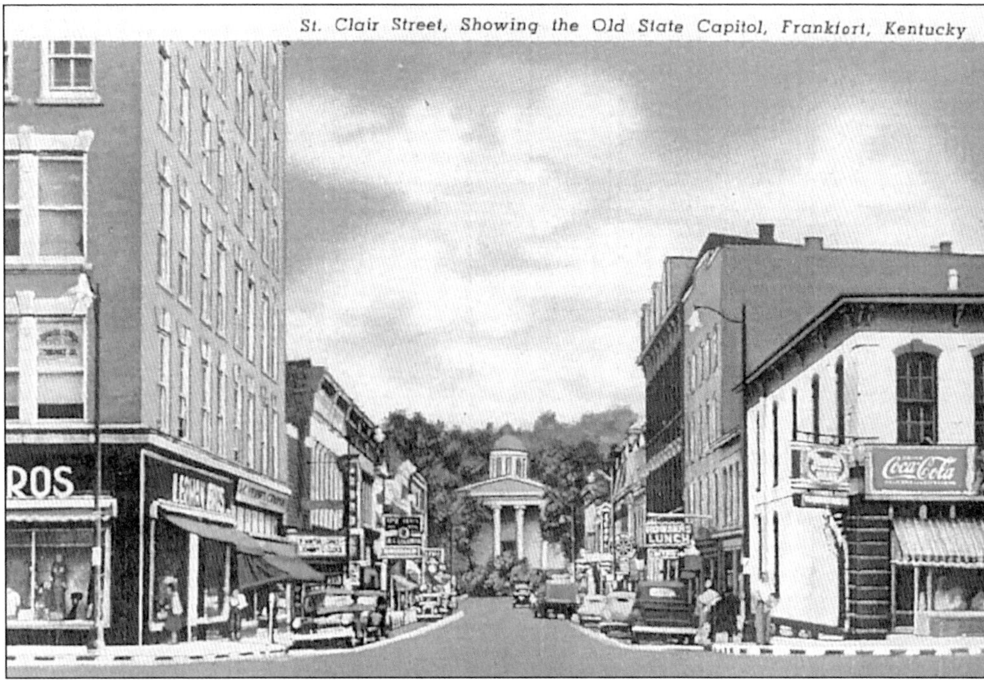

This postcard shows the first block of St. Clair Street between 1930 and 1945. Leaman Brothers Department Store was on the left, and a Furniture Store and Coca-Cola sign were on the right.

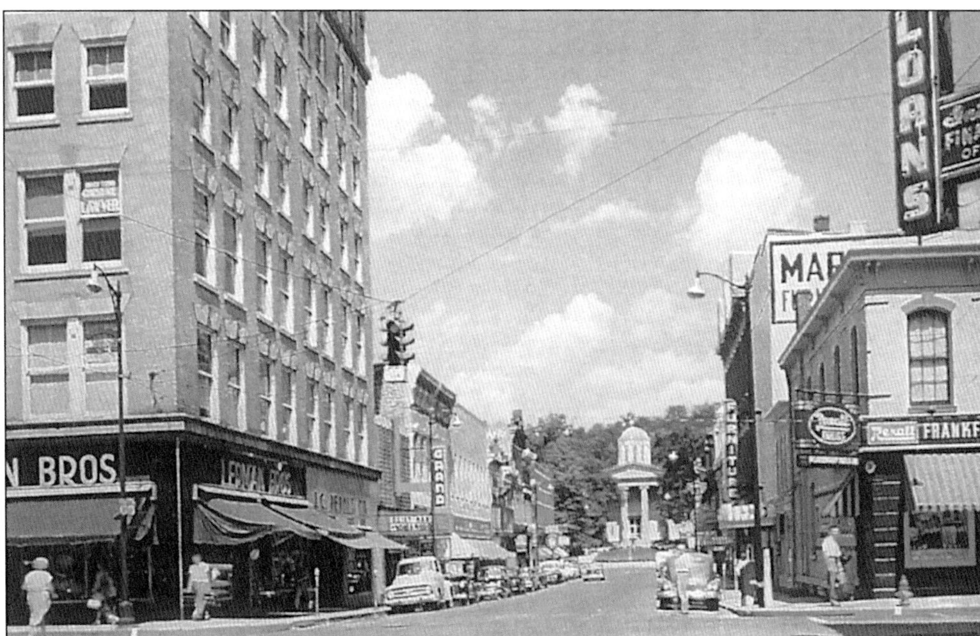

This postcard shows the same view of St. Clair Street around 1950, with Leaman Brothers still on the left and a furniture store on the right. A Rexall sign replaced the cola sign.

This postcard shows the city hall of Frankfort around 1909, with a horse and carriage in the front.

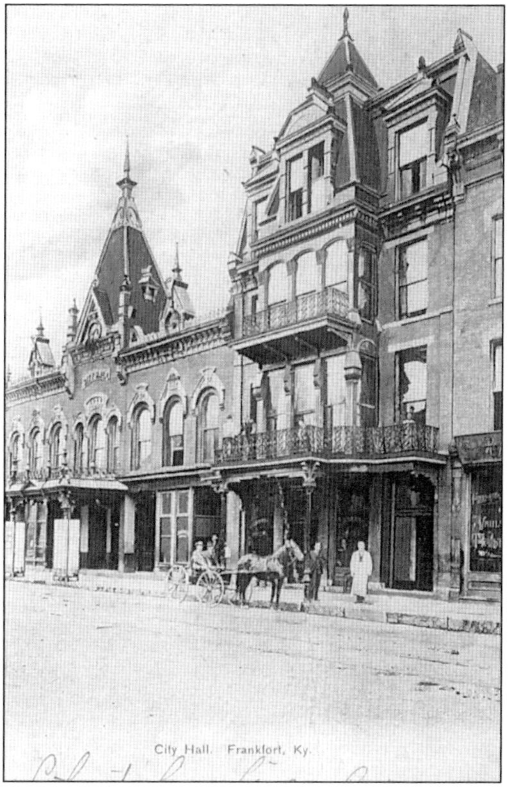

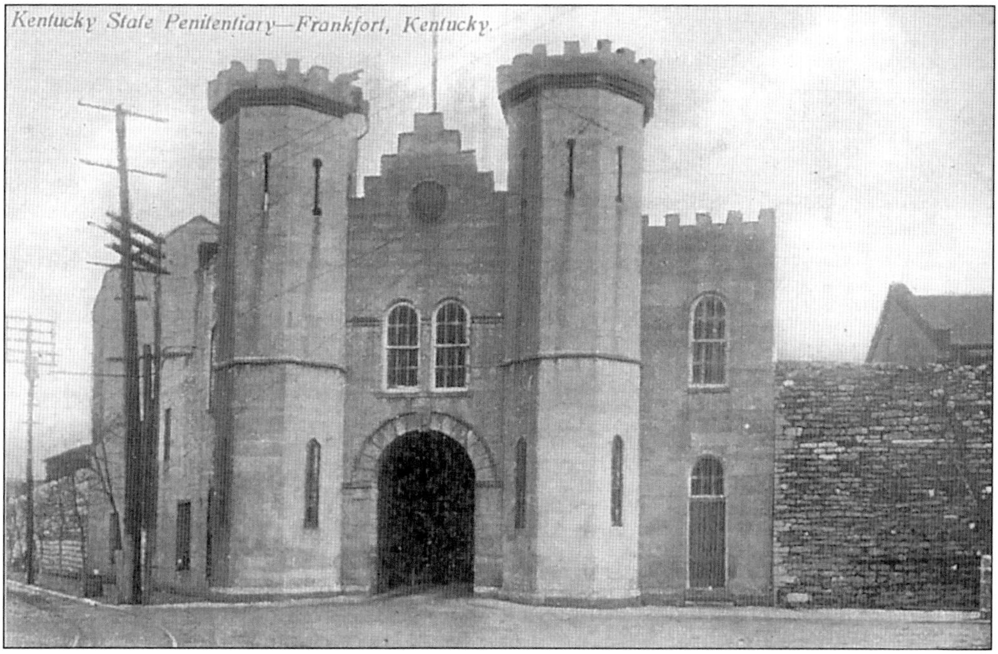

This view, published between 1907 and 1915, shows the Kentucky State Penitentiary, which had been in Frankfort since the beginning of the city. This penitentiary was destroyed in the 1937 flood that swept throughout the city.

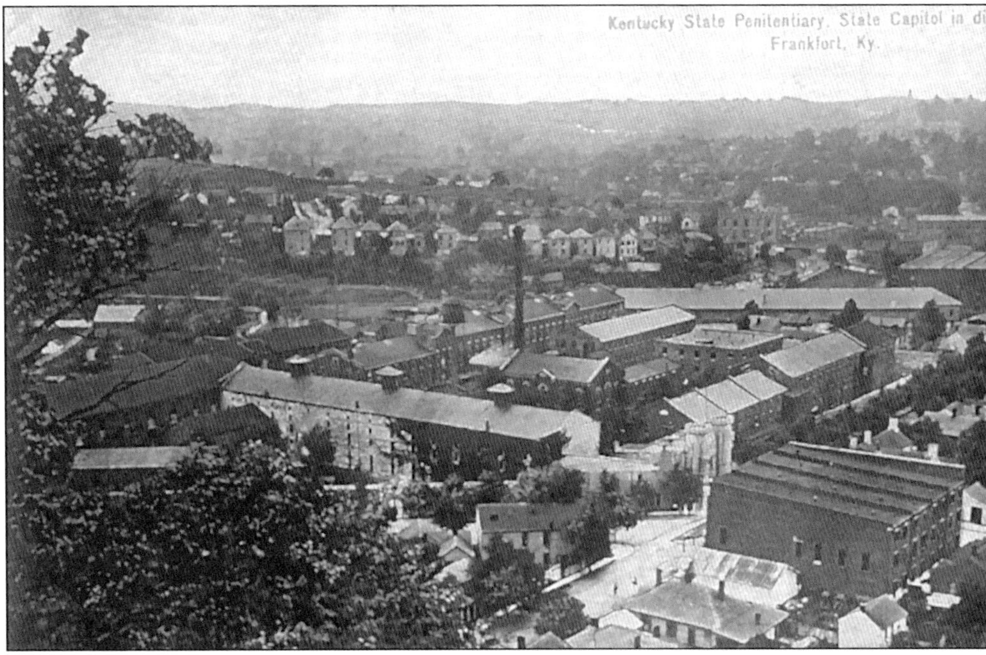

This view is an aerial view of the Kentucky State Penitentiary. When the grounds of this penitentiary were destroyed by flood, the prisoners were moved into surrounding facilities, and another penitentiary was created in a different part of the state.

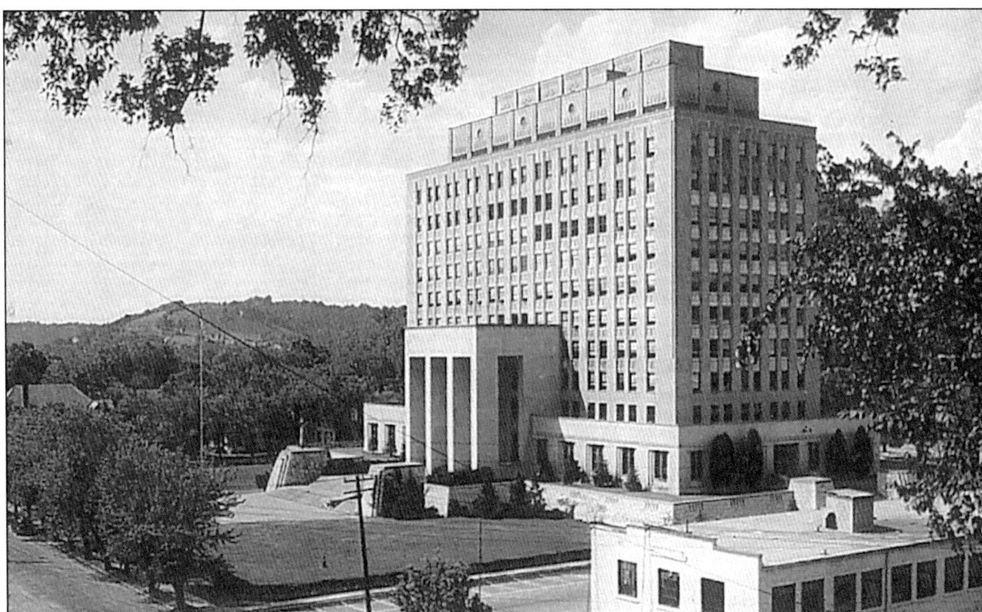

This State Office Building was erected in 1941 on the site of the old penitentiary and was 12 stories high. The building on the right was the old broom shop, the one remaining building of the penitentiary. It was occupied for many years by state employees until torn down. This author remembers the early Department of Mental Health offices occupying that broom shop at the beginning of her 31 years of employment in Kentucky.

This postcard shows the Franklin County Court House, which was completed in 1835. It is the second and current courthouse. It has gone through several renovations and is listed in the National Register of Historic Places.

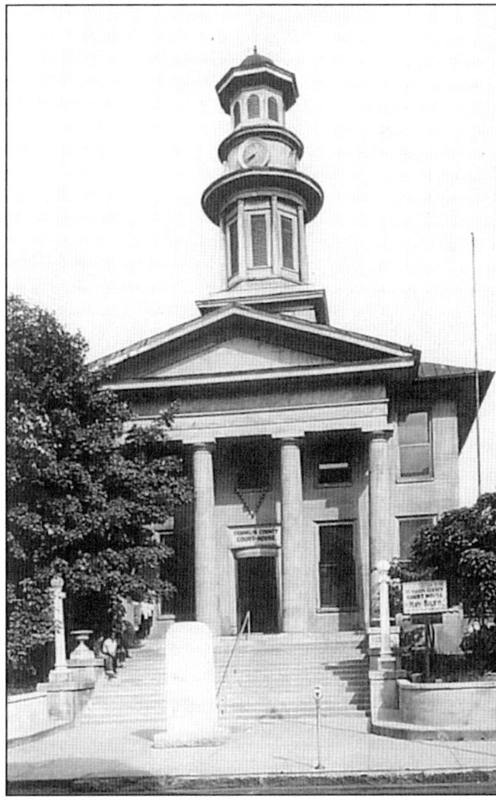

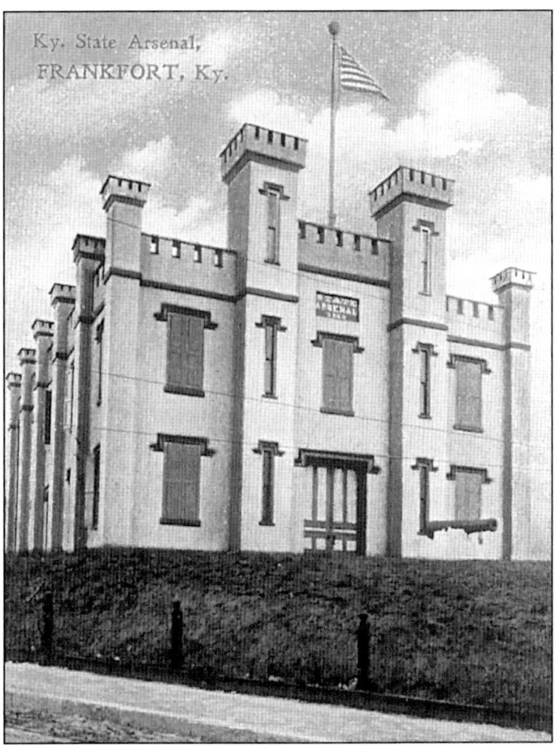

This postcard shows the Kentucky State Arsenal in Frankfort. Handwriting on the back states, "Built in 1850. The L & N Railroad runs under it. A cannon from the Spanish War is on the lawn." It is now a history museum that displays the Kentucky Historical Society's collection of weapons and uniforms.

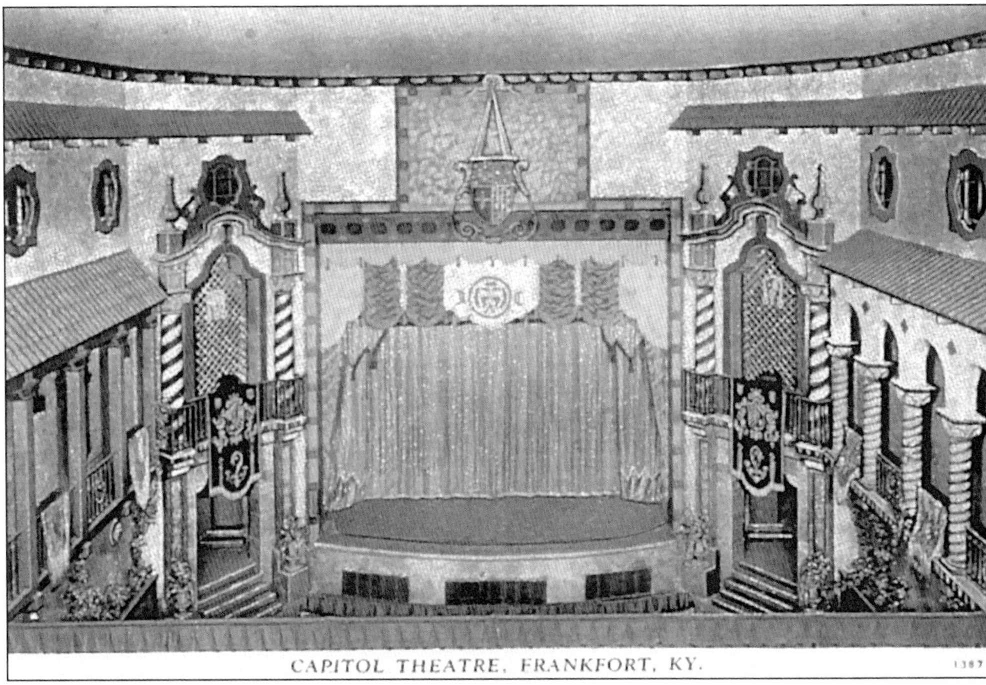

This view shows an inside view of the Capitol Theater in Frankfort, around 1920. This postcard was included because of the rarity of such a view.

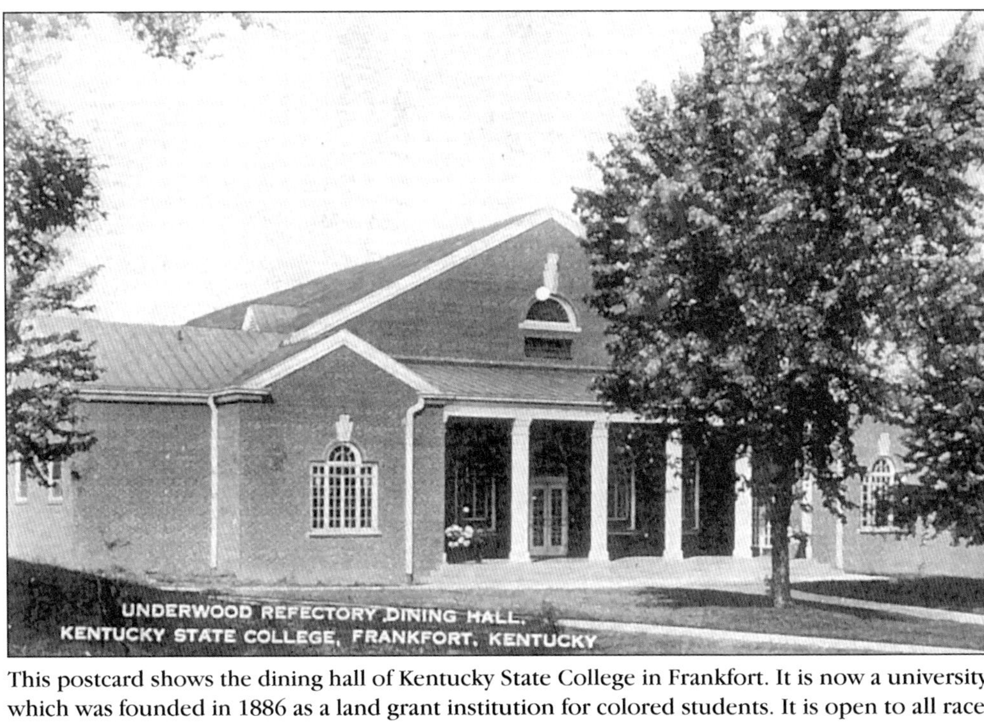

This postcard shows the dining hall of Kentucky State College in Frankfort. It is now a university, which was founded in 1886 as a land grant institution for colored students. It is open to all races to help resolve agricultural and social difficulties. It enrolls 2,500 students and has a 300-acre campus with 166 acres as a research farm.

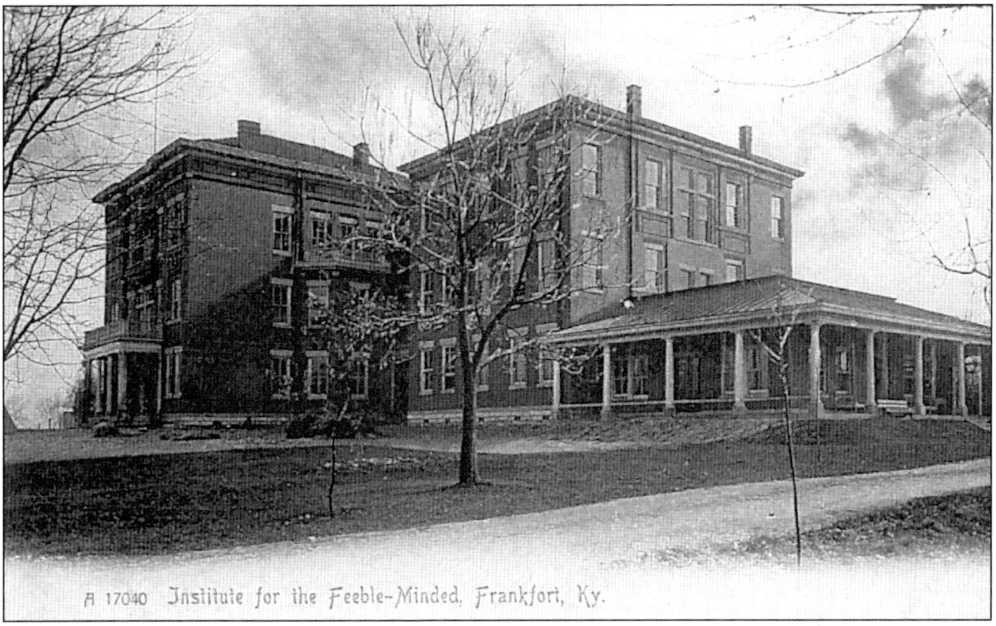

This postcard, published between 1901 and 1907, shows the Institute for the Feeble-Minded in Frankfort. It was the primary state-supported facility for the mentally retarded until the late 1900s. Facilities for the mentally retarded were moved to other areas of the state, and this has since been torn down. Several state office buildings have been built on the grounds.

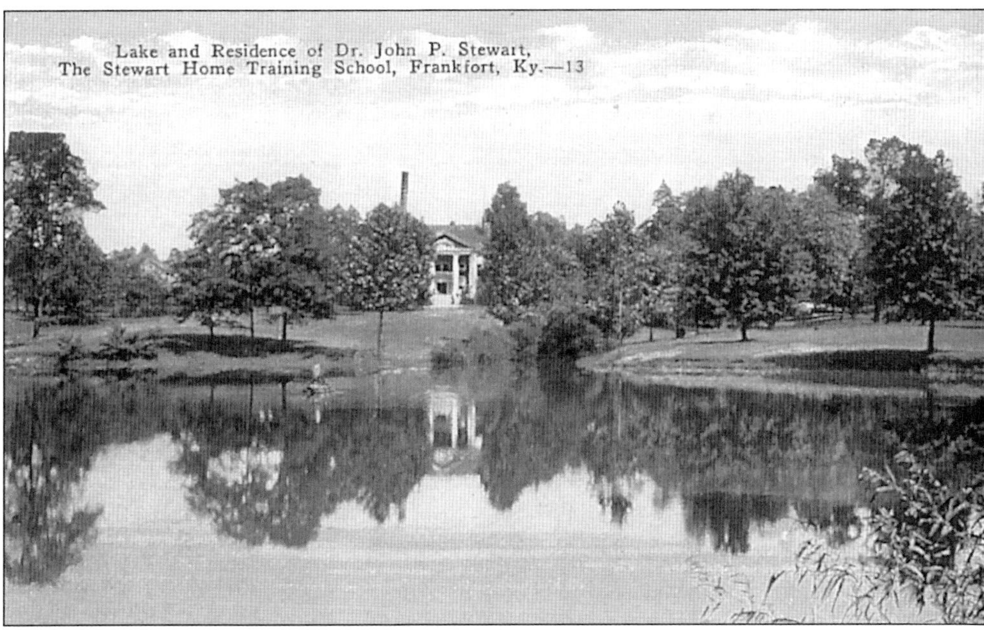

This postcard, published between 1915 and 1930, shows the residence of Dr. John P. Stewart and the Stewart Home Training School in Frankfort. This was a private facility for the mentally retarded during that same time period.

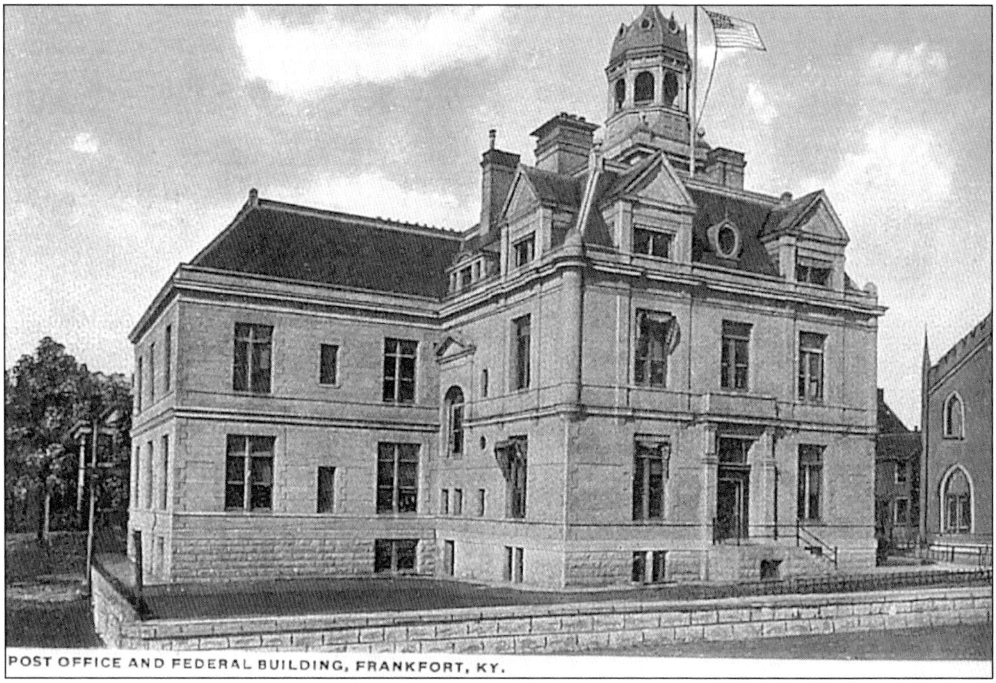

This *c.* 1920s view shows the U.S. Post Office and federal building. This same building can be seen with the bridge view and was called the Custom House at an earlier time.

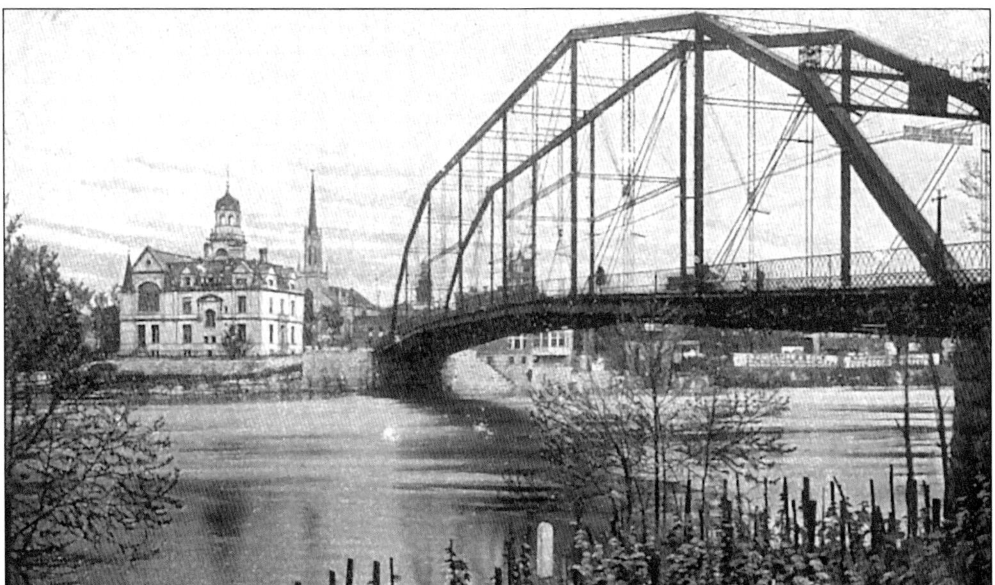

This view shows the State Bridge and Custom House in Frankfort and was published between 1907 and 1915. Notice the old bridge that has been a part of Frankfort for many years.

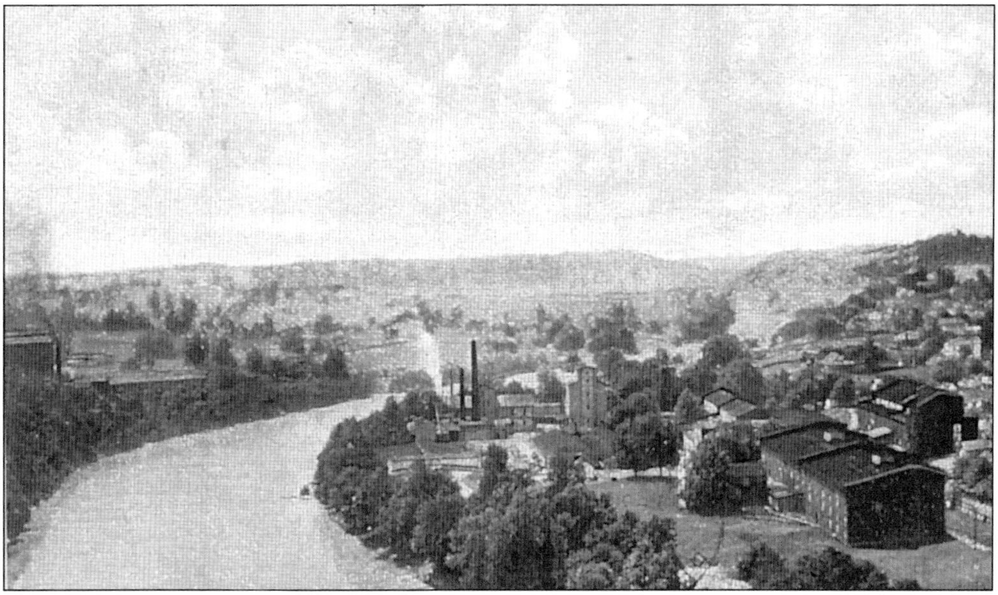

This is a bird's-eye view looking down the river into Frankfort. This postcard was mailed in 1907 with the handwritten message, "Compliments of Mr.and Mrs. Jefferson Cox."

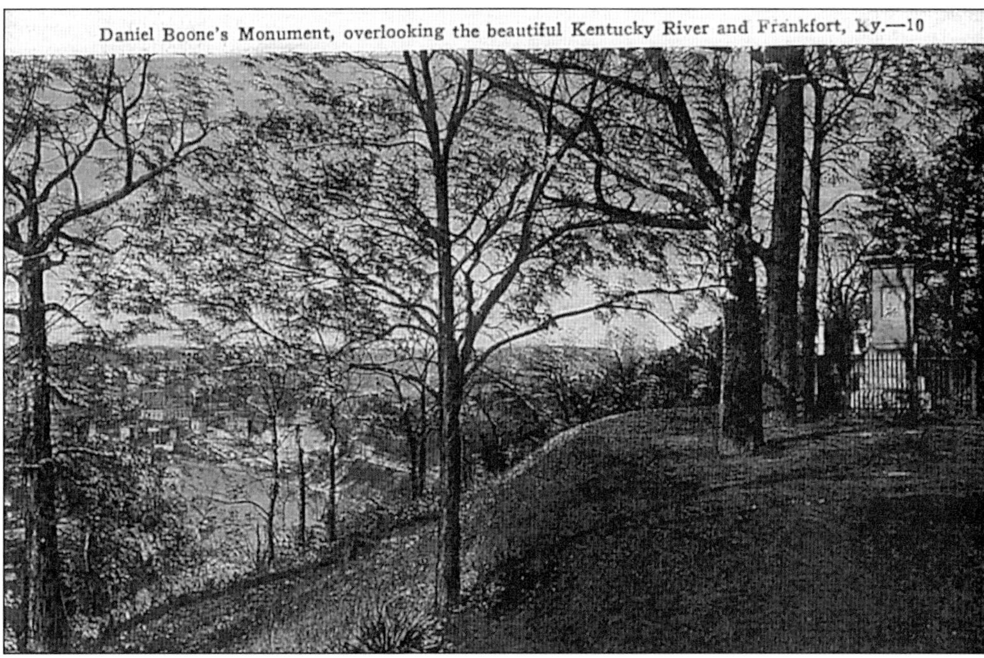

This postcard shows Daniel Boone's Monument overlooking the Kentucky River. This is where the first view of Frankfort was taken from on page 59 showing the spectacular scenery around Frankfort. While there is still some debate as to whether Daniel Boone was actually buried here, his grave is marked in the old Frankfort cemetery where many famous Kentuckians are buried. The cemetery was made a state shrine by the Kentucky legislature in 1844.

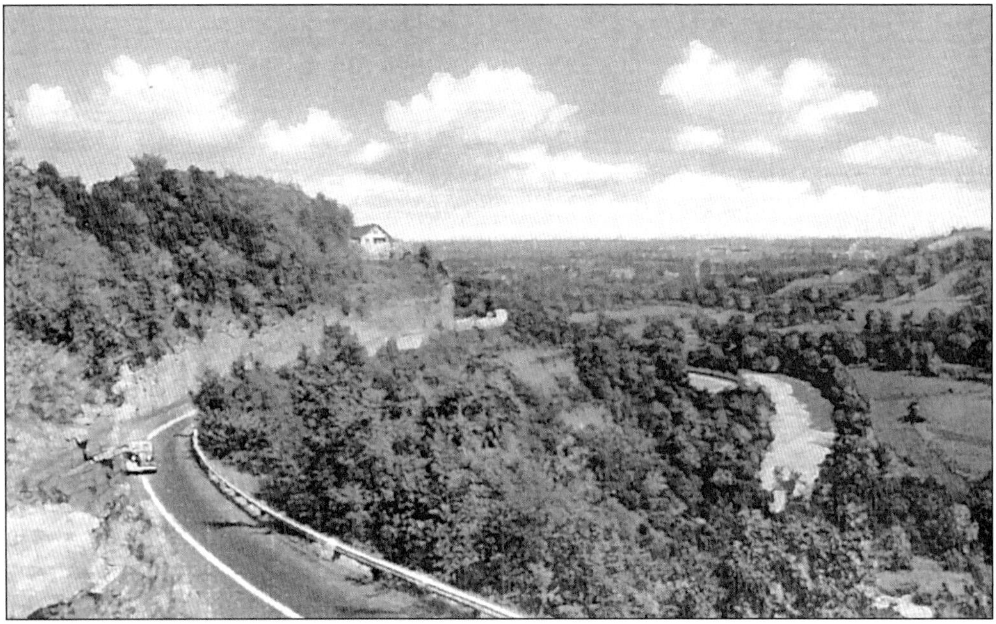

This postcard shows the scenic drive through Benson Valley, with Frankfort in the distance. This view was published between 1930 and 1945 and probably shows old U.S. 37.

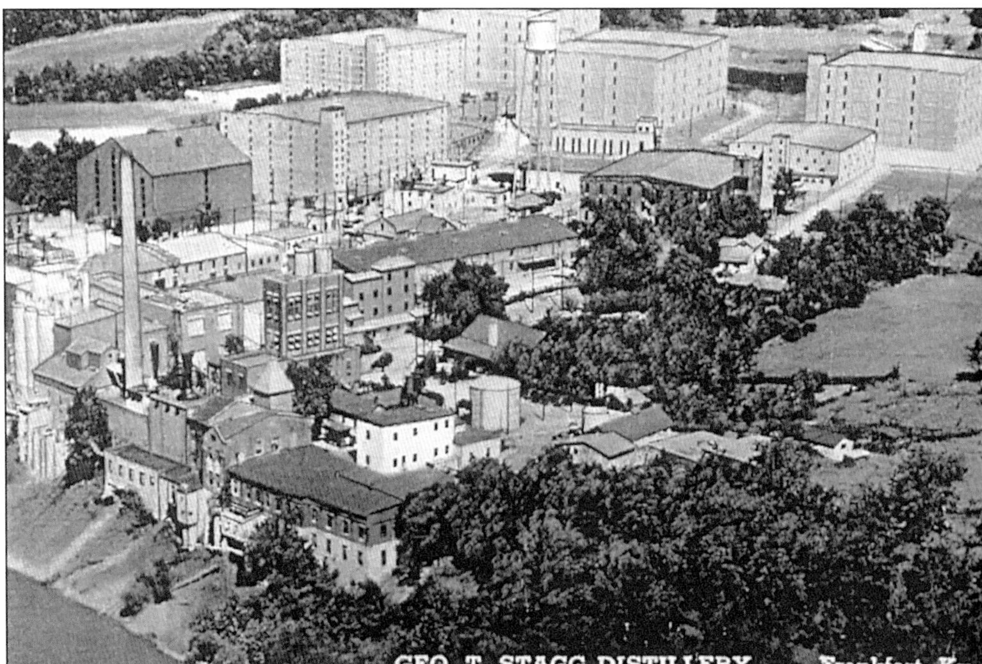

This postcard shows an aerial view of the George T. Stagg Company, the home of Bourbon Whiskey, founded in 1869. Kentucky is famous for its many distillers, with a claim that the hard limestone water imparts a flavor that only water in the Bluegrass can give.

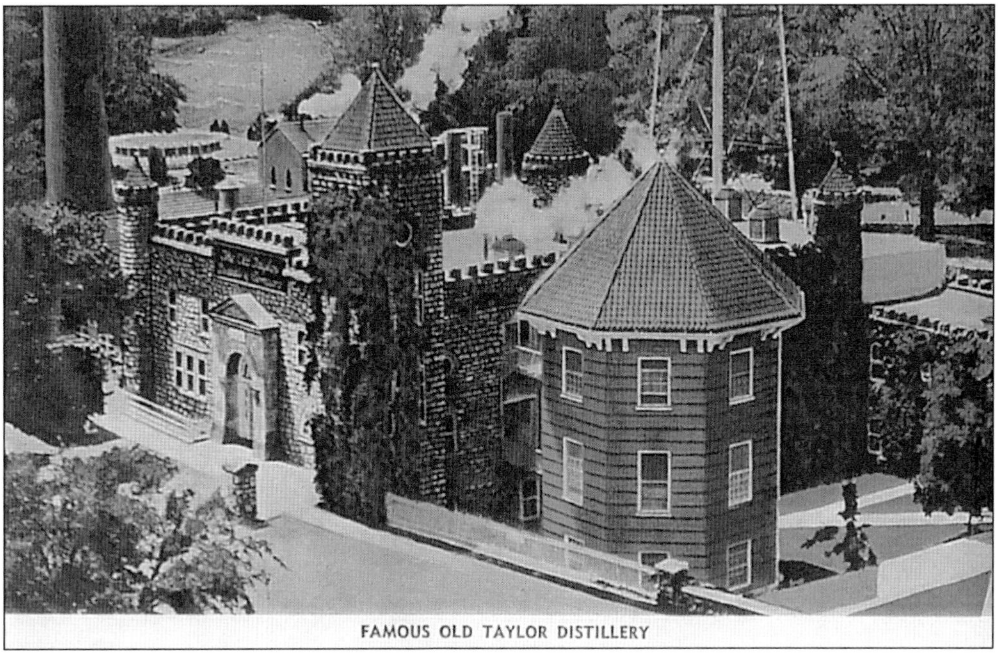

Old Taylor, bottled as Bond Kentucky Bourbon Whiskey, gets its name from Colonel Edmund H. Taylor Jr., who in his day was the nation's leading distiller. The distillery itself, on the outskirts of Frankfort, was founded just after the Civil War.

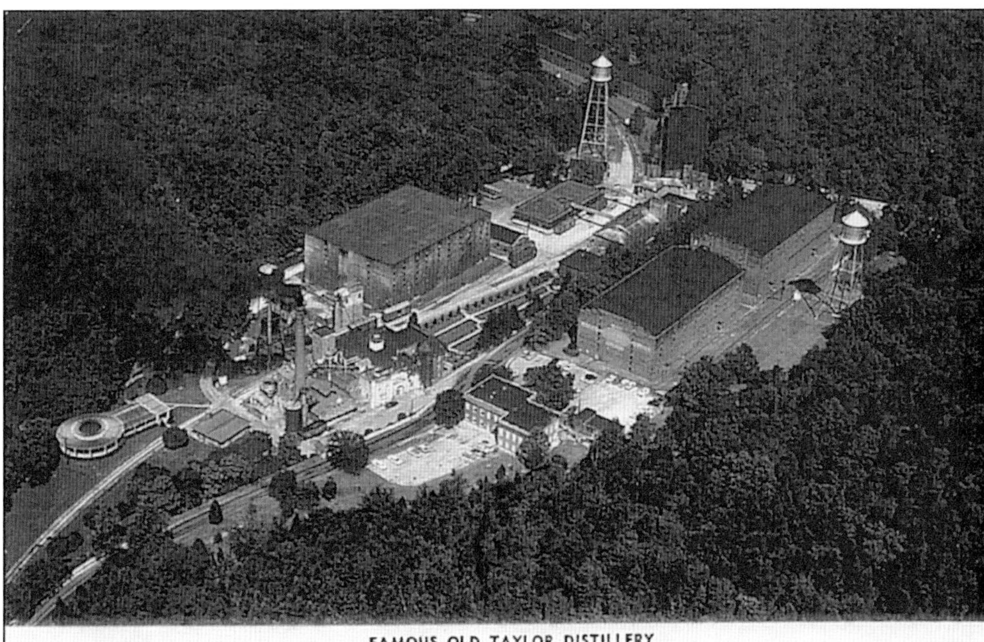

A more distant view of the Old Taylor Distillery can be seen in this postcard. The first of the present buildings was built in 1887. Visitors from every land come to see this turreted home of one of the world's greatest whiskeys.

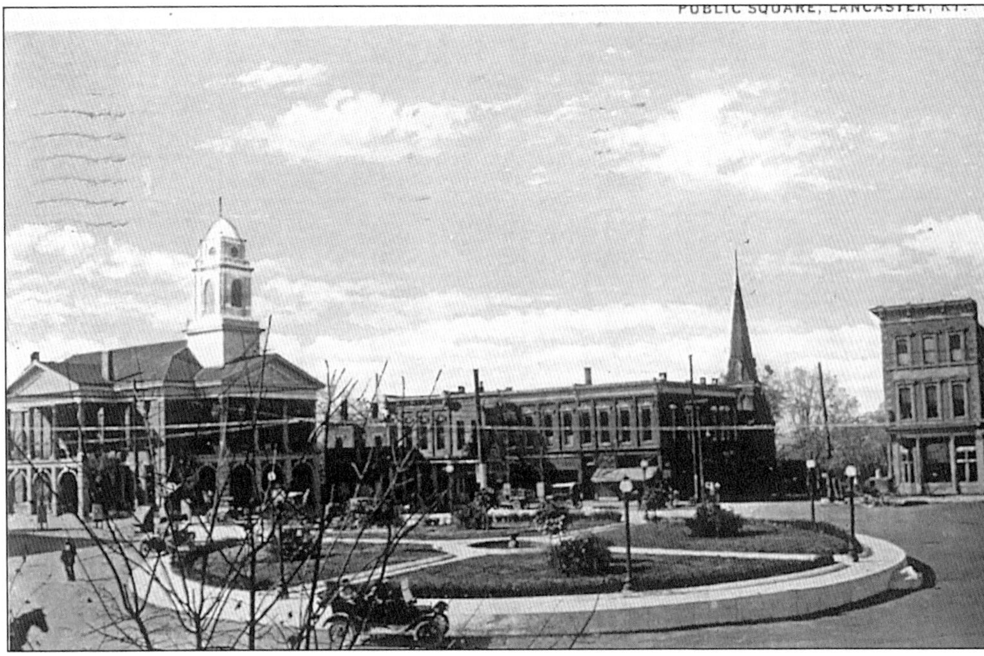

The next six old postcards will focus on Garrard County, starting with this one of Lancaster and the public square around the 1930s. This is the third and current county courthouse, having been built in 1868. The original cupola was an observation tower used for geological survey but has been replaced in this postcard.

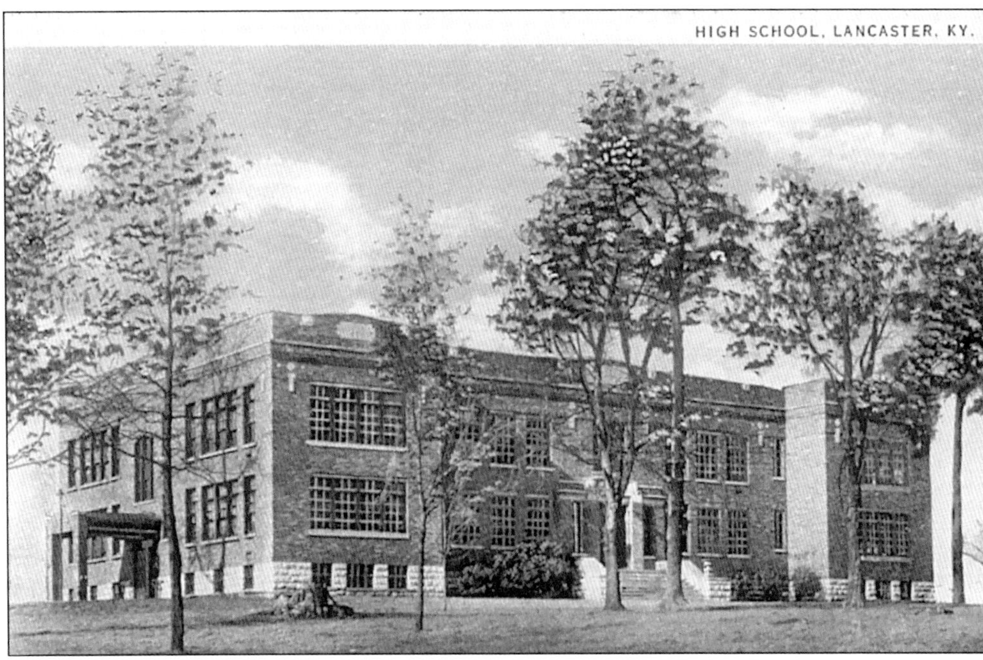

This postcard shows the high school in Lancaster *c.* 1915. The cupola of the courthouse was replaced with yellow brick left over from the construction of this Lancaster High School from 1914 to 1918.

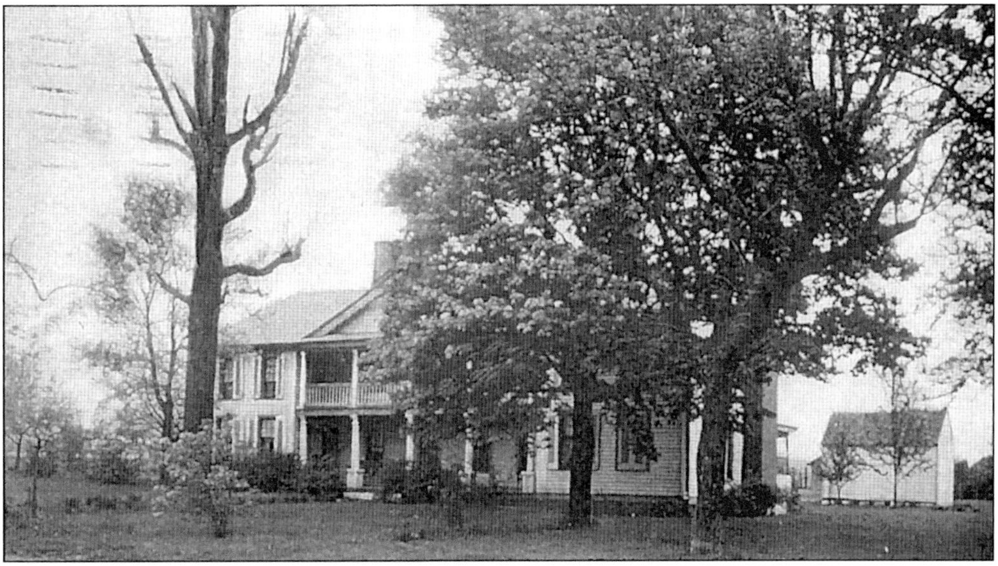

This is a 1945 view of Camp Dick Robinson on U.S. Highway 27, near Lancaster. Camp Dick Robinson was the federal recruiting station south of the Ohio River during the Civil War. This picture shows General William Nelson's headquarters. Twelfth Kentucky was organized here in 1861, and Granville Hacker, as part of the 12th Kentucky, was wounded here. He gained a pension of $4 a month for his injuries in 1889, and his widow collected his pension until her death in 1927, when the pension had increased to $30 a month.

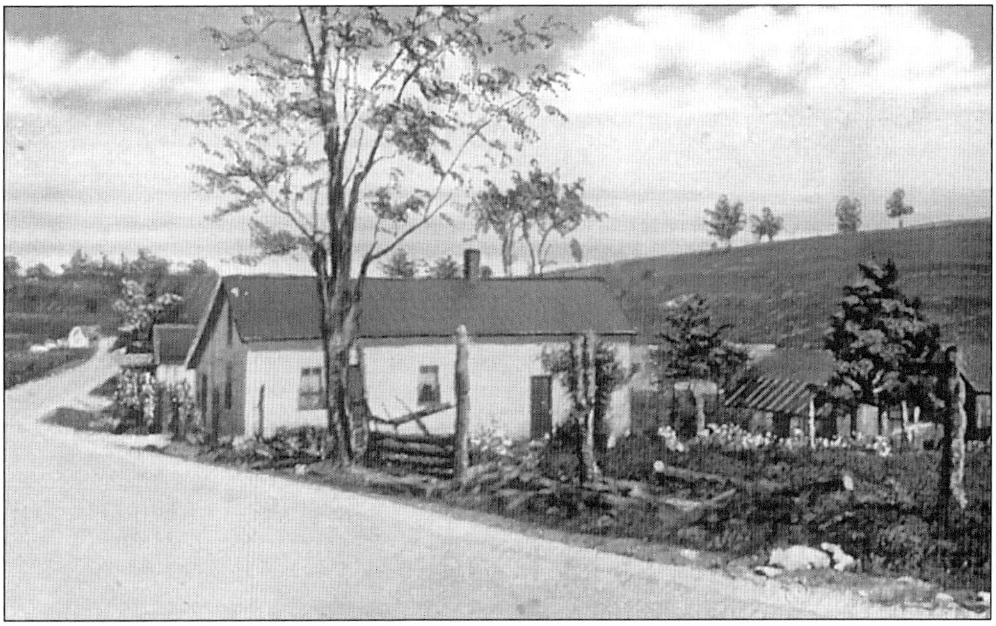

This postcard shows the birthplace of Bradley Kincaid, a famous old mountain ballad singer and pioneer radio entertainer. Bradley Kincaid was a native of Garrard County and put songs that had been handed down to him by word of mouth, into book form. He was born July 21, 1895, and died September 23, 1989. The house was near a village of Point Leavell, "in old Kentucky."

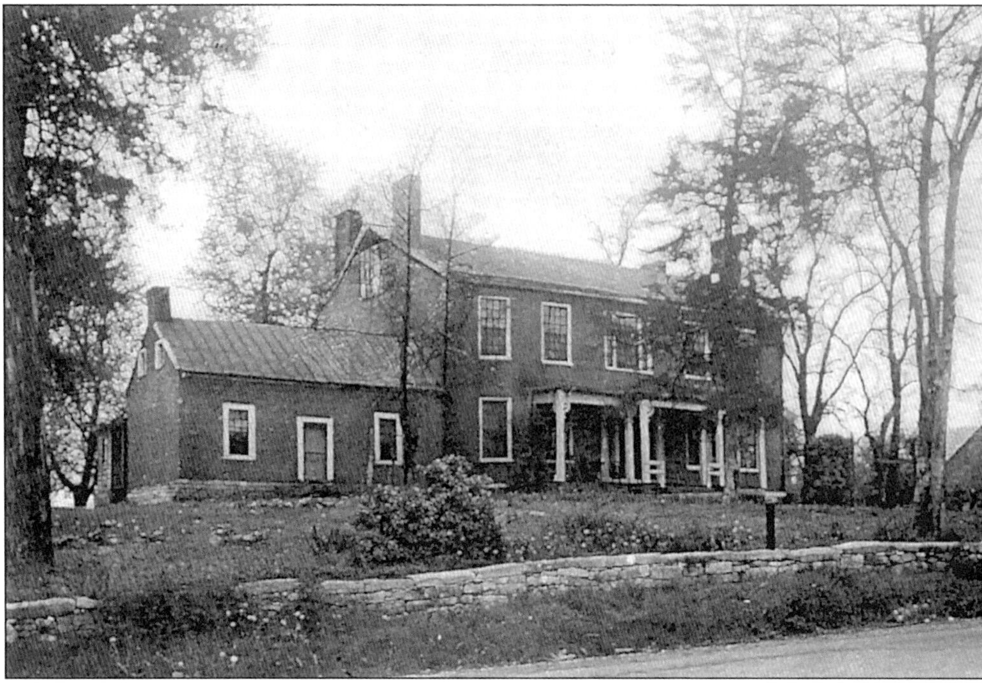

This postcard view, *c.* 1910, shows the Old Burnt Tavern on U S Highway 27, in Bryantsville. The left wing is more than 100 years old and was part of a stagecoach tavern on an older road from Nashville, Tennessee, to Zaneville, Ohio.

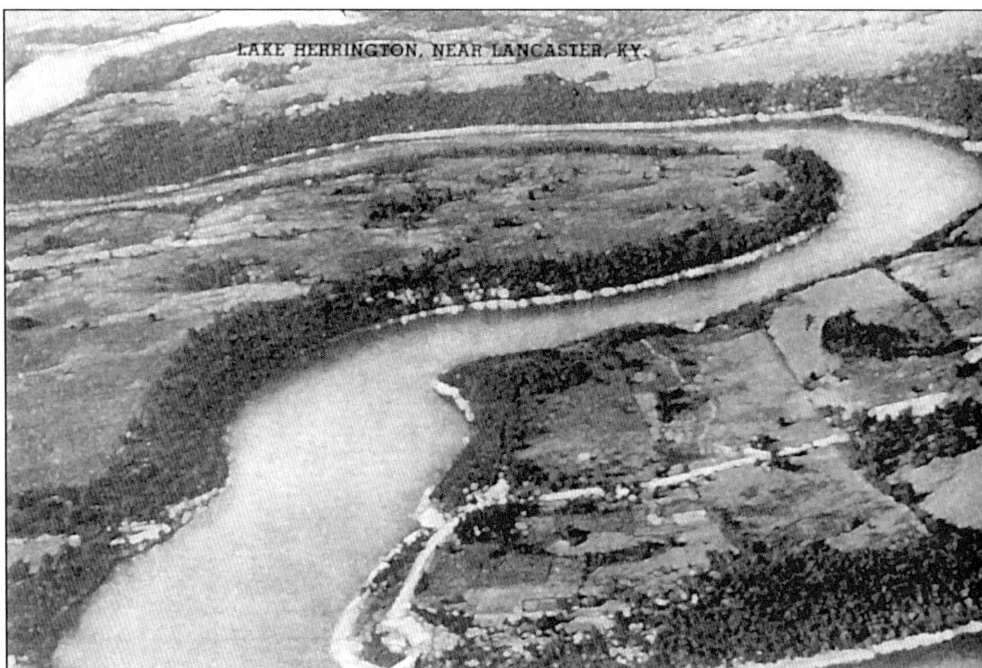

This panorama view, from *c.* 1910, shows 3 miles of Herrington Lake near Lancaster. The lower arrow points to the Kennedy Bridge.

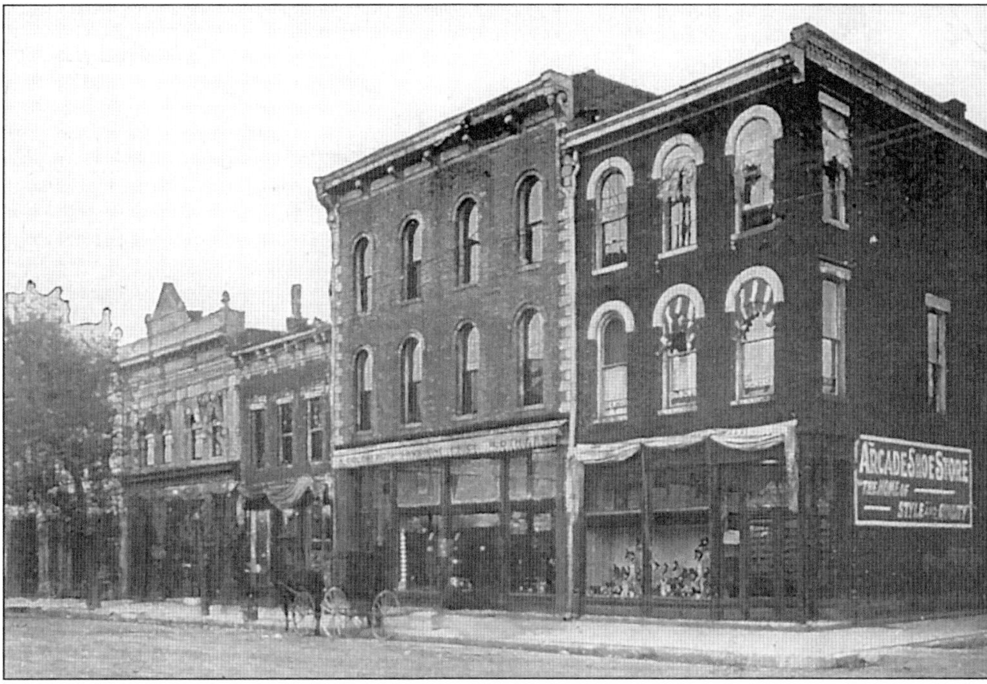

The next four old postcards will show views of Harrison County and the town of Cynthiana. This one shows main street looking north of Cynthiana, *c.* 1912. An Arcade Shoe Store is identified on the corner as "the home of style and quality." A dentist, Dr. Boyd, is listed above, in the front three windows. The next building has on its front, "A. Coldberg & Sons, One price clothiers."

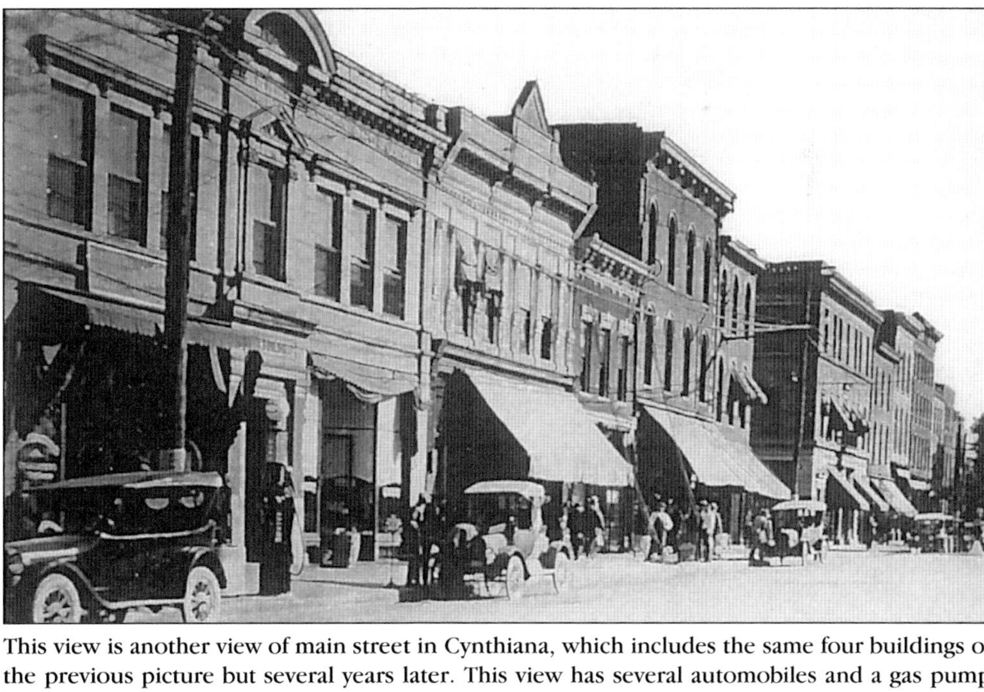

This view is another view of main street in Cynthiana, which includes the same four buildings of the previous picture but several years later. This view has several automobiles and a gas pump between two cars.

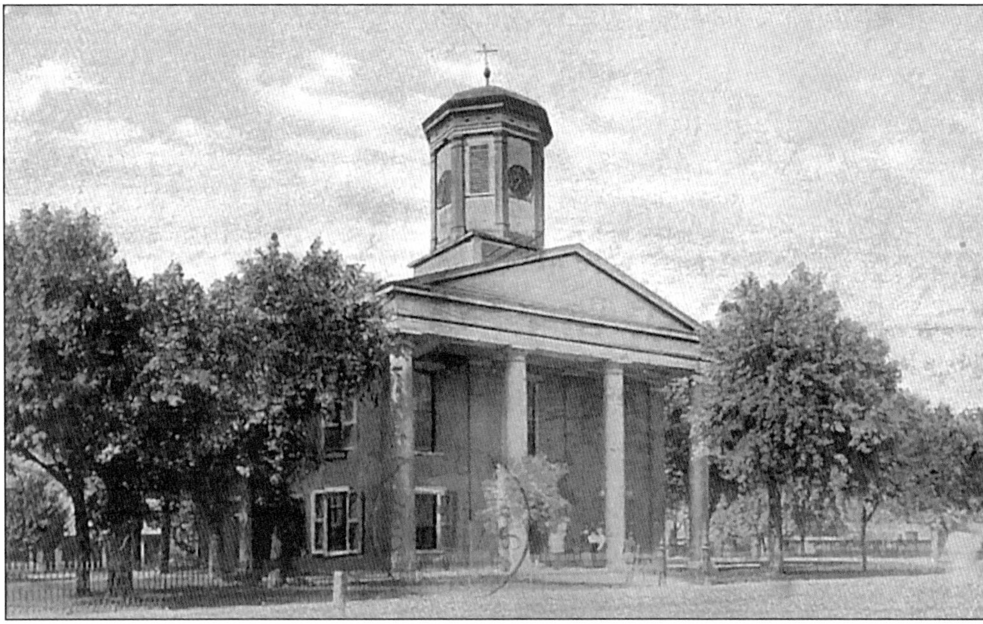

This is a *c*. 1910 view of the Harrison County Courthouse in Cynthiana. It is the third and present Harrison County Courthouse, which was finished in 1853. There have been many nationally known figures to try cases here, one of which was Henry Clay.

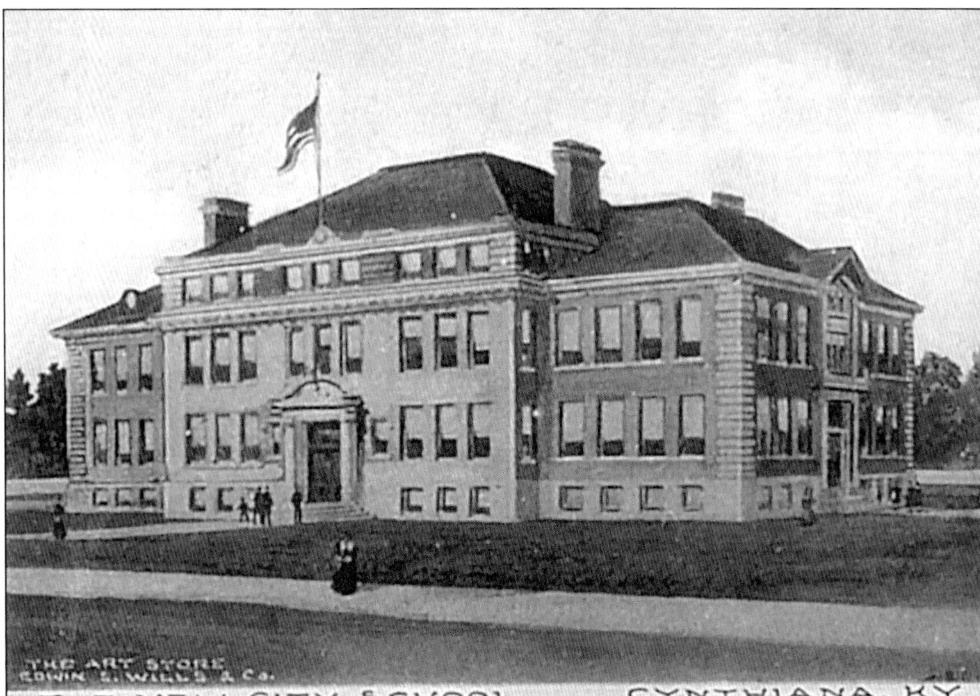

This view, with a postmark of 1911, is of the New City School in Cynthiana. Since the first U.S. Post Office in Cynthiana was established in 1801, Cynthiana must have had earlier schools but this one was captured on a postcard.

Five

Jessamine County

This whole chapter will center around Jessamine County, the 36th county erected in Kentucky, formed in 1798. The Kentucky River forms its southeast, southern, and southwest side. Nicholasville, the county seat, was established in 1812 as the terminus of the Kentucky Central Railroad, while another town, Wilmore, was established by the railroad in 1876 and became incorporated in 1918. Camp Nelson, a few miles south of Nicholasville, became a point of concentration for Union forces during the Civil War and is now a U.S. military cemetery where thousands of solders were buried after the Civil War.

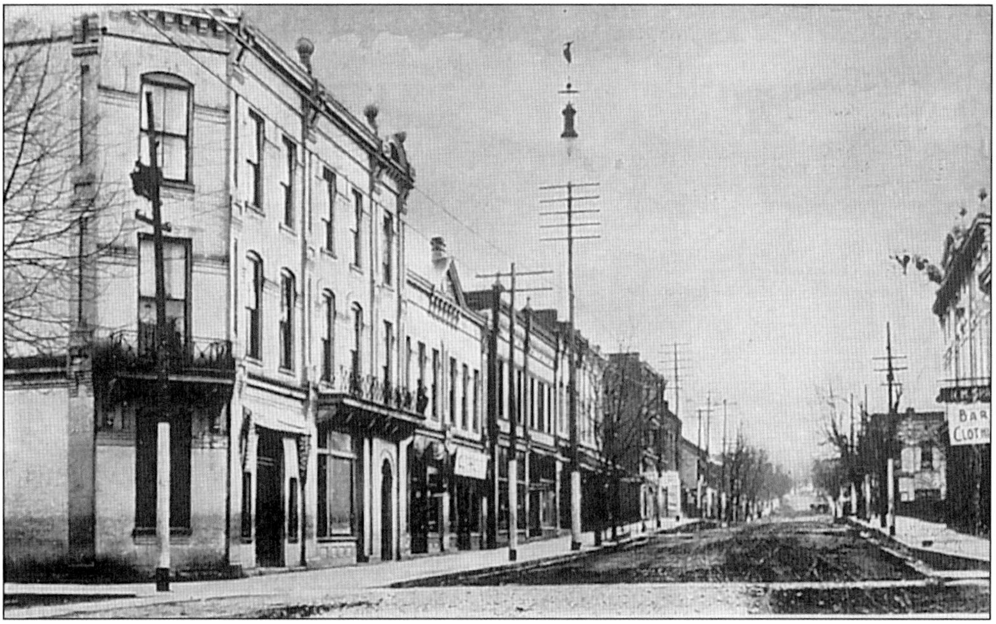

This view, probably around the 1920s, shows main street in Nicholasville looking south. On the right is the R.M. Sparks Bargain Clothing, and a stoplight in the center of the street.

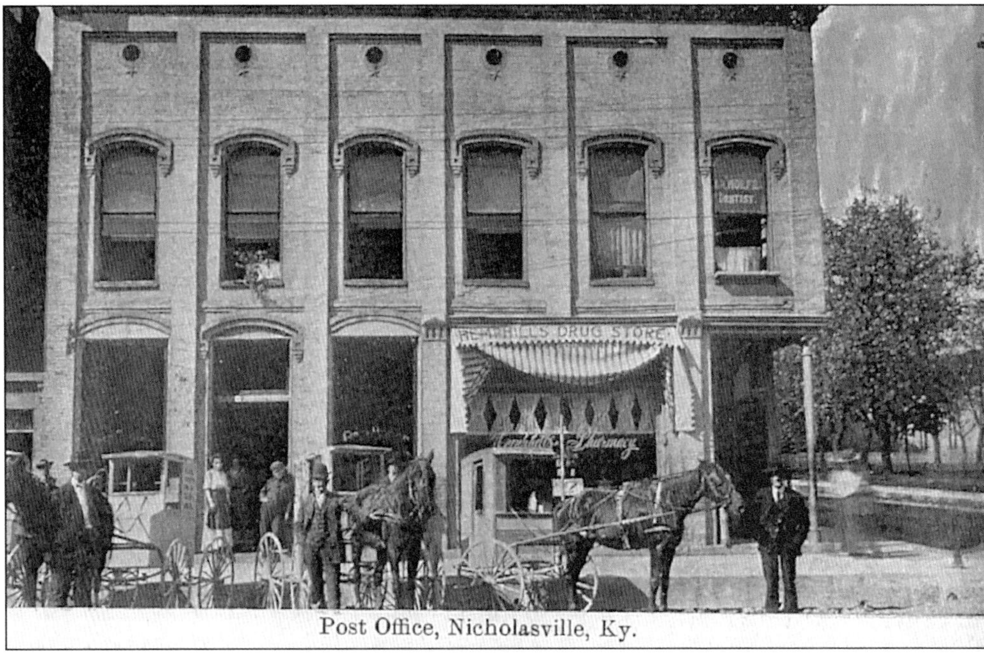

This postcard, postmarked 1909, shows the post office in Nicholasville. The three horses and carriages must be delivery carriages for mail. This card was sent to Lexington saying, "Will be in Lexington tomorrow night to attend opera at auditorium." On the corner can be seen "Hemphill's Drug Store," and the top right window has "Dr. Wolfe, Dentist."

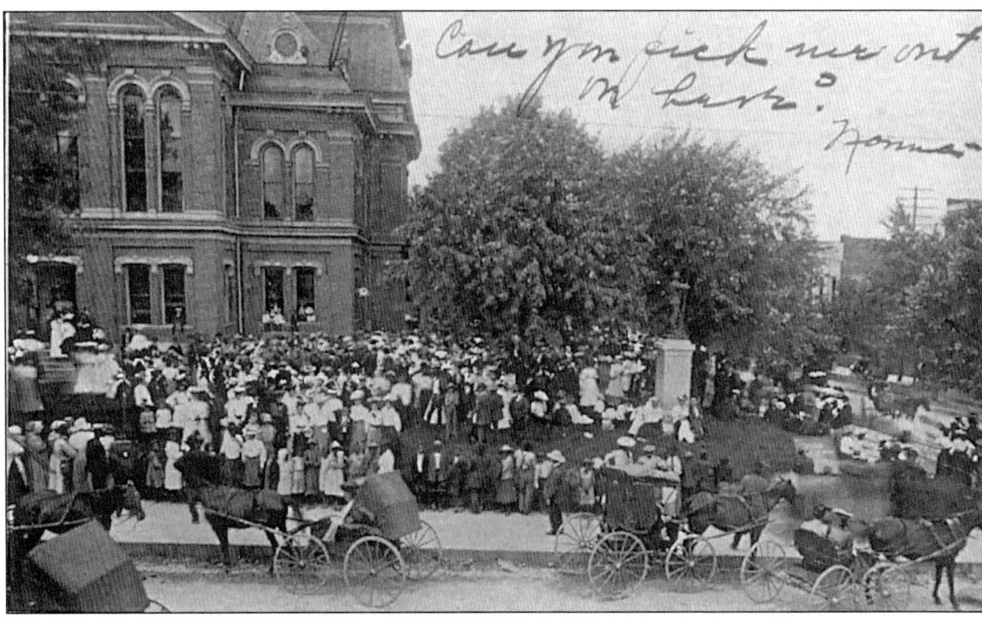

This postcard shows the courthouse in Nicholasville for a homecoming on June 20, 1906. The homecoming could have been a celebration of the first meeting of city trustees that started on June 19, 1824. This is the second courthouse in Nicholasville, being built in 1878.

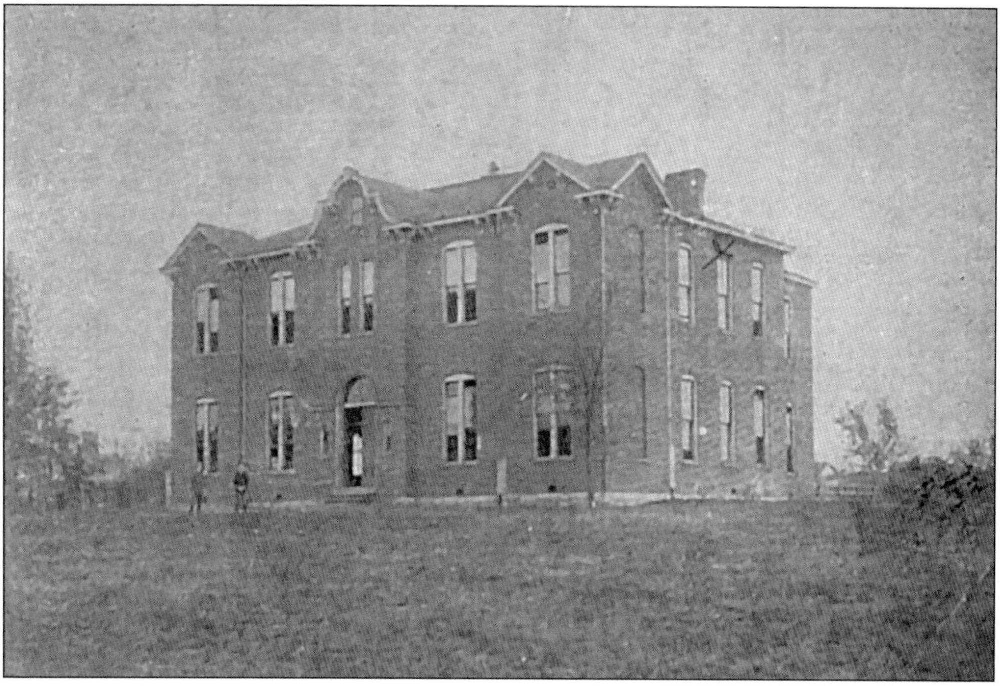

This postcard view, postmarked on September 5, 1908, was sent to England from Nicholasville. It shows the high school in that town and had a handwritten message reading, "Hetta teaches here, School begin Monday."

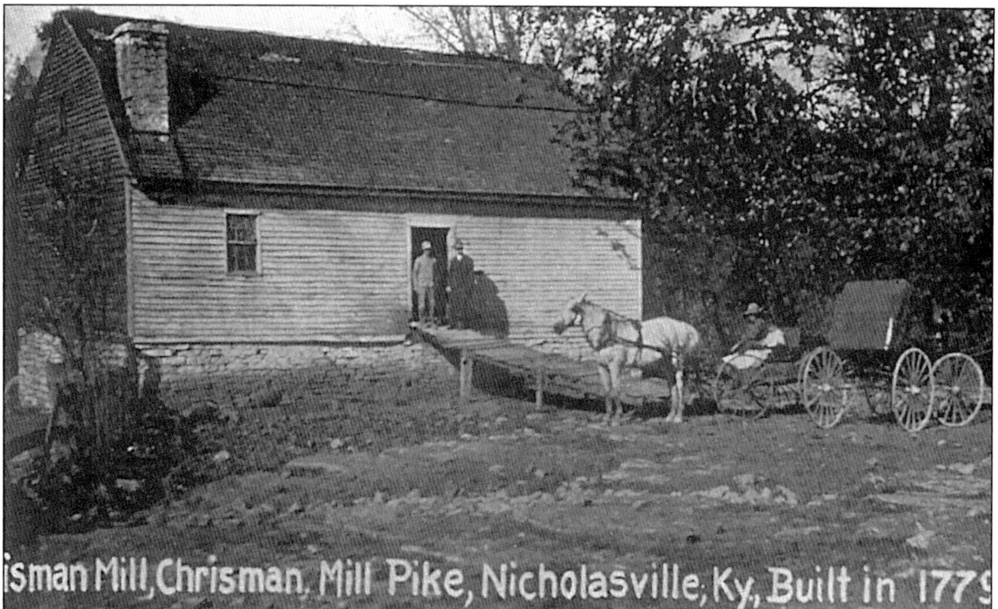

This postcard, published between 1907 and 1915, shows an early mill located on Chrisman Mill Pike. General Hugh Chrisman was the creator and operator of the mill for many years starting in 1779. It changed hands several times and became the last mill in Jessamine County where water ground meal could be bought. It was torn down in the 1940s.

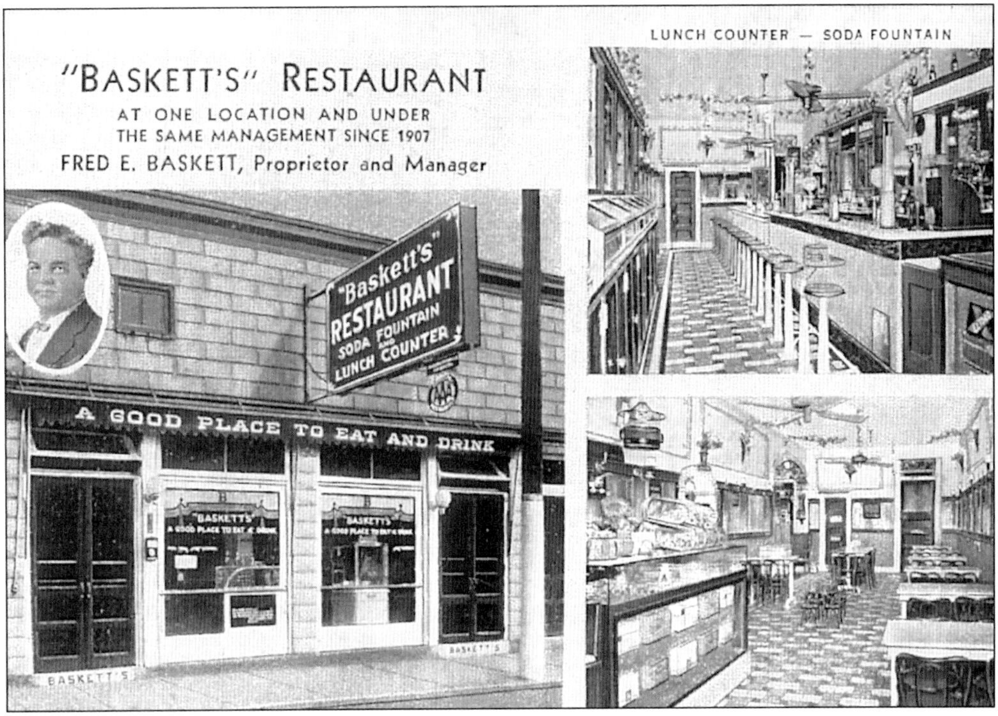

This is a double postcard showing the Baskett's Restaurant in Nicholasville ,with a map around 40 miles of Nicholasville. Baskett's was established in 1907 by Fred E. Baskett, and the double postcard could be obtained from the cashier for 5¢ each.

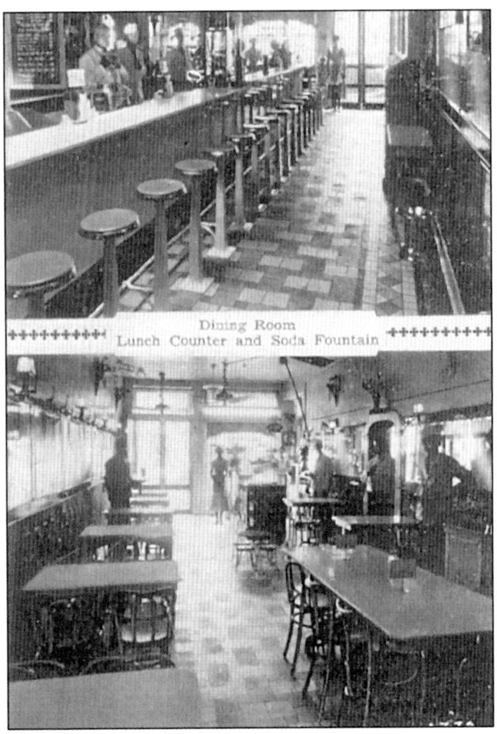

This postcard, published between 1907 and 1915, shows another look at Baskett's Restaurant, with the dining room, lunch counter, and soda fountain.

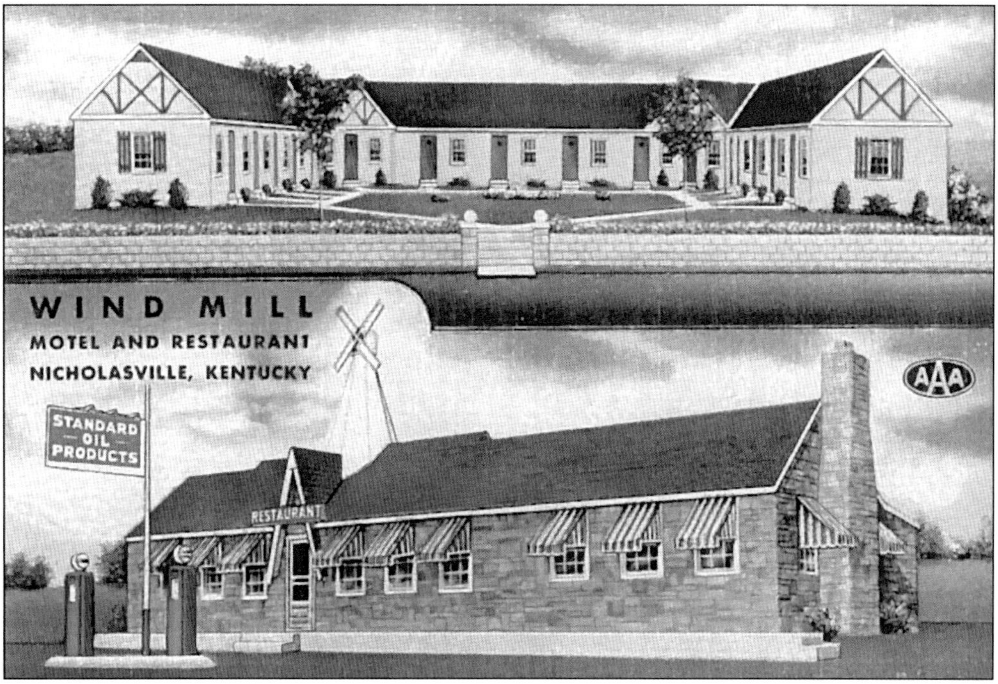

Postcards on this page are of the 1950s vintage, but were part of the long history of Nicholasville. This one, the Wind Mill, was a motel and restaurant on U.S. 27, 7 miles south of Lexington. It had 18 rooms with steam heat, radios, and a bath in each room.

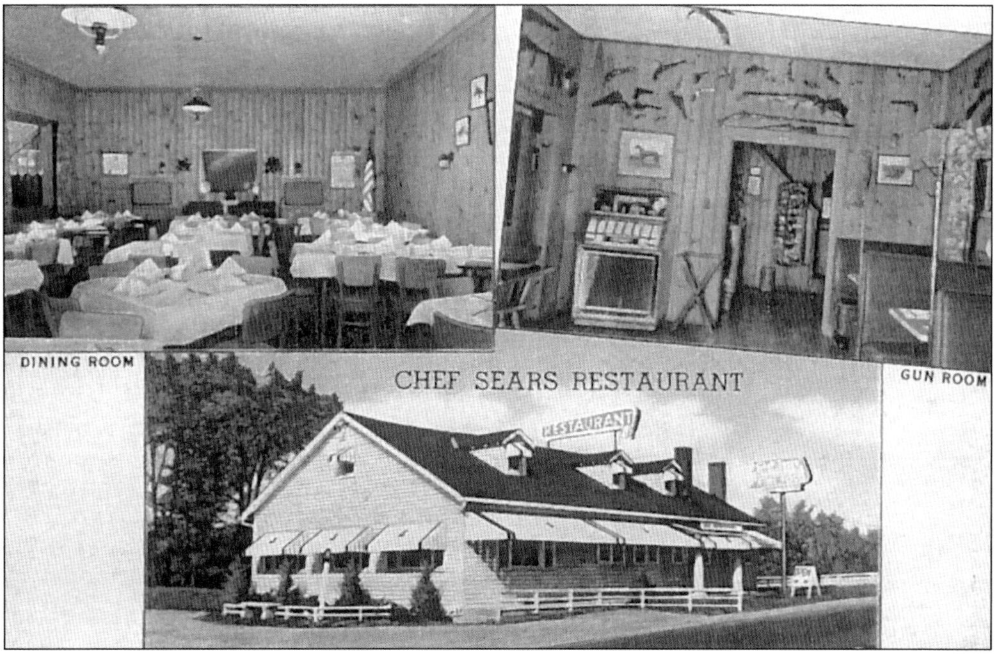

This postcard shows Chef Sears Restaurant, south of Lexington on U.S. 27. The restaurant was noted for old hams, beaten biscuits, fried chicken, sea food, and steaks.

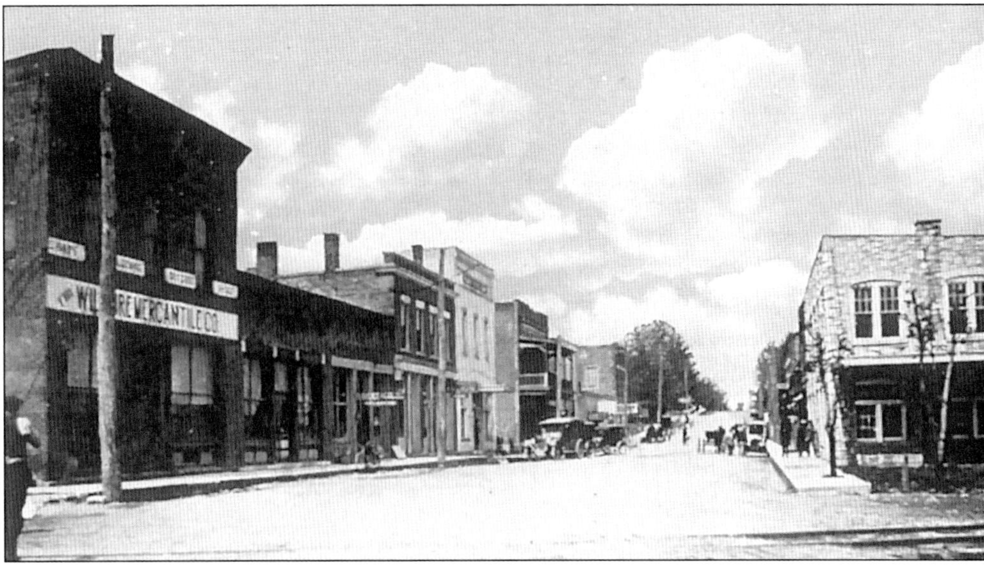

The next seven postcards will show the town and homes of Wilmore, Kentucky. It is unusual that so many postcards were made of such a small town and survived. This one shows the downtown when it was published, between 1915 and 1930. The railroad tracks can be seen at the bottom where the depot was constructed in 1882.

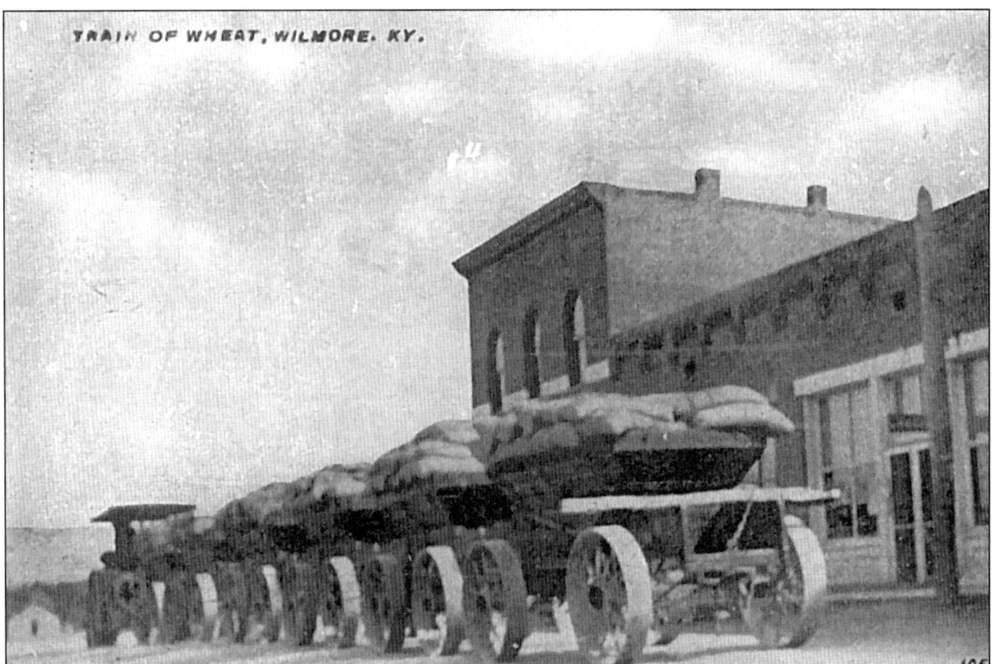

This postcard shows a train of wheat in Wilmore, with the Wilmore Mercantile Company building showing. This postcard was postmarked in 1914, after the 1911 fire, which destroyed much of the town.

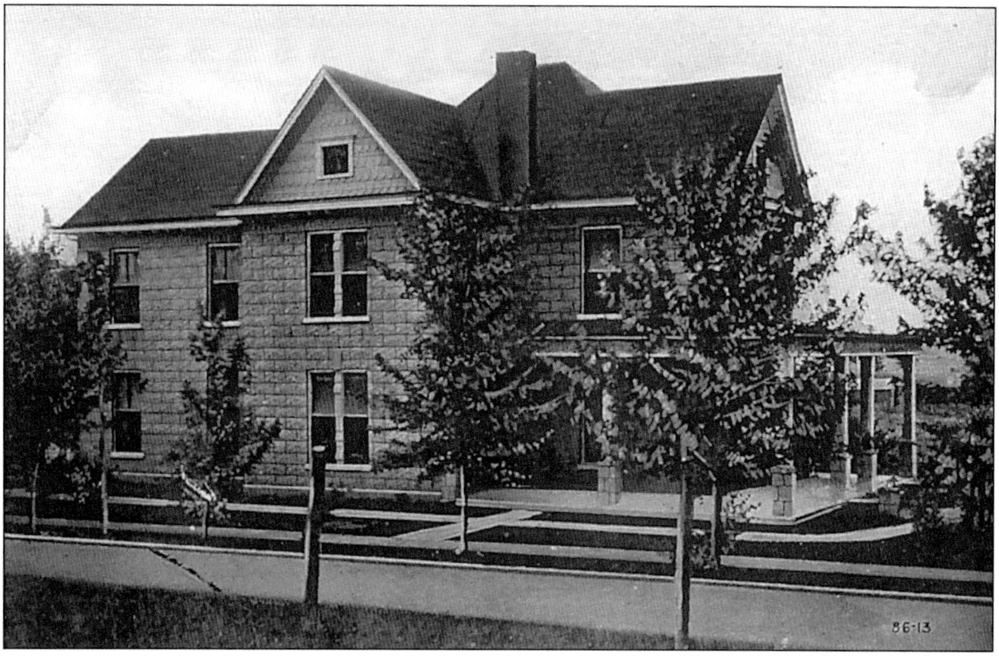

This postcard shows the residence of H.W. Bromley, D.D., in Wilmore. This building later became part of Asbury College.

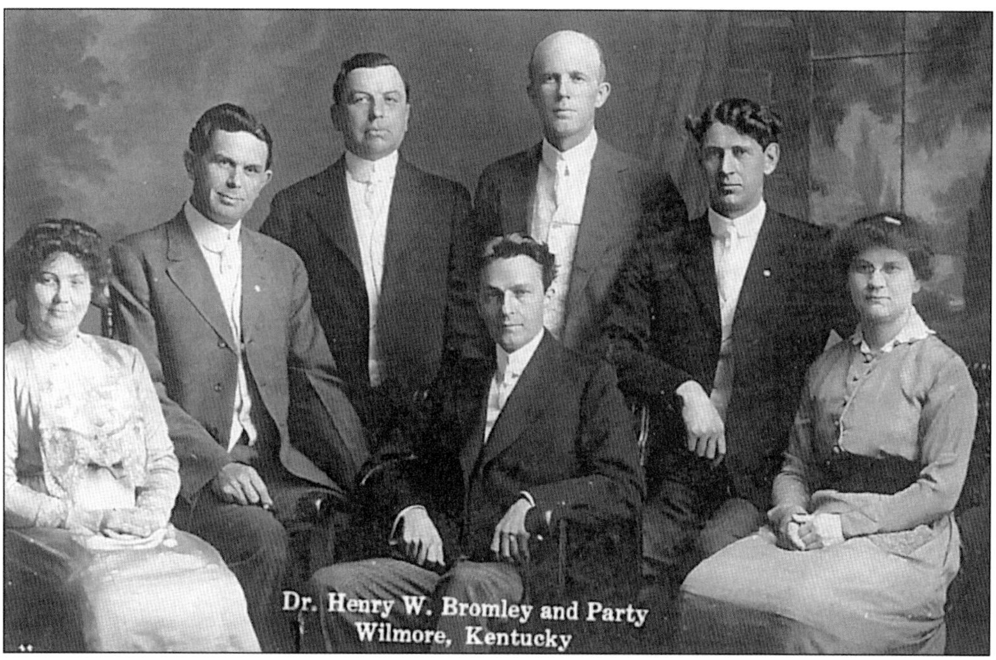

This photo-postcard shows the party of Dr. Henry W. Bromley, taken between 1907 and 1915. He was a professor at Asbury College in 1905. Dr. Bromley was involved in evangelistic work, and the postcard could have been made for his work.

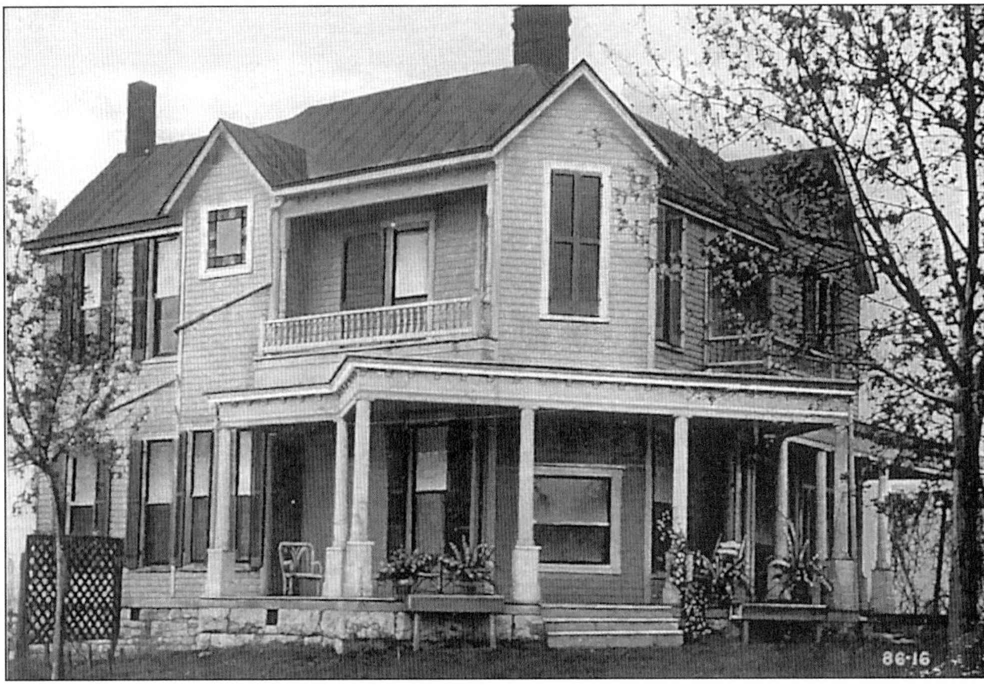

This is the residence of R.A. Dodd in Wilmore. Colonel R.A. Dodd was a presbyterian living in Wilmore, and the home was later reported to be the Duncan family home on South Maple Street.

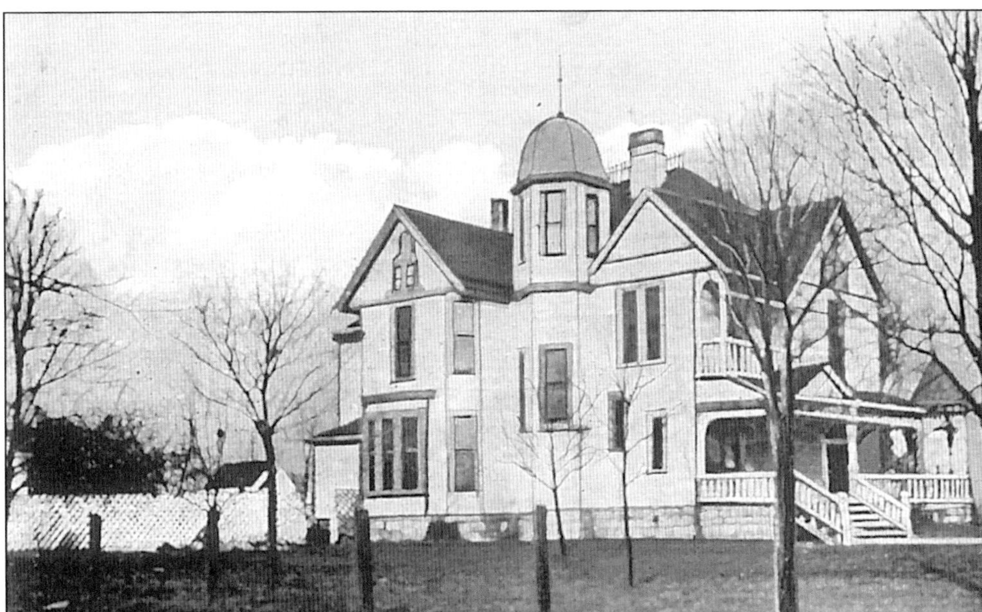

This view shows the Arnold Homestead in Wilmore. Mr. F.T. Arnold was on the Asbury College Board from 1906 to 1907.

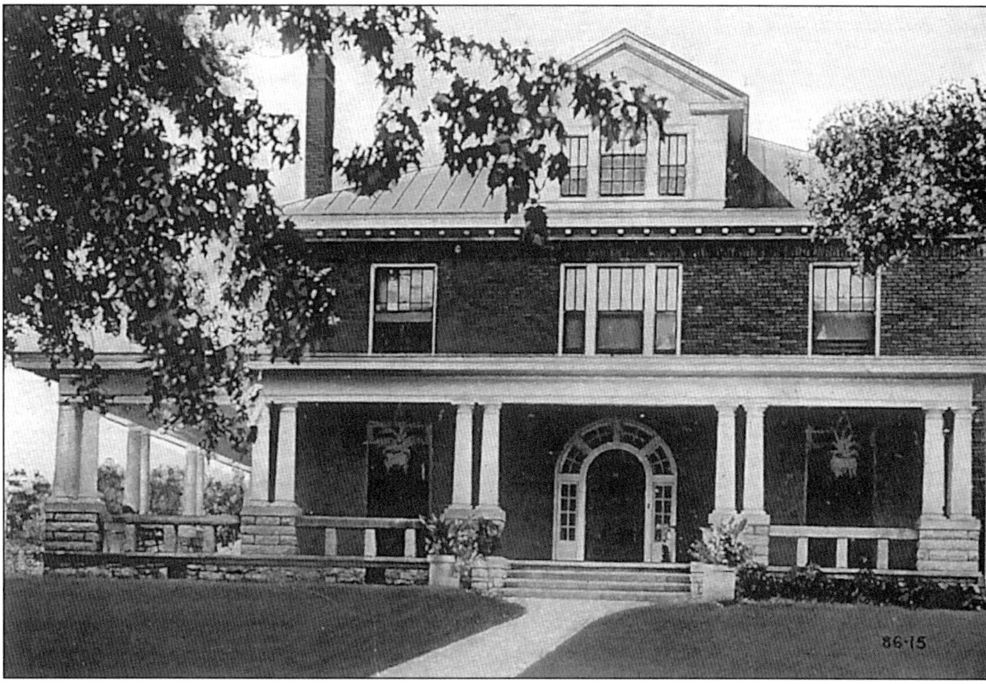

This was the residence of J.S. Lowry. The postcard was published between 1907 and 1915.

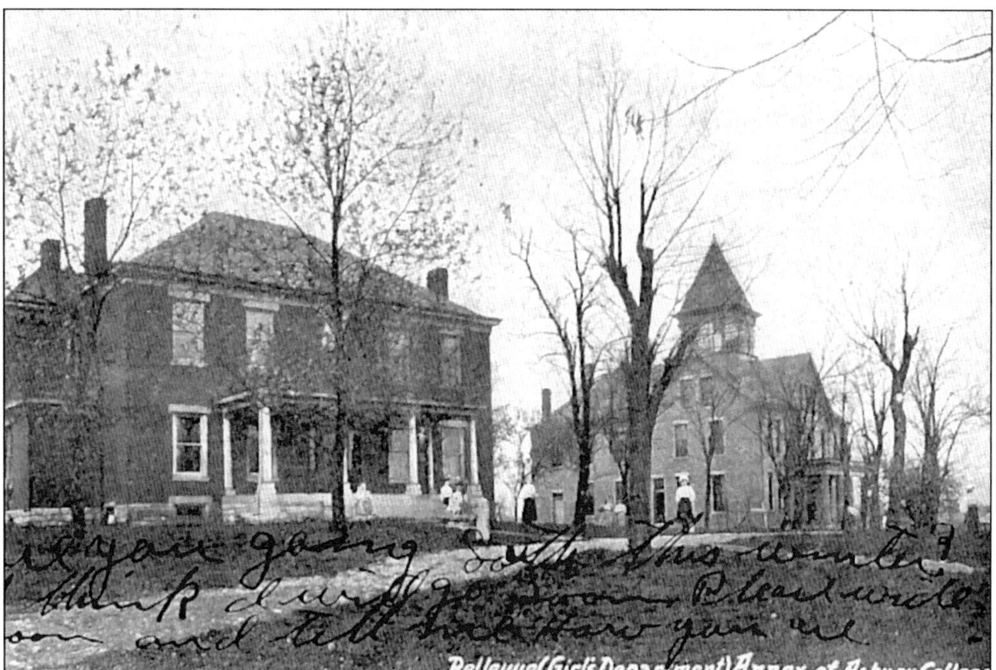

This postcard, with a postmark of 1908, shows the old Bellevue School in Wilmore. The school was purchased by Asbury College in 1905. The Bellevue School was started in 1898 in the home of John R. Scott, one of the original land owners.

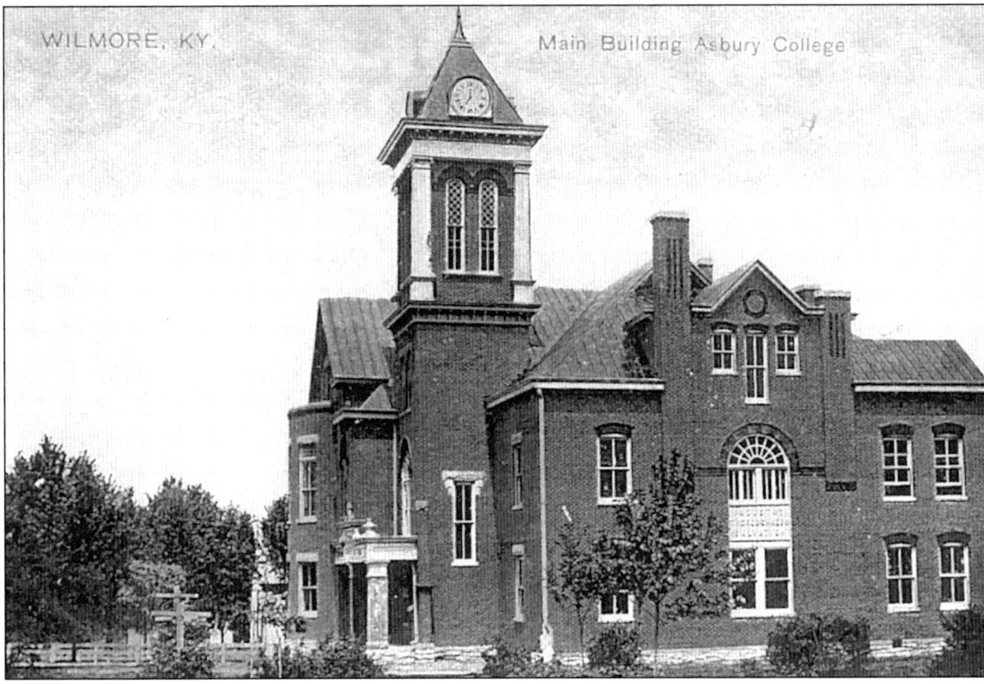

This postcard, with a postmark of 1907, shows the administration building of Asbury College, established in 1890, in Wilmore. This building burned in 1908. The reason that so many Asbury College and Wilmore old postcards have survived is that this author graduated from Asbury College and devotedly collected them for many years.

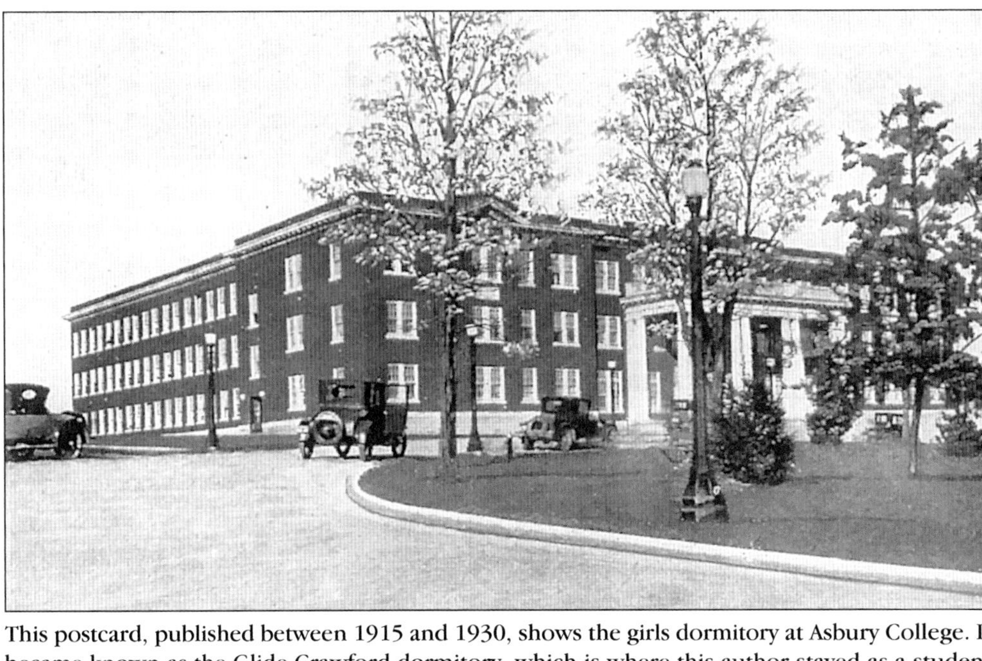

This postcard, published between 1915 and 1930, shows the girls dormitory at Asbury College. It became known as the Glide Crawford dormitory, which is where this author stayed as a student many years later.

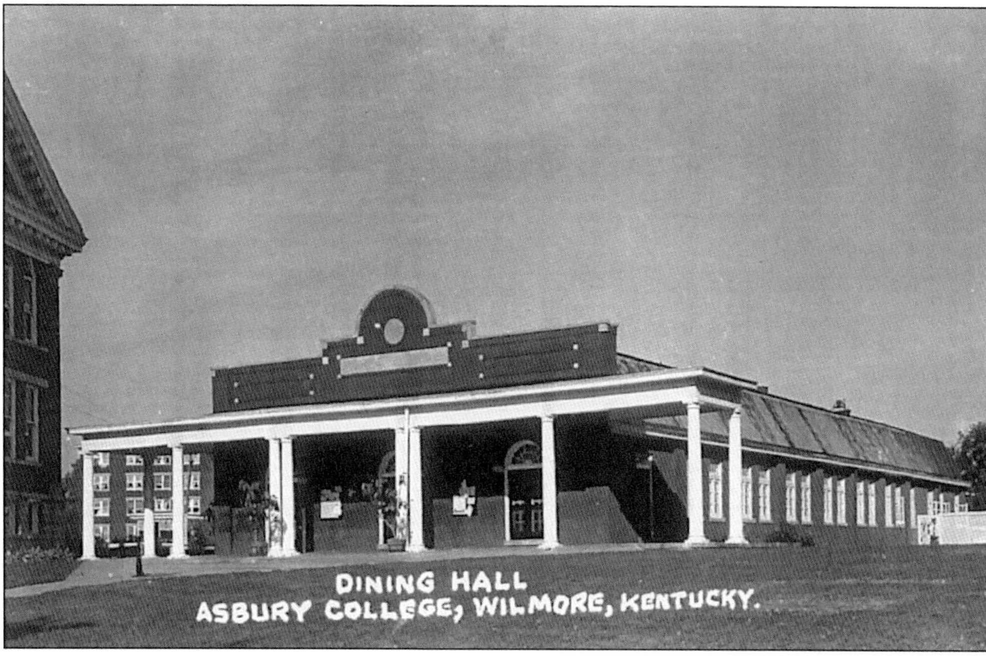

This photo shows the early dining hall at Asbury College, which was replaced in later years.

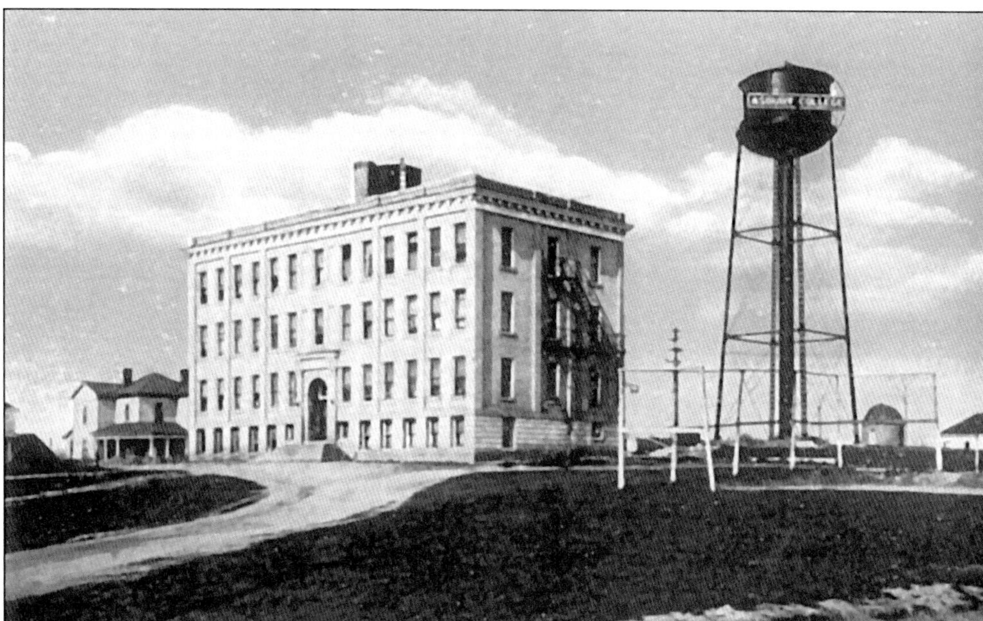

This postcard, published between 1915 and 1930, shows a view of the men's dormitory at Asbury. The water tower is on the right and was donated by the senior class of 1925. The dirt road leading to the dormitory was later paved as other buildings were added.

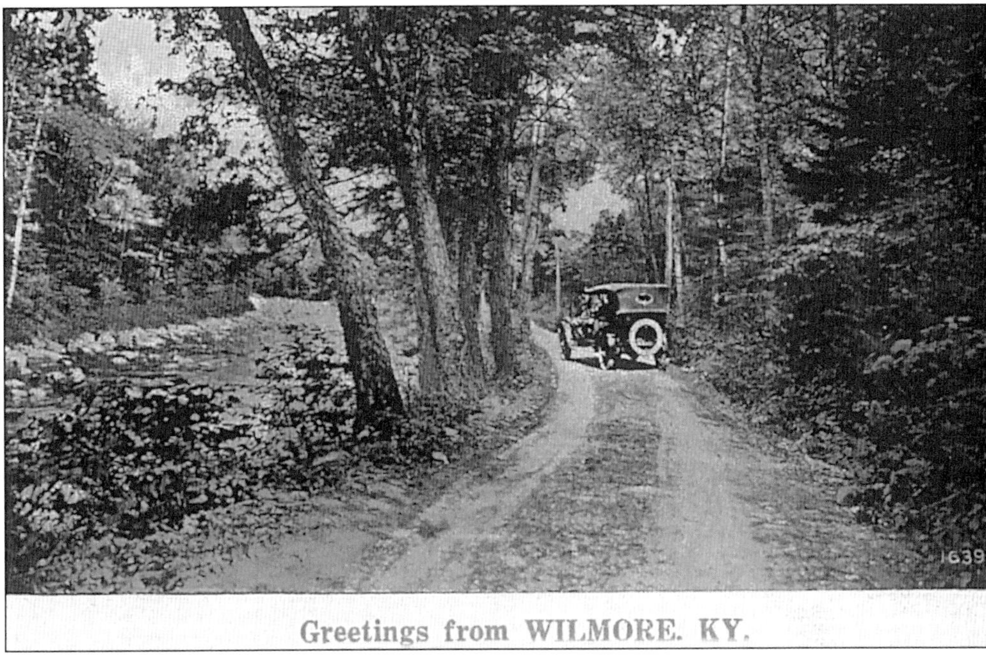

This postcard, published *c.* 1915, shows the area and road around Wilmore. The stream with a one-lane road shows the early 1900s Bluegrass.

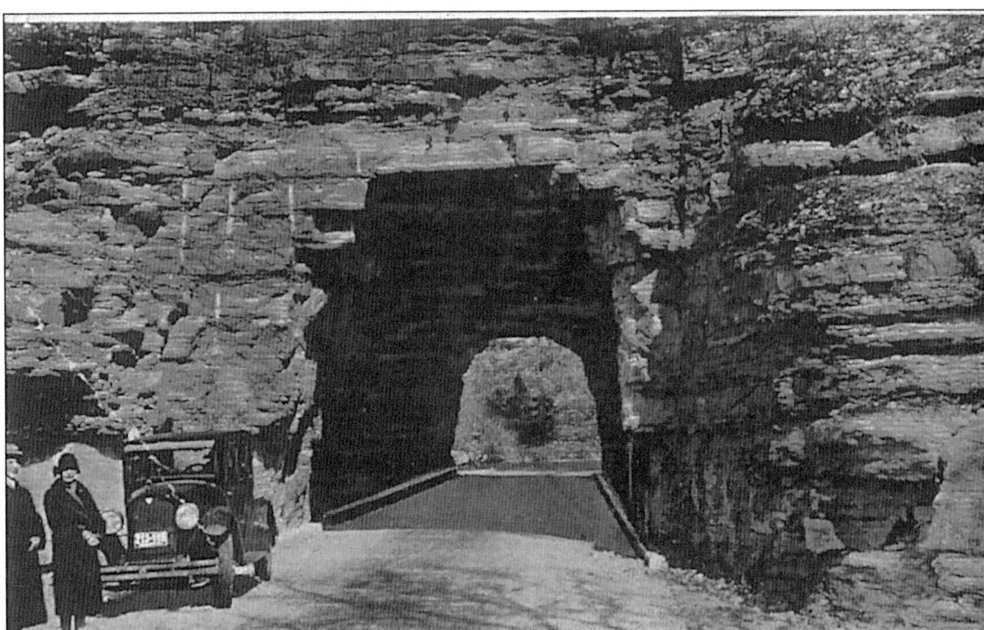

This view of the Boone's Tunnel is on U.S. 68, about 3 1/2 miles south of Wilmore. This postcard has a postmark of 1931. Boone's Tunnel lead to what was called the Brooklyn Bridge, as it continued into Mercer County and was captured in old postcards of Mercer County.

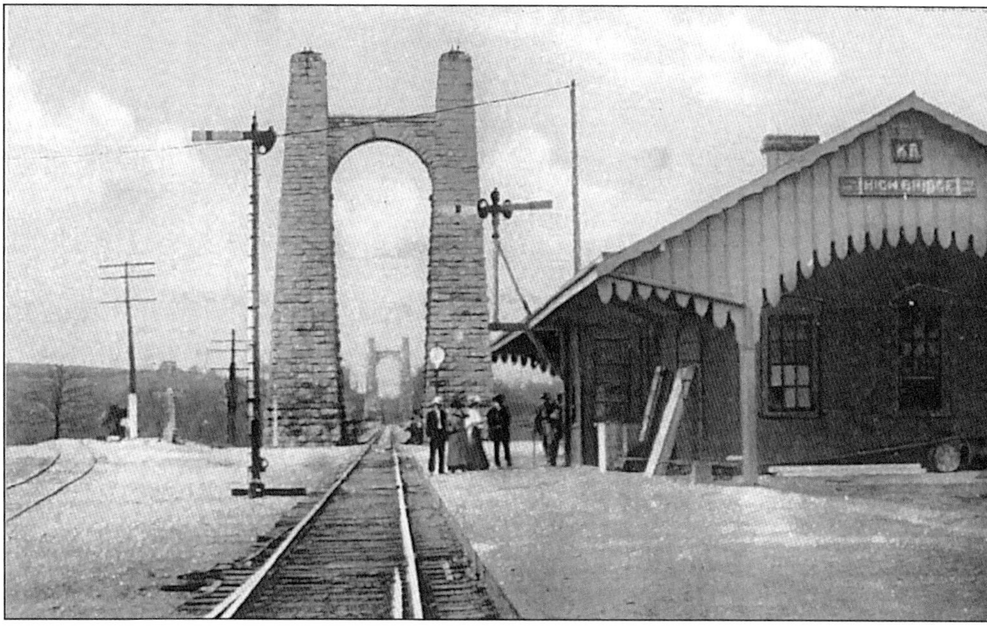

The next seven postcards will show the area around High Bridge, Kentucky, that grew up around a train station. This postcard, from *c.* 1907, shows the train station and beginning of the bridge. The massive towering piers were attempts in 1876 at a suspension bridge. John A. Roebling, famed as the builder of the Brooklyn Bridge, stopped that construction and resumed with the present truss structure rather than the suspension type.

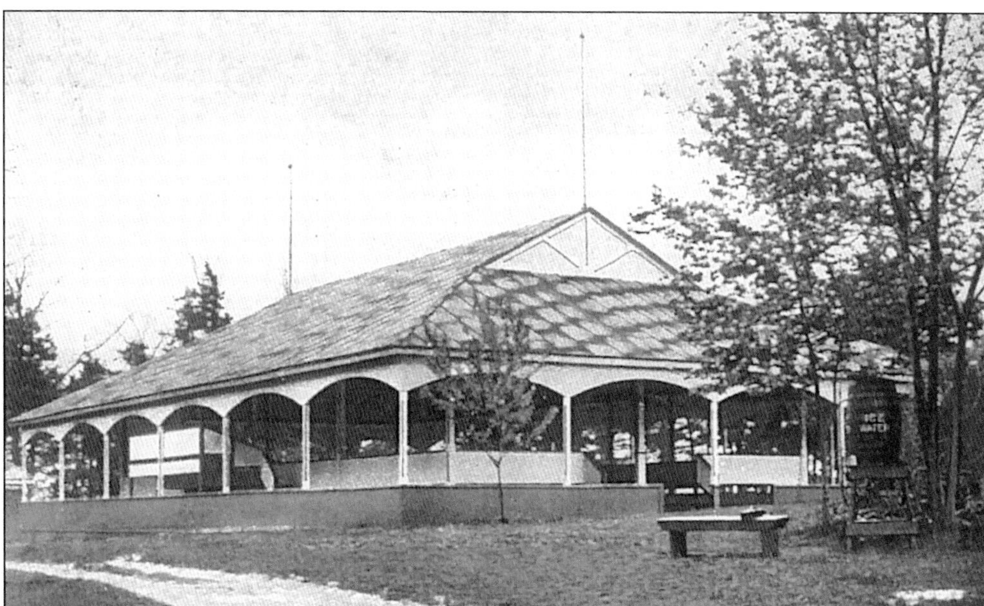

This *c.* 1907 view shows the dancing pavilion at High Bridge Park. The park consisted of a few acres, with a dance floor as recreation for residents of the area.

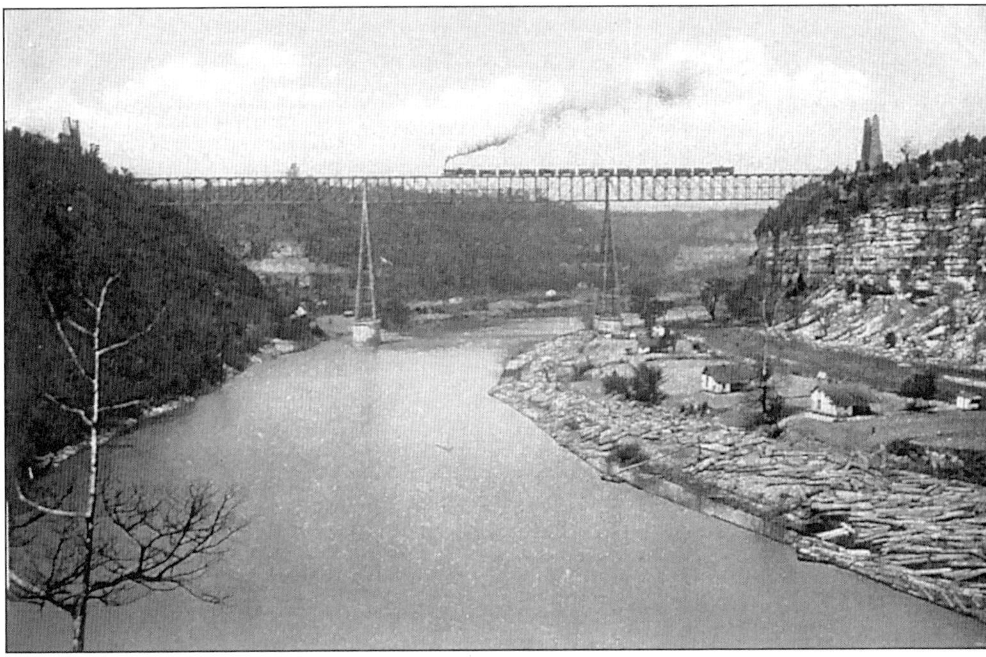

This view from between 1907 and 1915 shows High Bridge over the Kentucky River. This height of the bridge was 285 feet, and it was 1,100 feet long. No highway crossing was provided when this bridge was built, so the road ends at the bridge.

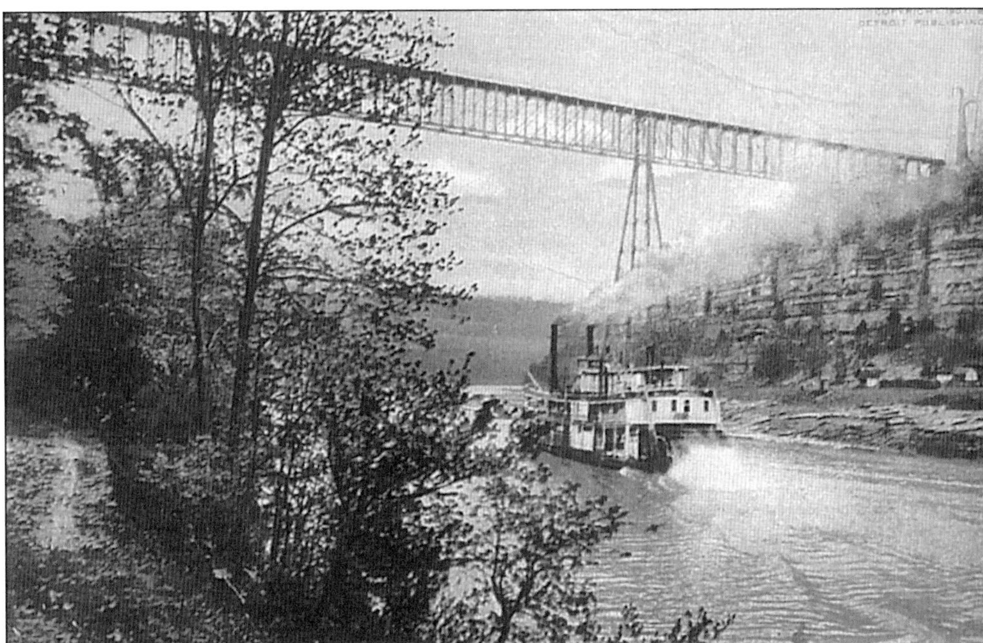

This view during the same time period shows High Bridge from land looking toward the Kentucky River. The steamer *Falls City* is passing under High Bridge. Notice the dirt road on the left side and the houses on the right side. Many early farmers grew hemp in narrow fields that bordered on one side with walls of limestone and the other with the river.

This postcard, from around 1909, shows a stairway at High Bridge from the top to the bottom of cliffs with a height of 250 feet. This is a very unusual view, since the stairway was discontinued after a few years.

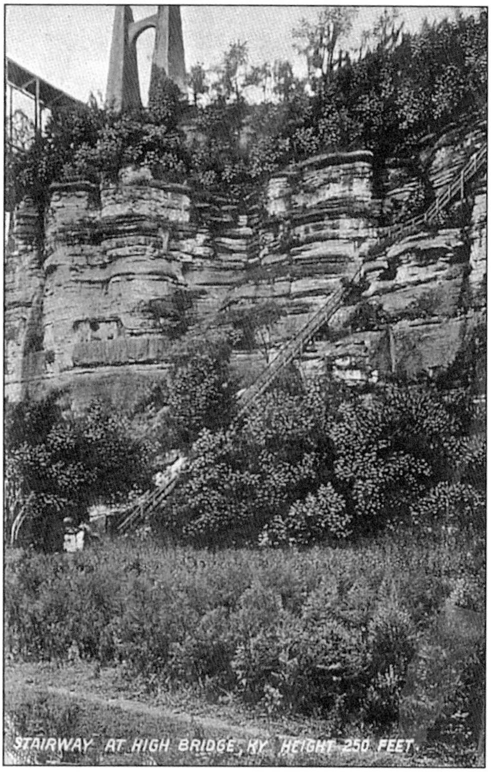

STAIRWAY AT HIGH BRIDGE, KY. HEIGHT 250 FEET.

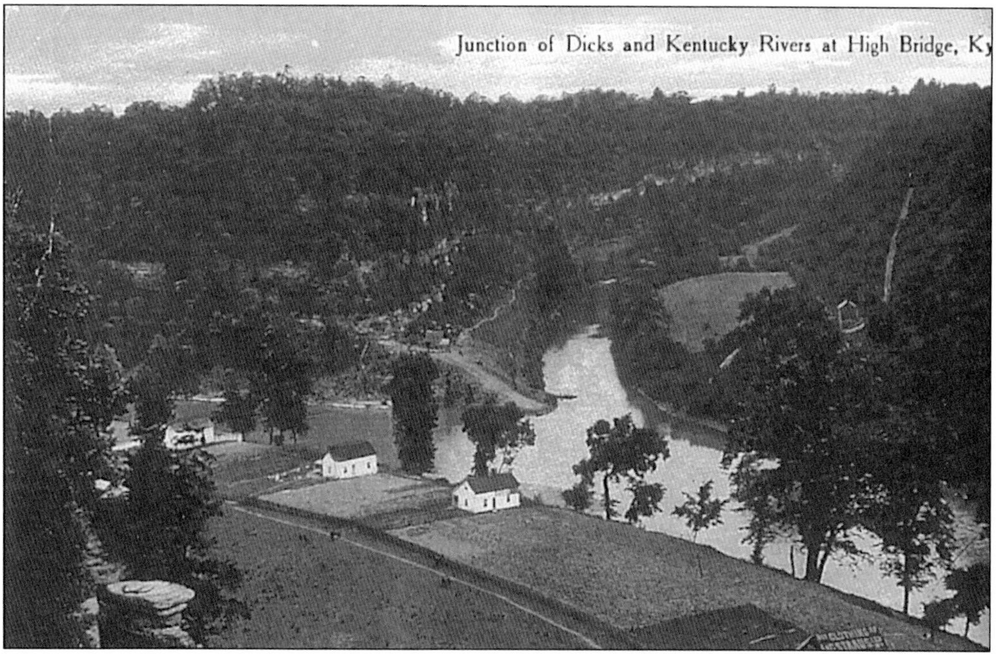

Junction of Dicks and Kentucky Rivers at High Bridge, Ky

This view, taken around 1907, shows the junction of Dicks and Kentucky Rivers at High Bridge. The Dicks River became known as Dix River, and Dix Dam in later years. Notice the homes at the bottom of the cliffs.

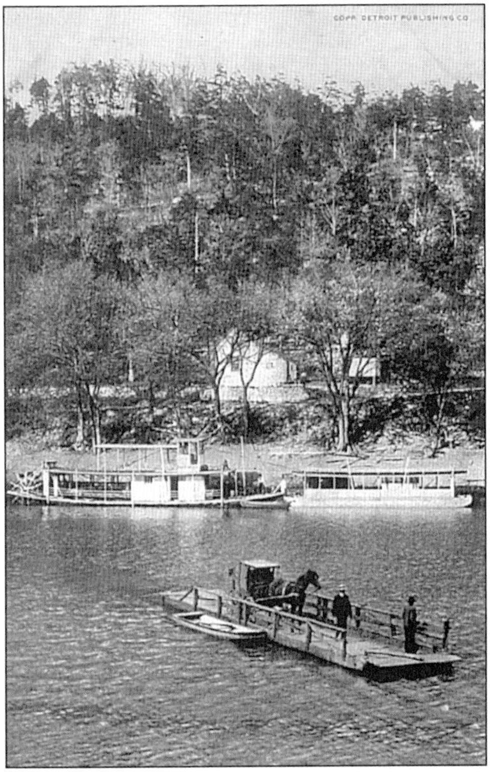

This view shows the ferry at High Bridge around 1910. Ferries were very common in "old Kentucky." The horse and carriage on the ferry shows how primitive transportation was at that time.

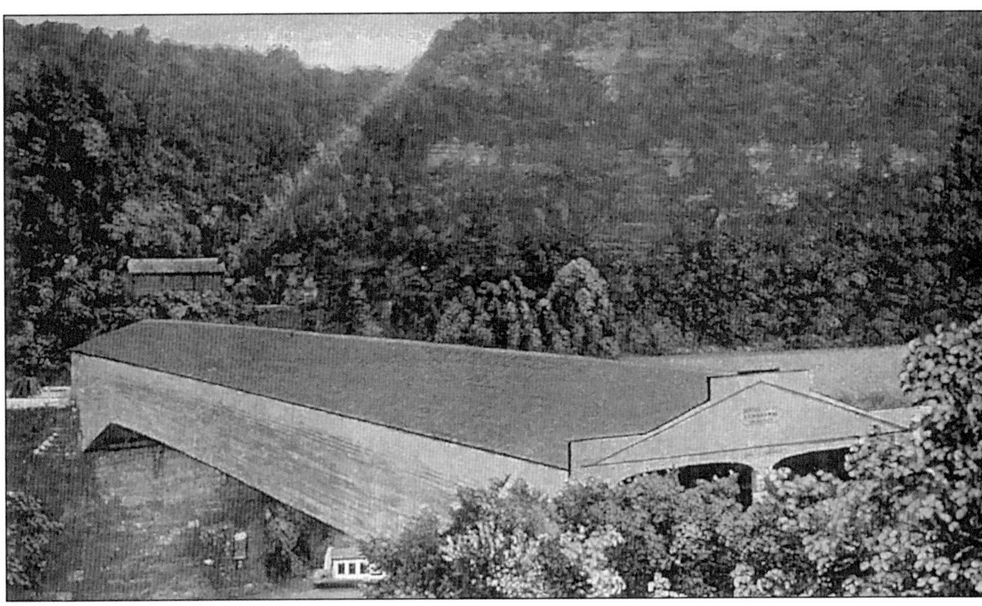

This view shows the Hickman Bridge over the Kentucky River at Camp Nelson. This small village became General William Nelson's headquarters during the war. It later became the United States Military Cemetery, with many Civil War soldiers buried there. The bridge was erected in 1838 and became part of US Highway 27. It was condemned in 1926 and was razed in 1933. It was the longest wooden cantilever bridge in America.

Six

Lincoln and Madison Counties

This chapter will include old postcards of Lincoln and Madison Counties. Lincoln County was established in 1780 as one of the original three counties in the district of Kentucky. It comprised a third of the area before being divided numerous times into smaller counties for residents forced to travel long distances to the nearest courthouse. The county seat is Stanford, located on the Louisville and Nashville Railroad, while other towns in this county will include Crab Orchard and Halls Gap.

Madison County was formed in 1785, before Kentucky became a state in 1792. All the principal streams of the county flow into the Kentucky River, and they were all named by Daniel Boone. Richmond, the county seat, was settled in 1785 but was not incorporated until 1809. Other towns include Berea, the seat of a college.

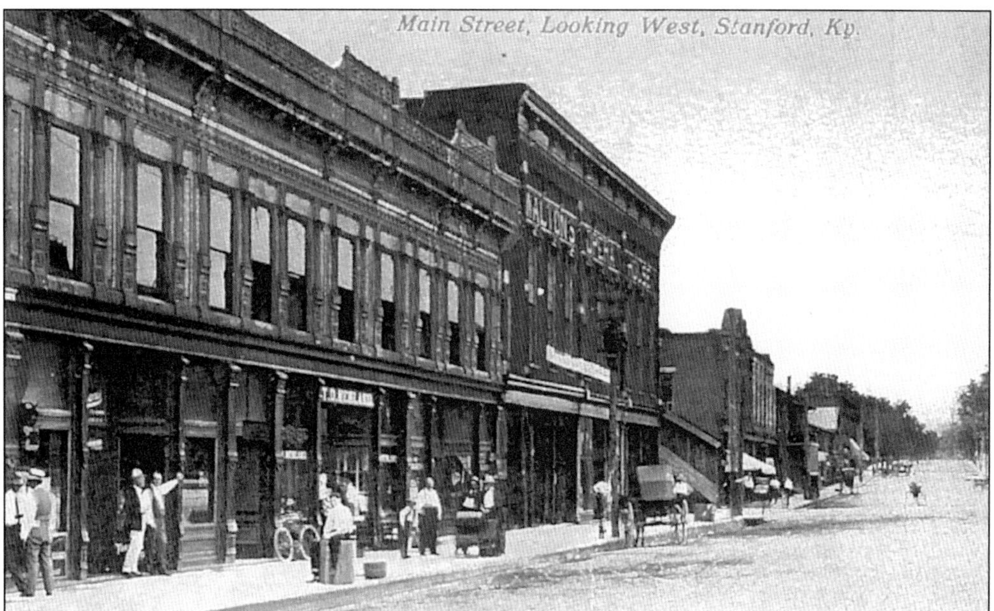

The following 11 old postcards will show Lincoln County, with six related to Stanford, Kentucky. This view of Stanford, postmarked 1912, shows main street looking west. The taller building is an opera house, and the name T.D. Newland can be seen above the door.

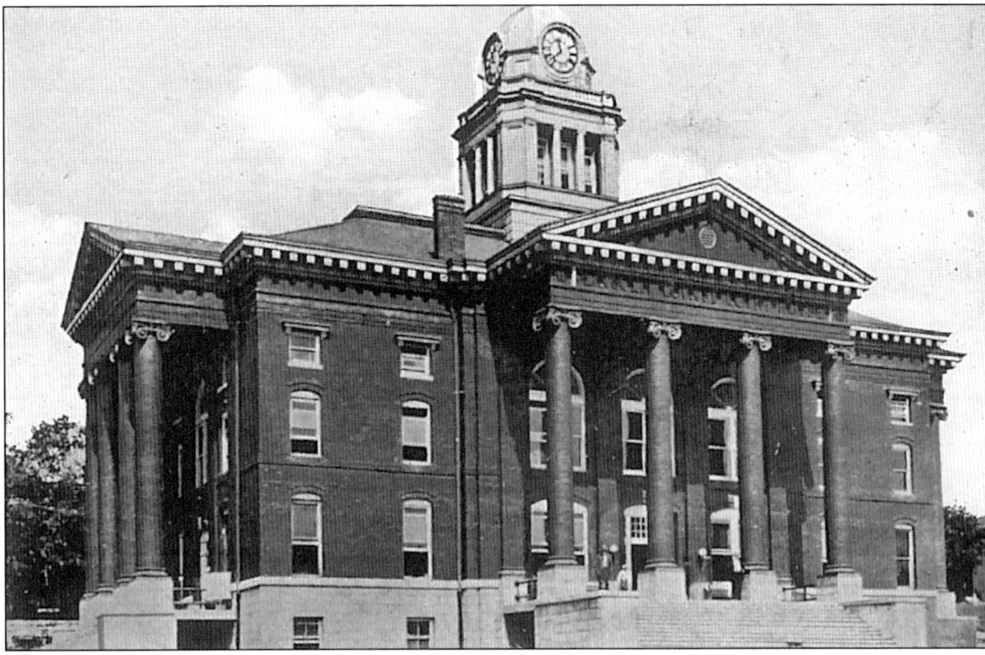

This view of the fourth and present Lincoln County Courthouse was built in 1909, while the postcard was published between 1915 and 1930. An annex was added to the building in the 1940s, and the original building is listed on the National Register of Historic Places.

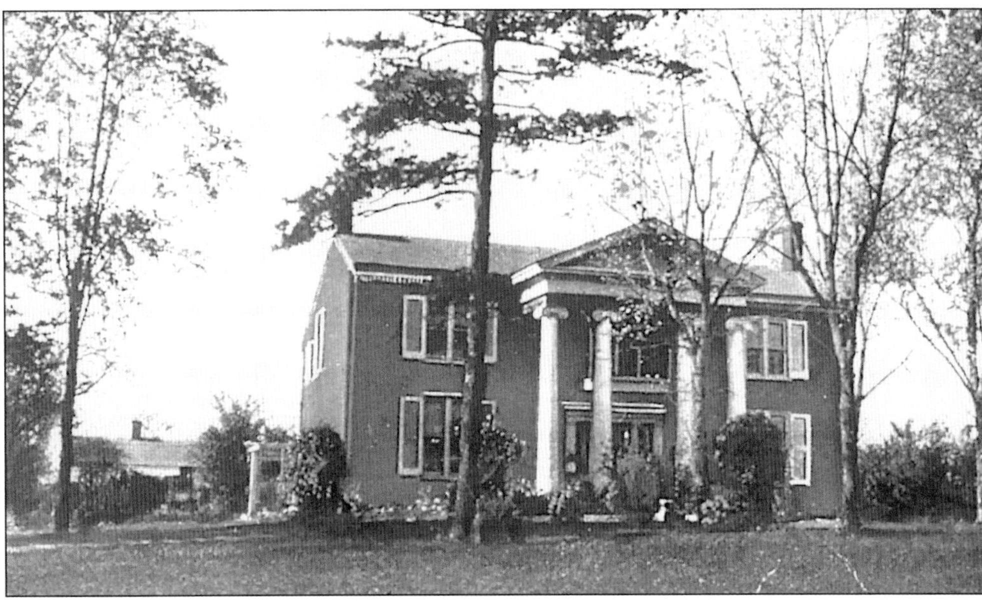

This postcard shows the residence of H.G. Harris Baughman at Somerset Street in Stanford, with a handwritten date of 1913. Handwritten on the message side was, "this is formerly the home of Dr. Thos. Montgomery, an ancestor of sender. Xmas greetings from your cousin fond, Mrs. J. Harris Baughman."

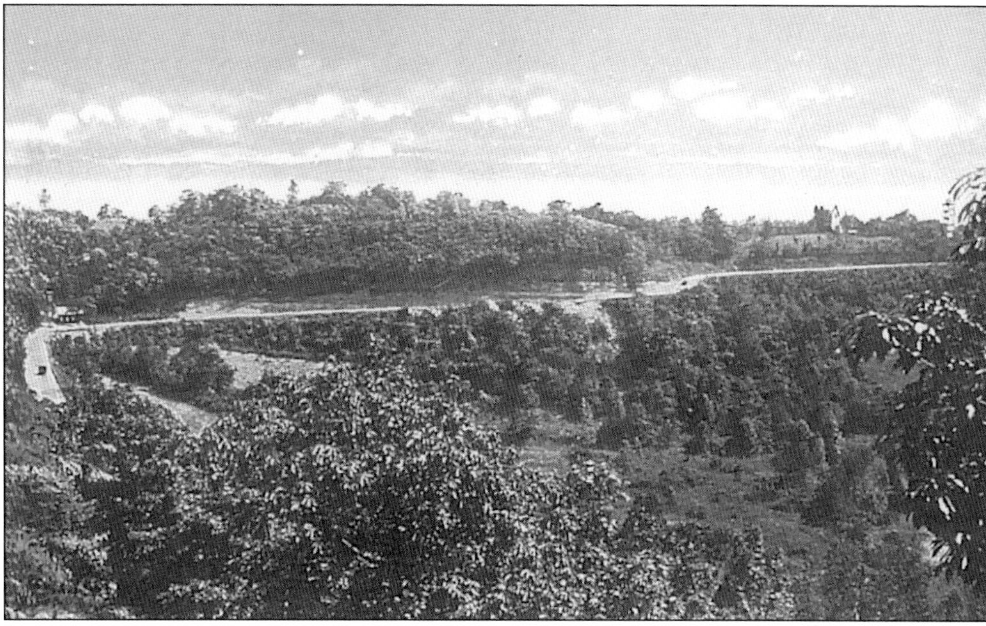

This is a view of Halls Gap, Kentucky, near Stanford. It is also a view of old U.S. Highway 27 with a postmark of October, 1951. The sender wrote a message, "Here for the night, dinner in Stanford and came over this road. Have had perfect weather and fine roads. Scenery gorgeous, not many leaves off and brilliant colors." Halls Gap was settled around the 1880s by immigrants who developed productive farms.

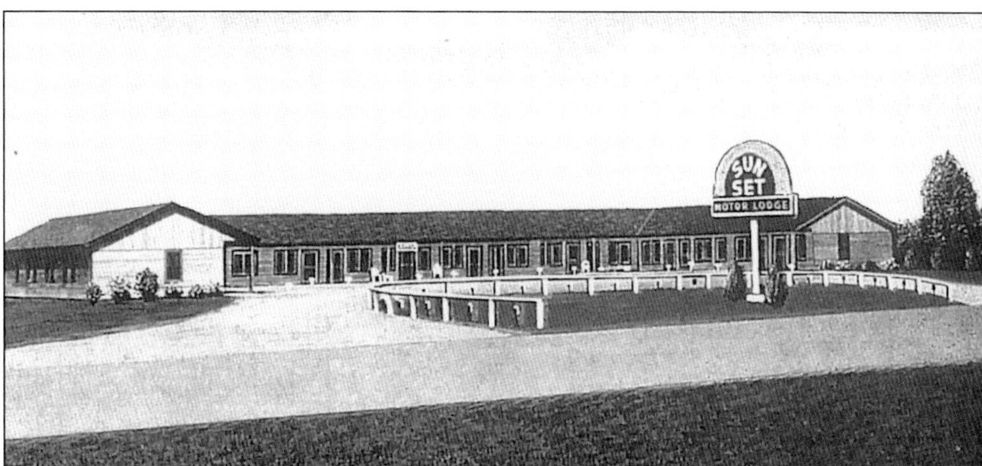

This postcard of the same vintage shows the ranch-style Sunset Motor Lodge, one mile north of Stanford on U.S. 150. Each unit in this Motor Lodge had tile baths, cross ventilation, central heat, and parking in front of the unit. It had the Triple A (AAA) designation.

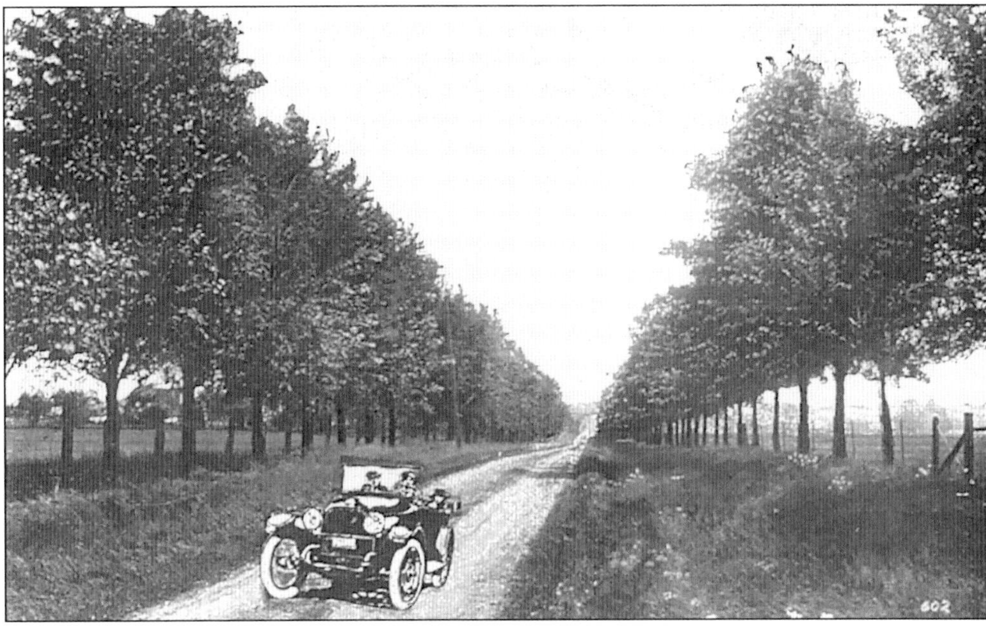

This view, with a postmark of 1923, shows a county road around Stanford. Actually the first road in Kentucky was the Old Wilderness Trail and it ran through Stanford.

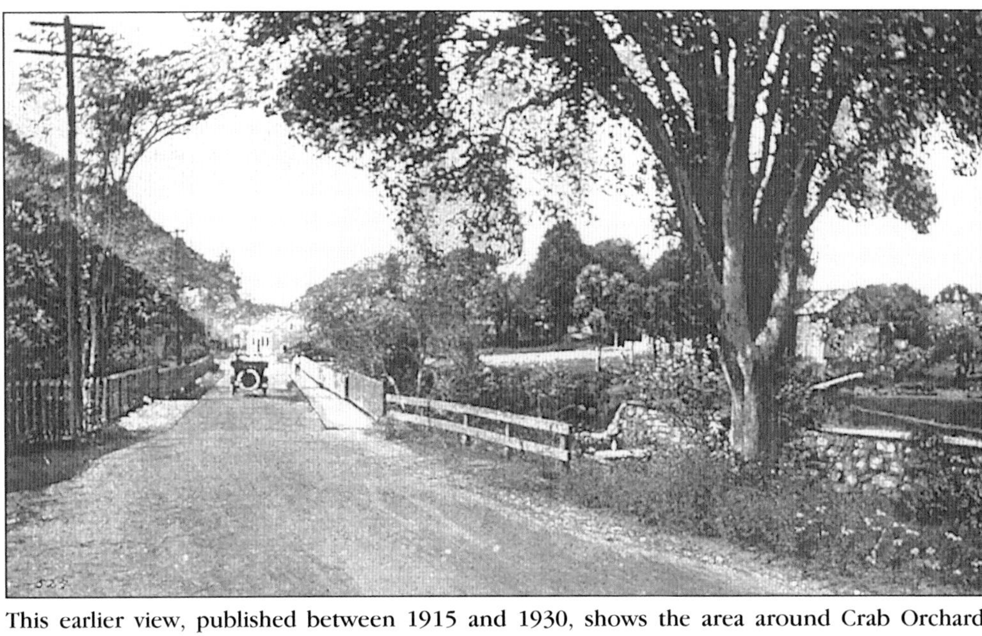

This earlier view, published between 1915 and 1930, shows the area around Crab Orchard, Kentucky. Notice the stone fence. The town of Crab Orchard was an early Wilderness Road town that flourished for over 100 years as a famous resort springs.

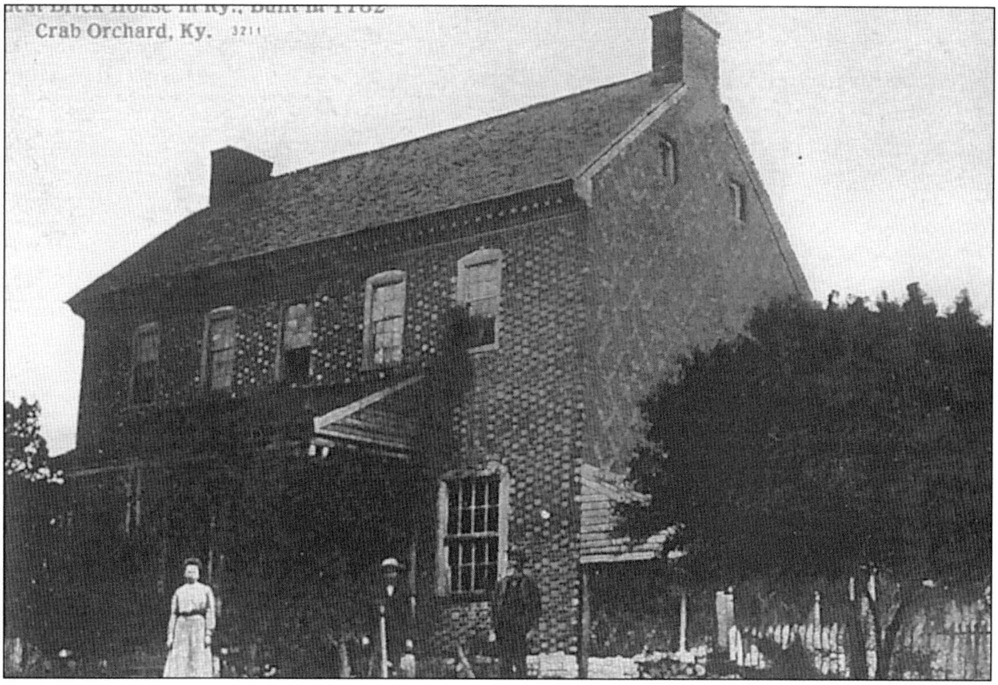

These two postcards show the oldest house in Kentucky, located in Crab Orchard, Kentucky; however, the porches are different. This postcard was postmarked 1910. Notice the people in front. This house and "Traveler's Rest," now part of Boyle County (on page 30) but part of the original Lincoln County when this was a frontier, were the finest homes built in the area. Most homes were small, single-room cabins when this house was built and the area was a wilderness.

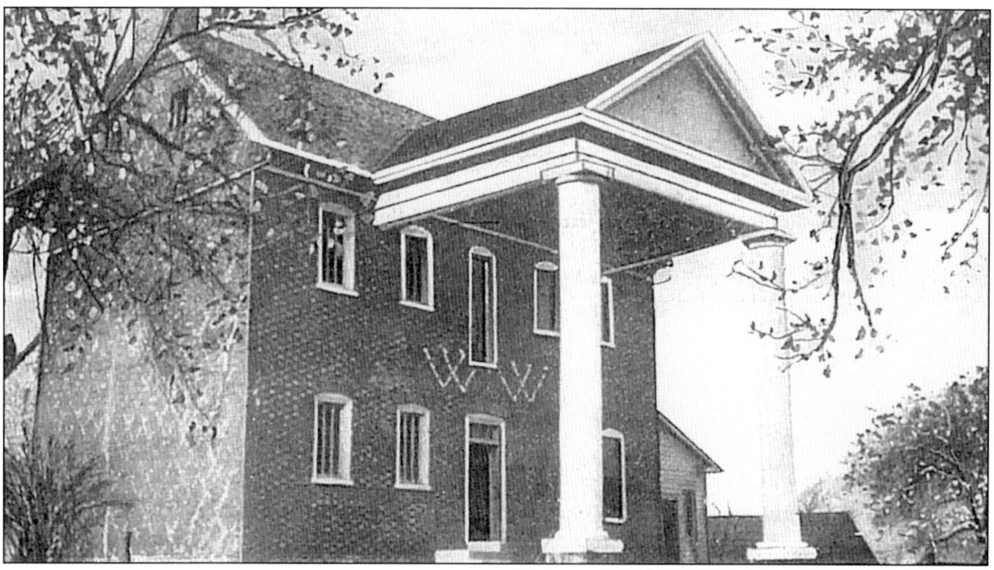

This postcard has a later postmark of 1933, with the front porch changed. This house was the first brick house in Kentucky, having been constructed in 1782 by Colonel William Whitley. He hosted lavish barbecues for area residents. The house is located southeast of Stanford with secret rooms built to hide the family from danger.

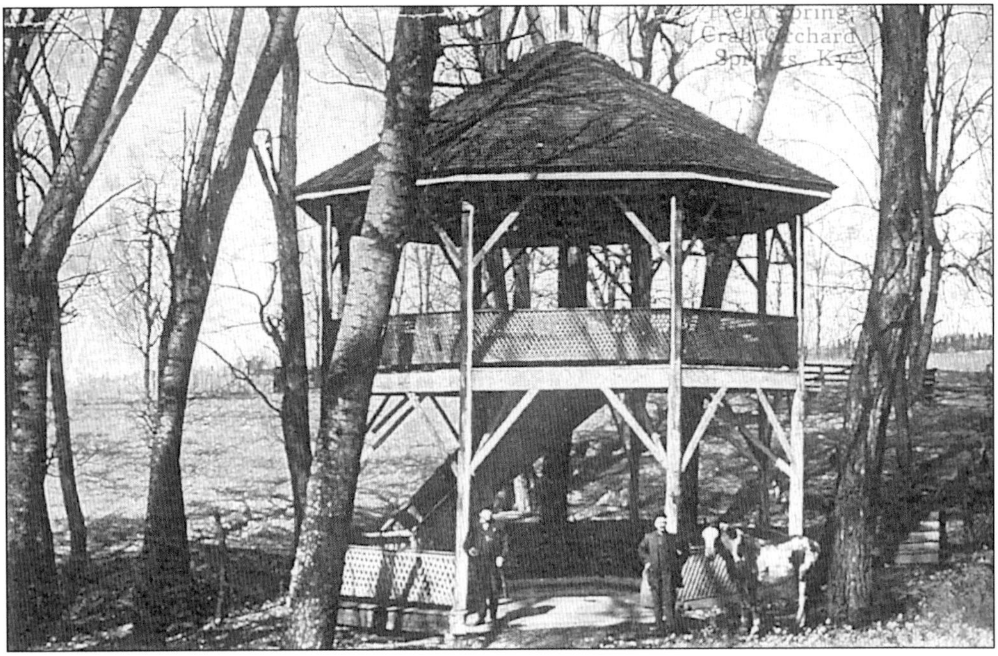

This postcard, postmarked 1912, shows the Field Spring of Crab Orchard Springs. Being a site of numerous mineral springs, Crab Orchard was a popular resort stop, from its founding until the 1930s. Crab Orchard is southeast of the Whitley House.

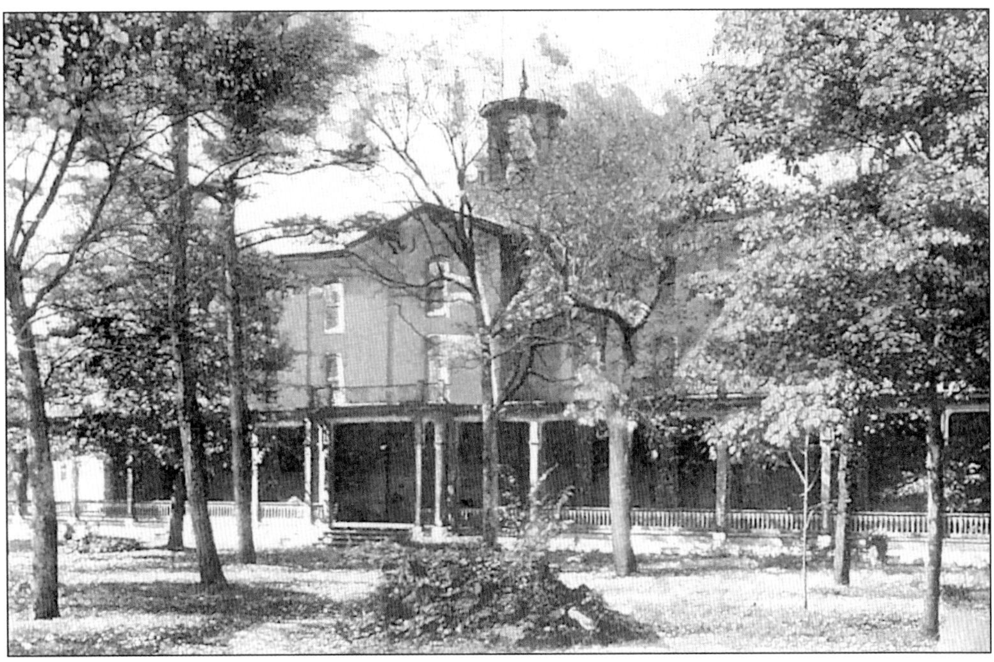

This view, postmarked 1922, shows the main building to the Springs Hotel in Crab Orchard. Handwritten on the message side was, "Sister dear, I wish you were with us. This is Fine."

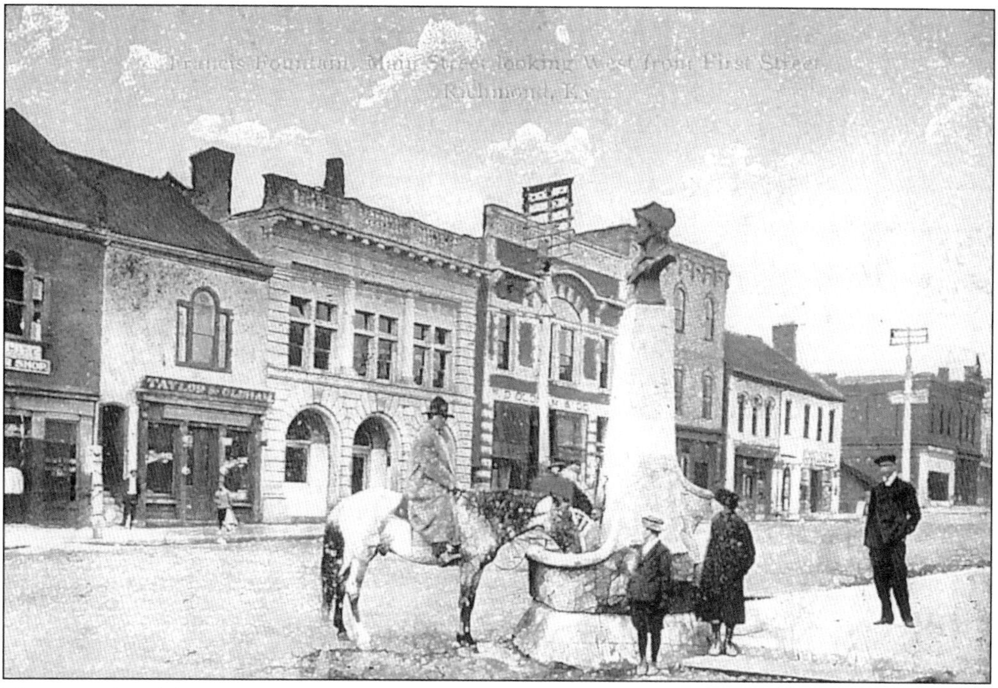

The next 20 old postcards are related to Madison County. This one starts with Richmond, Kentucky, and the Francis Fountain on main street, looking west from first street. The card was postmarked March 8, 1922.

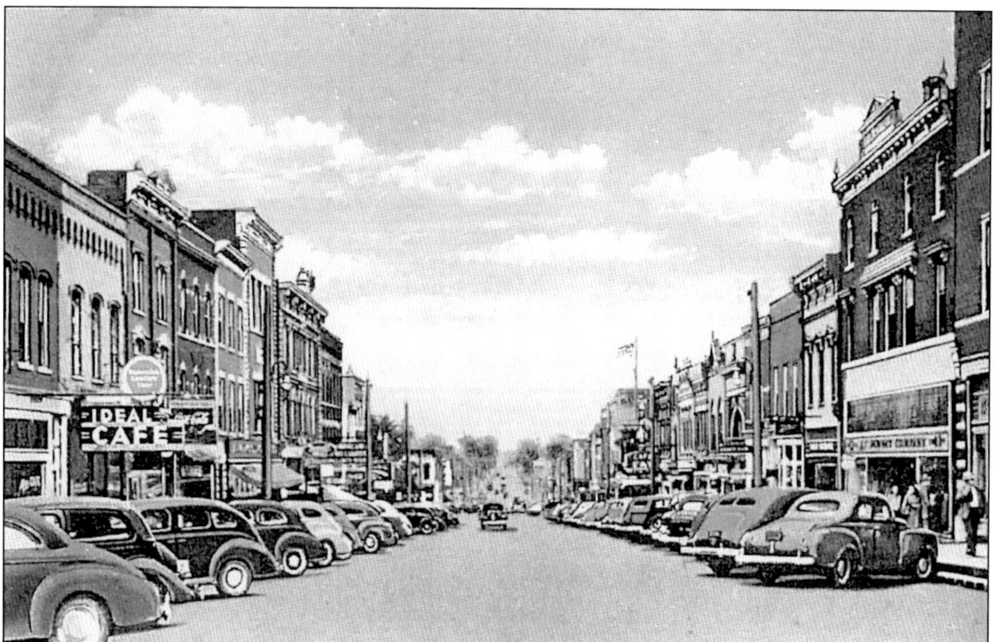

This view, published between 1930 and 1945, shows downtown Richmond on main street looking east. On the left is the Ideal Cafe, the Western Auto Associate Store, and on the right, the J.C. Penny Company can be identified.

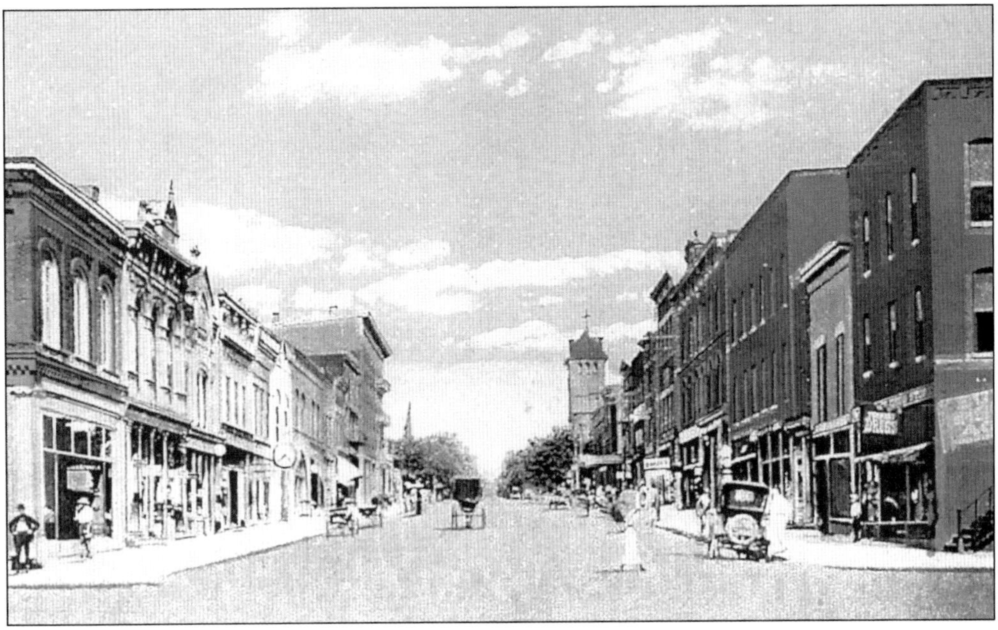

This view, earlier than the last view, shows main street in Richmond. Notice the tall building on the far right. It is similar to the next postcard.

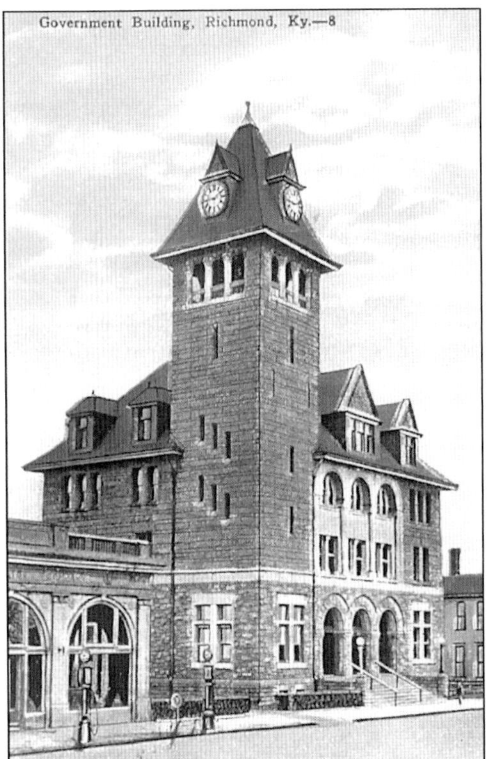

This card, with a postmark of 1932, is the Government Building in Richmond. Notice the gas pumps on the street.

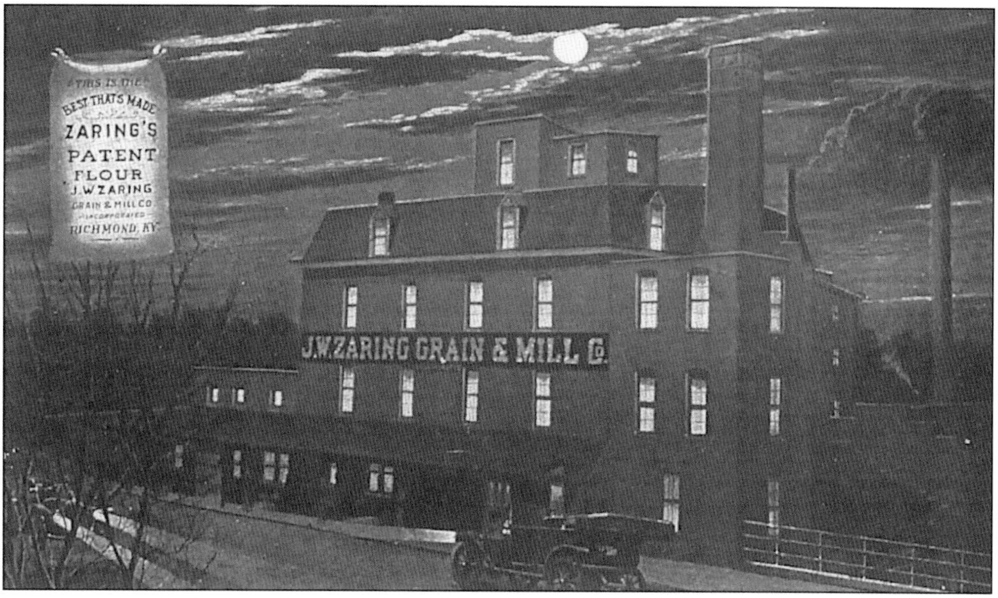

This postcard, published between 1907 and 1915, shows the J.W. Zaring Grain and Mill Company, Inc. at night.

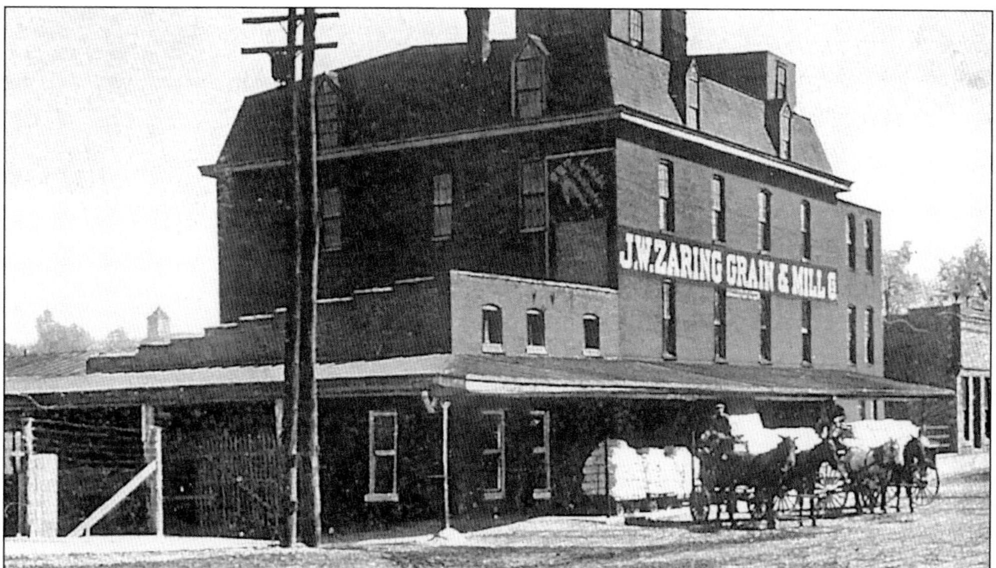

This postcard of the same time period shows a day picture of the same company. This is where Zaring's Patent Flour was made, and notice the horses and carriages.

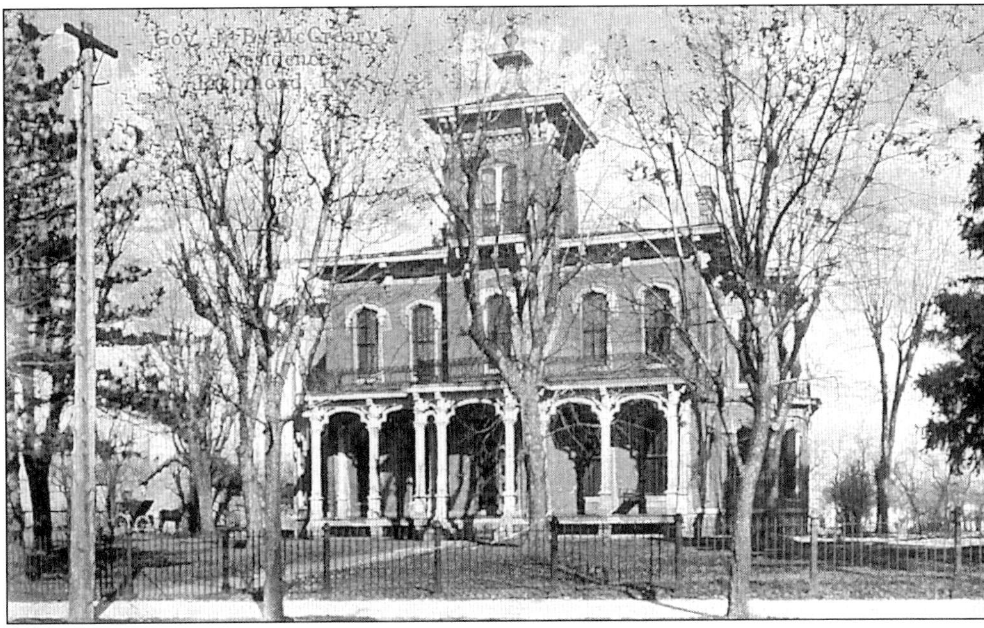

This home was the residence of Governor J.B McCreary in Richmond. James Bennett McCreary was a two-term governor of Kentucky. He was born in Madison County and served during the Civil War in the Confederate Army as cavalry major and lieutenant colonel. He served 12 years in the United States House of Representatives and one term in the United States Senate. He continued to work as a private attorney in Richmond until his death in Richmond.

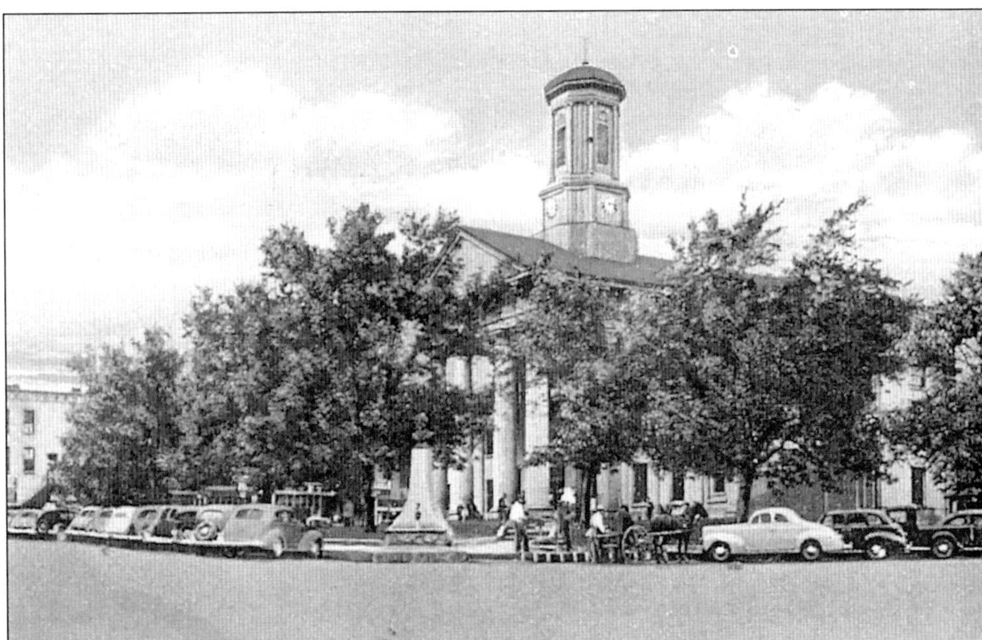

This is a *c.* 1930 view of the Madison County Courthouse in Richmond. This third and present county courthouse was built between 1848 and 1850.

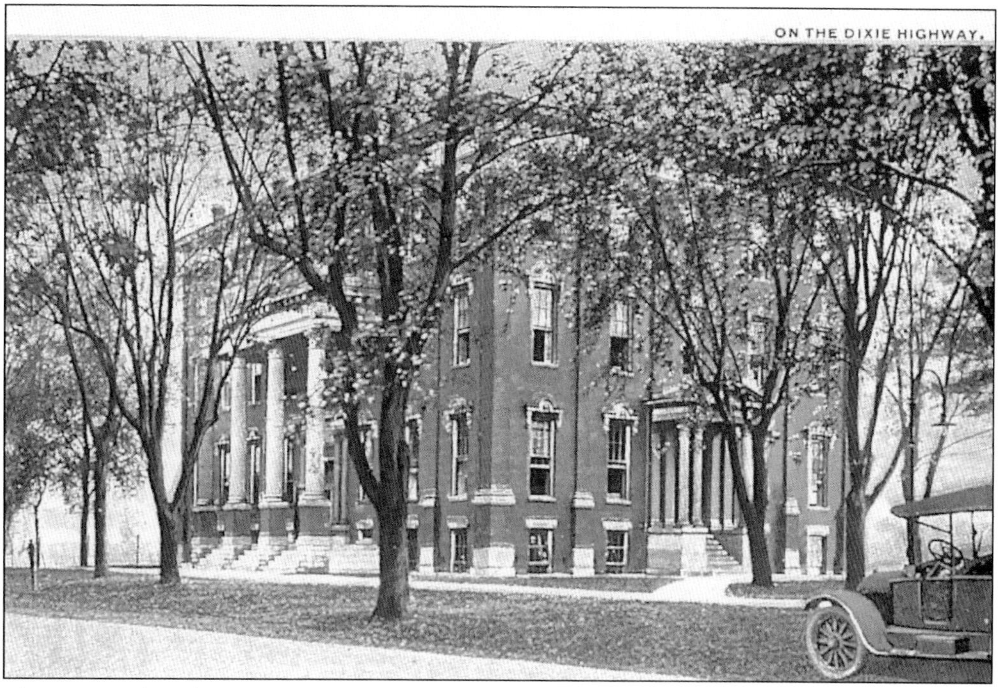

This postcard, published between 1907 and 1915, shows the University Hall of what was called the State Normal School for Teachers. It was, later, Eastern Kentucky State Teacher's College and is now Eastern Kentucky University. It was located near the Dixie Highway, or old U.S. 25 going south.

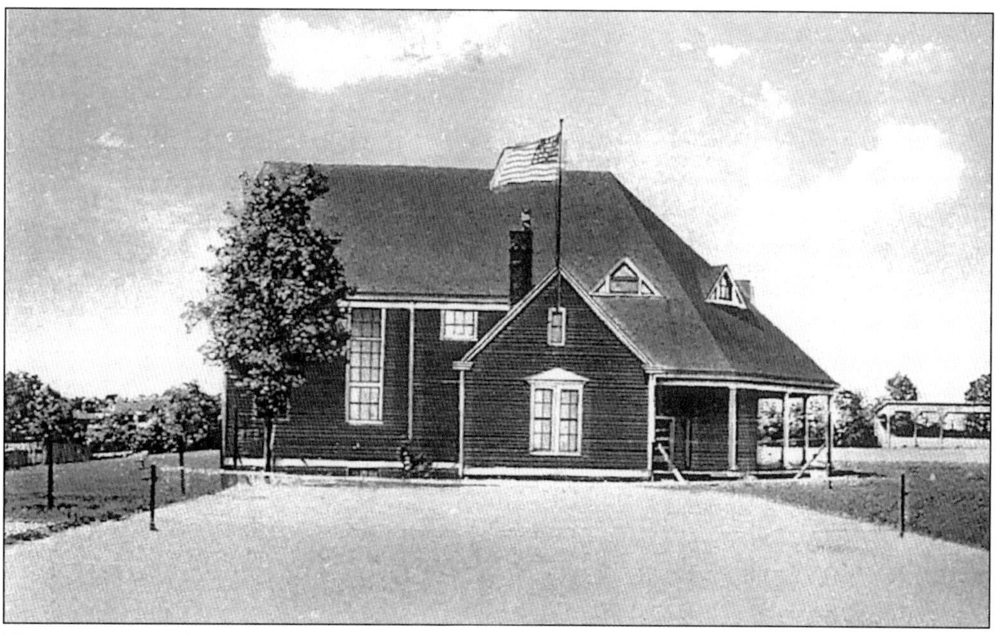

This postcard, with a postmark of 1914, shows the Miller Gymnasium at what was part of the State Normal School in Richmond. The school was started in 1874 by the Presbyterian Church, then became part of Central College in 1901, and a State Normal School for Teachers in 1906.

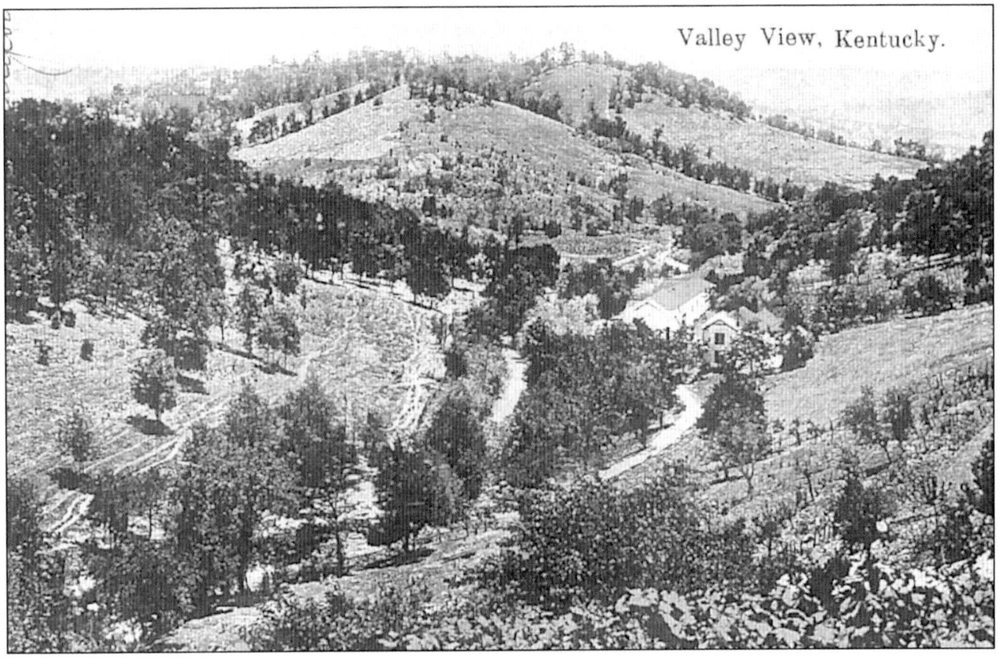

This *c.* 1907 card shows Valley View, Kentucky, in the northern part of Madison County, at the junction of Ky 169 and Tates Creek Road in Fayette County. Although not visible, Madison County joins the Kentucky River past the hills, with Jessamine and Fayette Counties on the other side. A Valley View Ferry has operated at this location for many years, being franchised by the Virginia legislature in 1785, and continues to operate today.

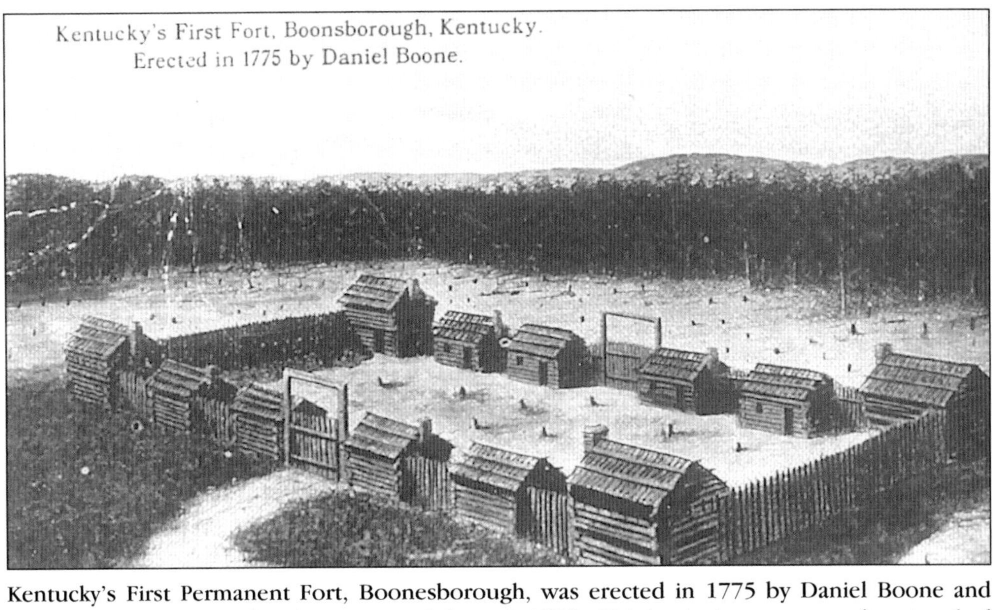

Kentucky's First Permanent Fort, Boonesborough, was erected in 1775 by Daniel Boone and continued as a village and trade center until the early 1800s. This fort is shown on a card postmarked 1912. It has since been reconstructed and opened as a working Fort open to tourists. Notice the misspelling of Boonesborough on the card, and its status as the First Fort is debatable.

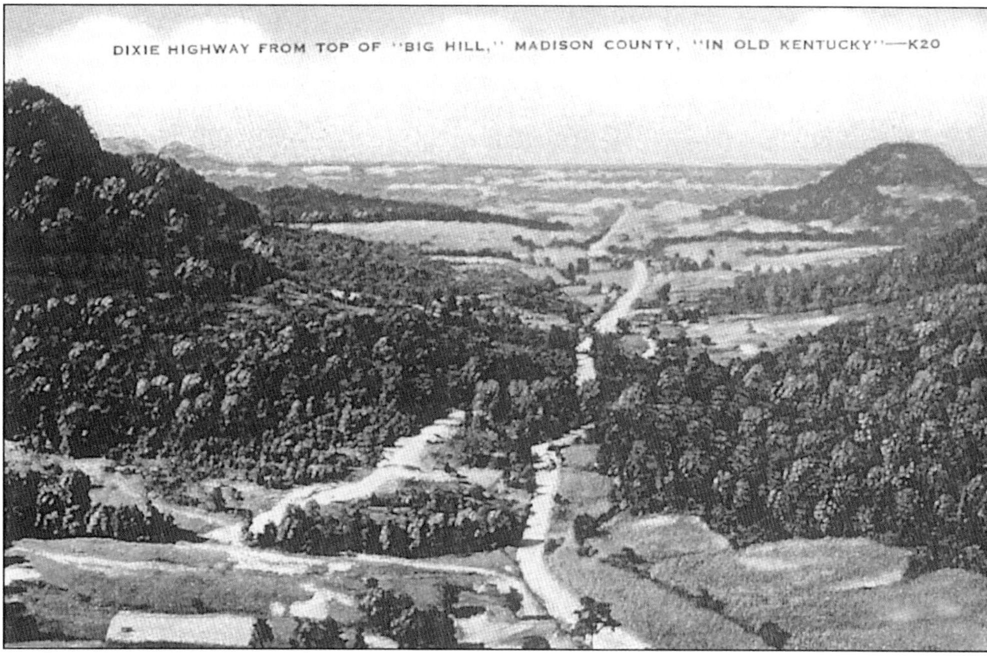

This view shows the Dixie Highway from the top of a big hill in Madison County. Dixie Highway was the old U.S. 25 going north and south through Kentucky. This postcard was published between 1915 and 1930. The first Clay's Ferry Bridge for U.S. 25 over the Kentucky River was constructed in 1869, while in 1946, it became two lanes and one of the highest bridges in the country. More lanes have been added in later years.

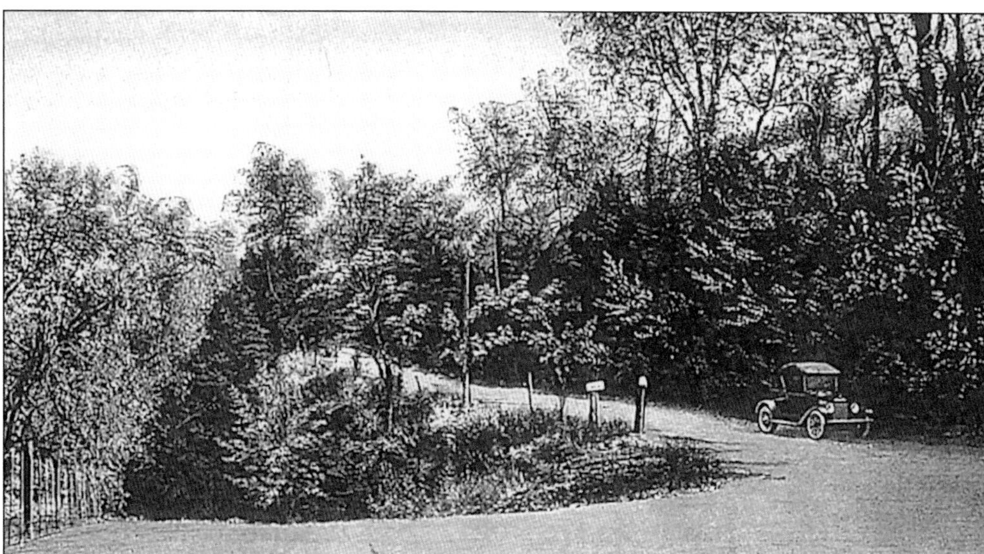

This is an earlier view (between 1915 and 1930) of Dixie Highway, near Richmond on River Hill at Hair Pin Curve, before the highway was paved.

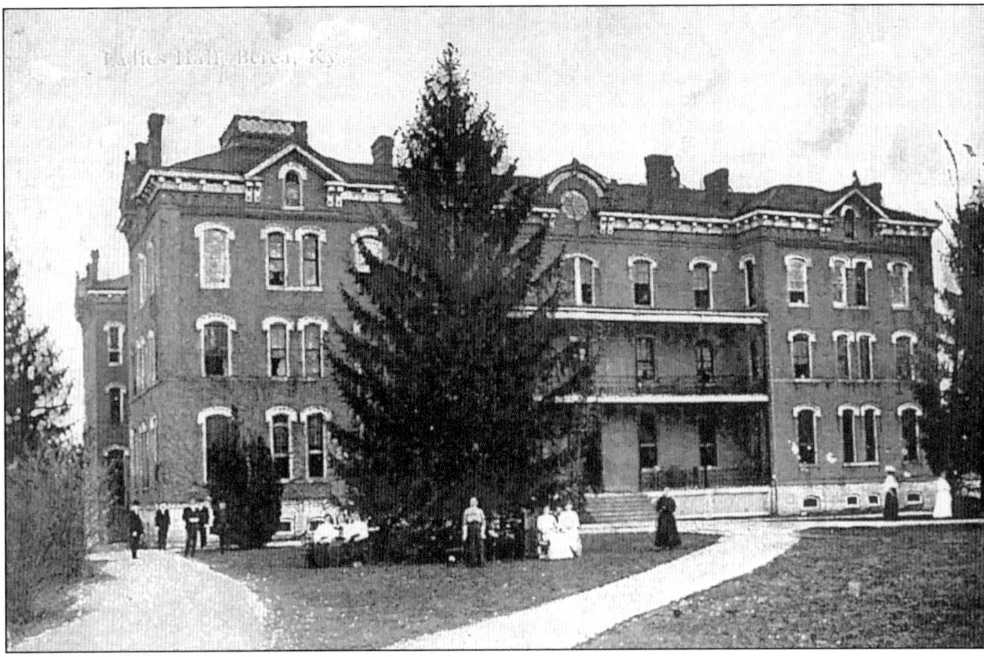

The next six postcards are more specific to Berea, Kentucky. This picture, postmarked 1912, reveals the Ladies Hall at Berea College. The College opened in 1853 to provide scholastic education for the needs of the mountain people and provided each student the opportunity to defray parts of their expenses with their own labor.

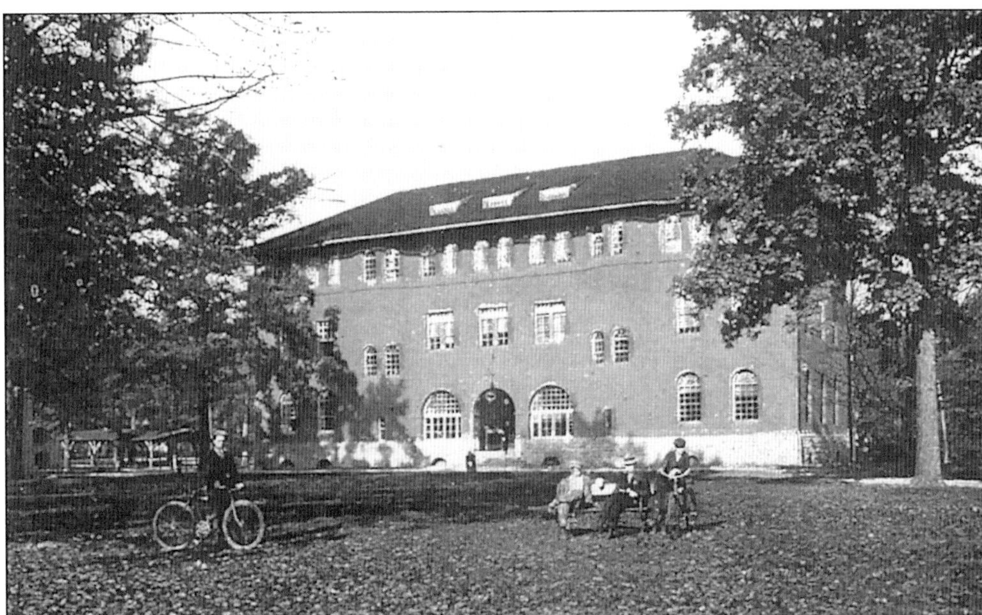

This view, published between 1907 and 1915, was taken of Lincoln Hall at Berea College. Students were employed in a broom factory, furniture shop, laundry, bakery, store, print shop, or on farms in the area.

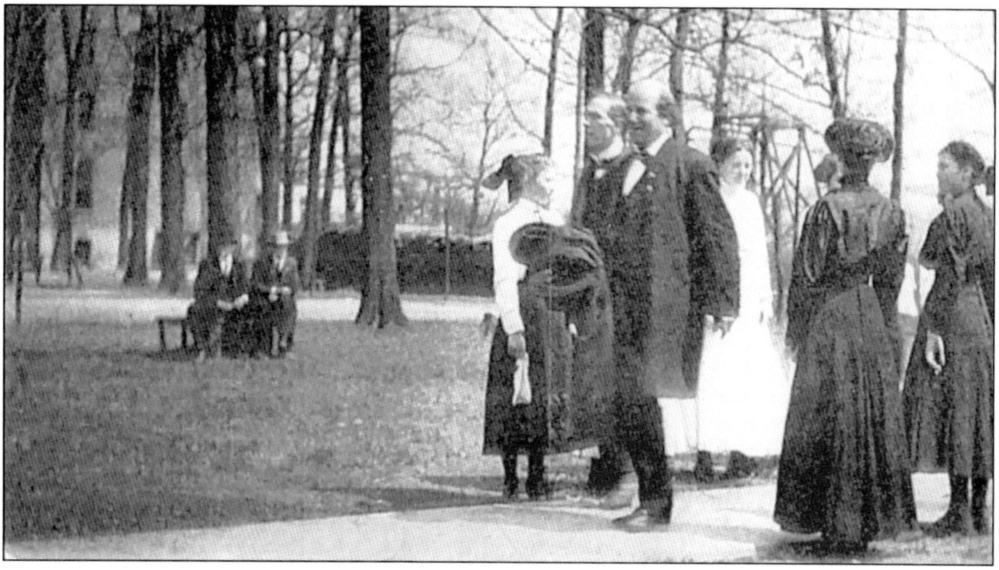

This photo postcard was taken in 1911, when William Jennings Bryan visited Berea College. Lennie Alcorn was lined on the sidewalk in front of President Frost's home, and her picture was made as William Jennings Bryan walked by. What a family treasure!

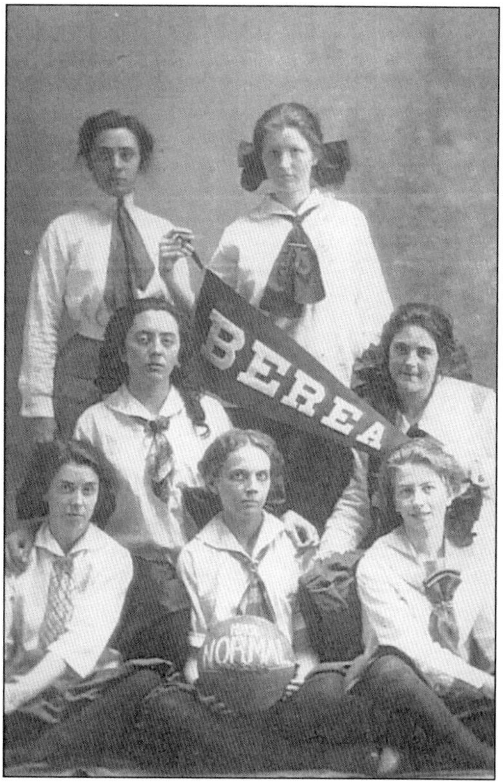

This is a photo postcard, taken in 1912, of Lennie Alcorn, Blanche Nichola, Oleo Morgan, Ruth ?, Edith Harvey, and Lorena Harvey, all students at Berea College. Lennie Alcorn later became a teacher and aunt to Peggy Brown, a fellow postcard collector and friend to the author.

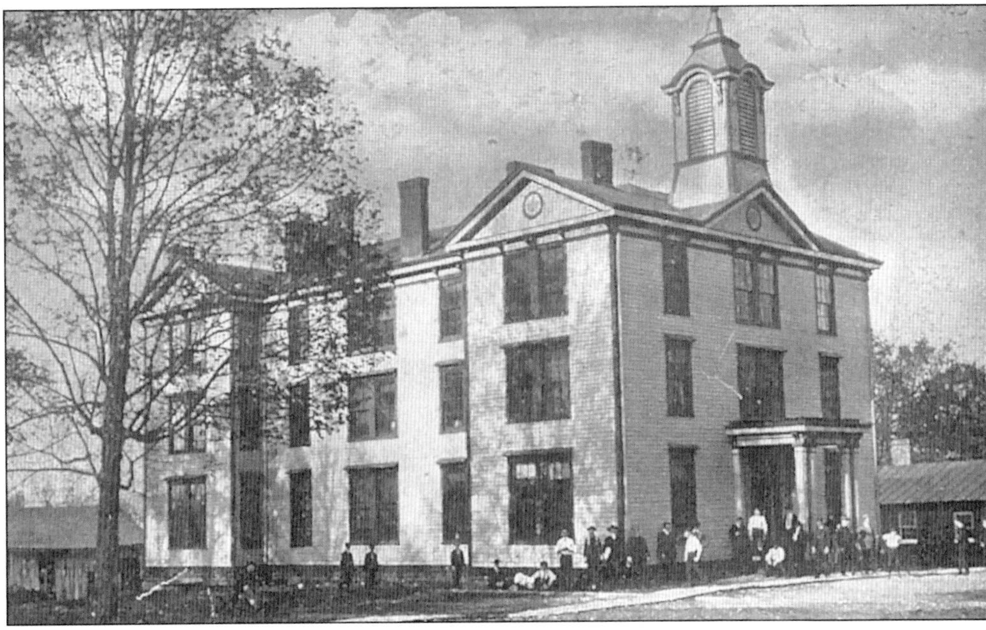

This view, published later between 1915 and 1930, was taken of Howard Hall at Berea College. A hotel called Boone Tavern, operated by Berea College, provided students additional opportunities to work their way through school.

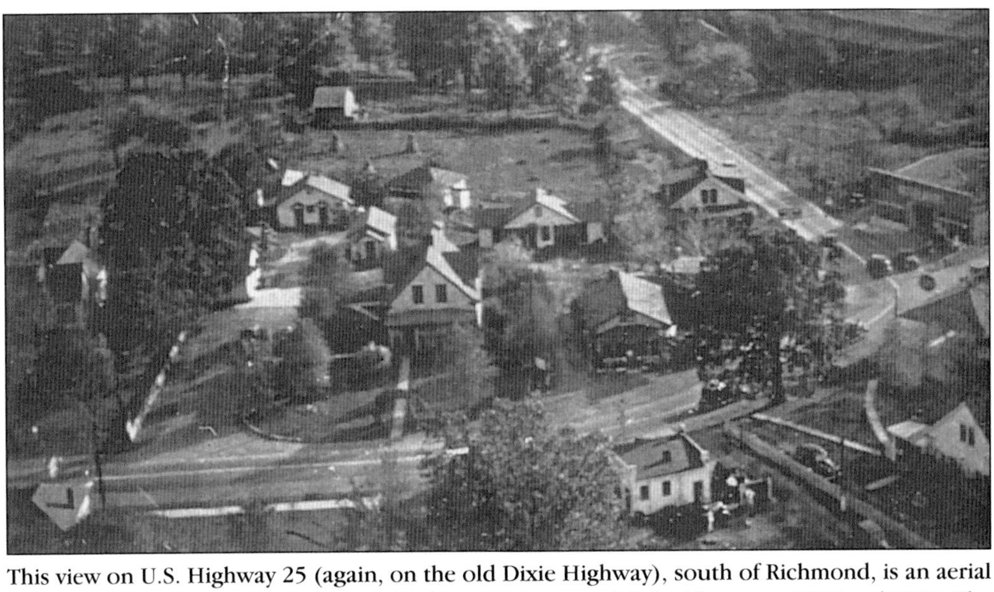

This view on U.S. Highway 25 (again, on the old Dixie Highway), south of Richmond, is an aerial view of the Sunset Inn, cabins on U.S. Highway 25. It was published between 1915 and 1930. The proprietor was M.H. Oliver.

Seven

Mercer, Nicholas, and Powell Counties

This chapter features old postcards for three counties: Mercer, Nicholas, and Powell. Mercer County was one of the nine counties erected by the legislature of Virginia before Kentucky was a state. Mercer was established in 1785, and Dicks' River, later called Dix, formed the east boundary on the Kentucky River. Harrodsburg, originally part of Lincoln County, is the oldest county seat and the oldest town in the state, now the county seat of Mercer County.

Nicholas County, the 42nd in order of formation, was formed in 1799. The Licking River flows through the county in a northwest direction and forms the northeast boundary. Carlisle is the county seat, situated on the Maysville and Lexington Railroad.

Powell County, the 101st county formed in Kentucky, was established in 1852. The Red River runs from east to west through the county, providing water power and recreation areas. The county seat and town is Stanton.

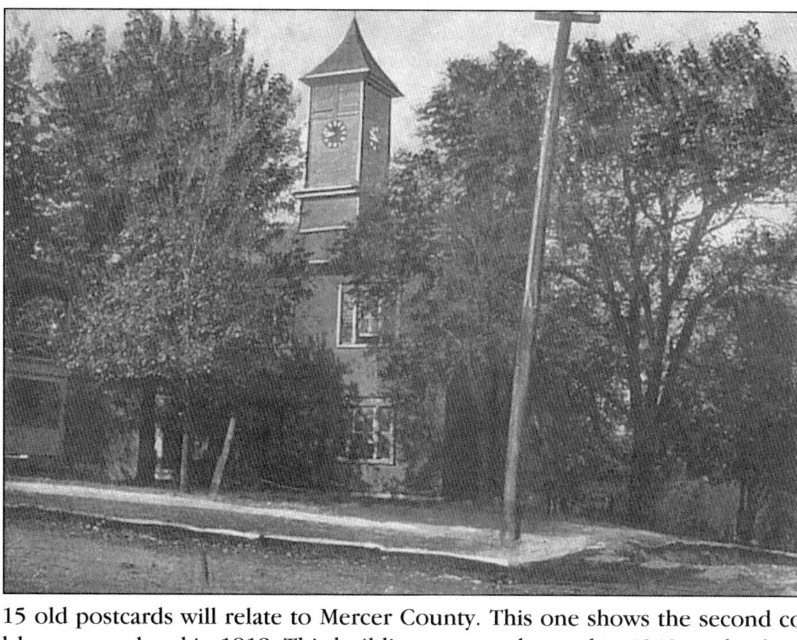

The first 15 old postcards will relate to Mercer County. This one shows the second courthouse in Harrodsburg, completed in 1818. This building was condemned in 1910, and a third one, the current one, was built from 1912 to 1913.

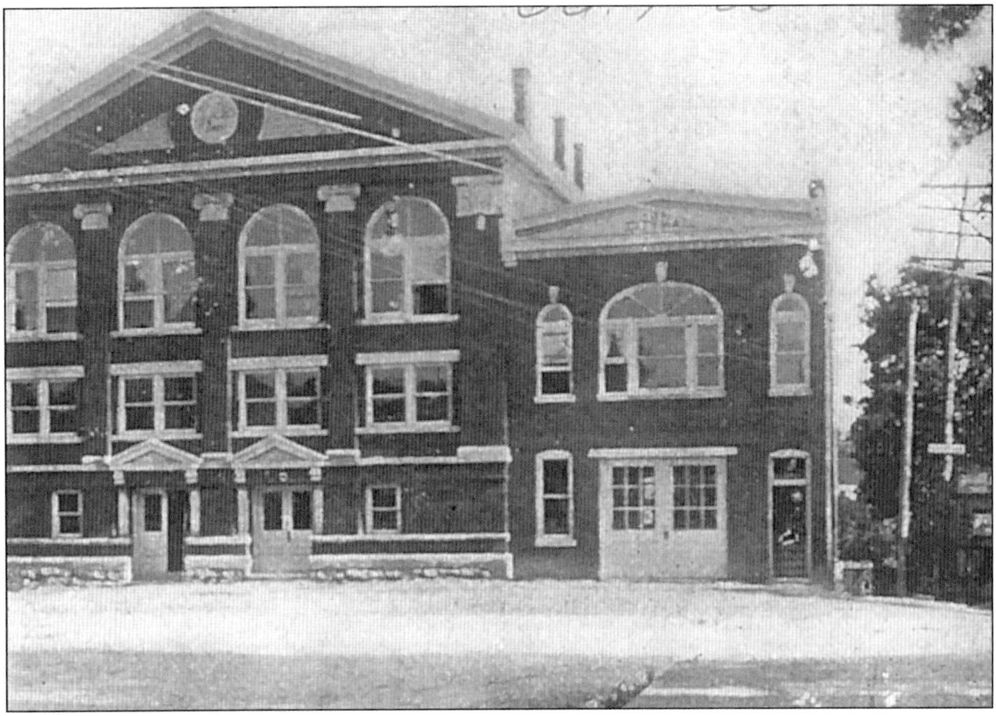

This postcard, with a handwritten date of October 9, 1906, shows the I.O. of O.F. Temple, opera house, and city hall in Harrodsburg.

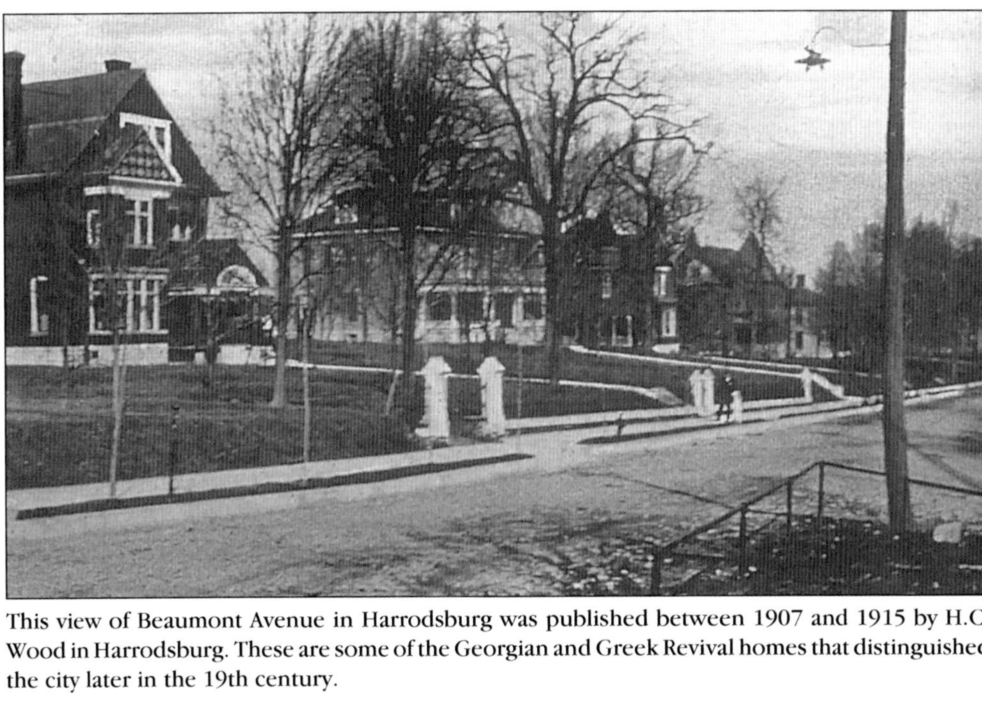

This view of Beaumont Avenue in Harrodsburg was published between 1907 and 1915 by H.C. Wood in Harrodsburg. These are some of the Georgian and Greek Revival homes that distinguished the city later in the 19th century.

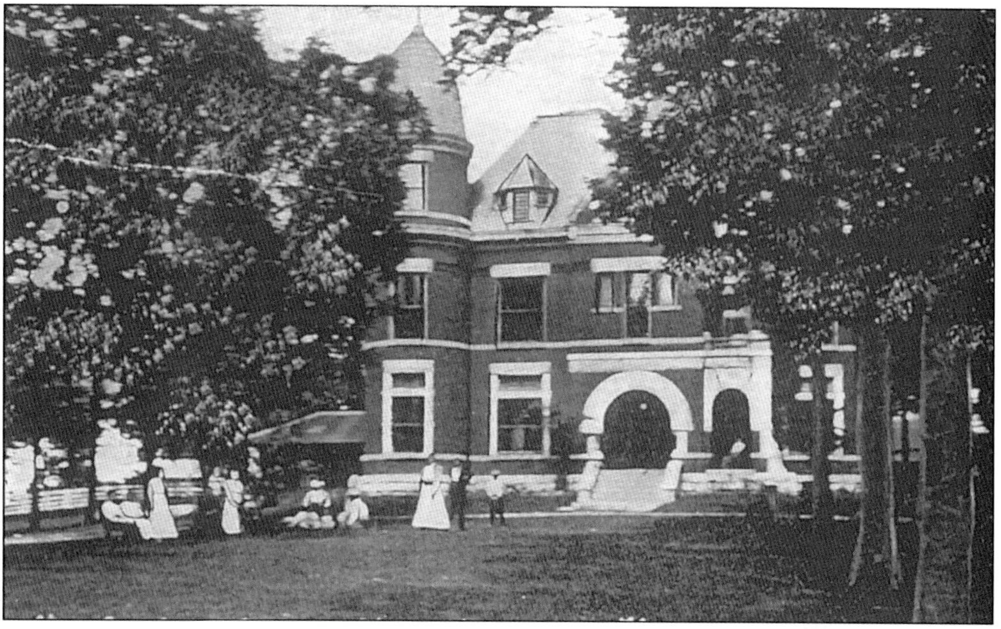

This postcard, showing the New Graham Springs Hotel in Harrodsburg, was published *c.* 1907.

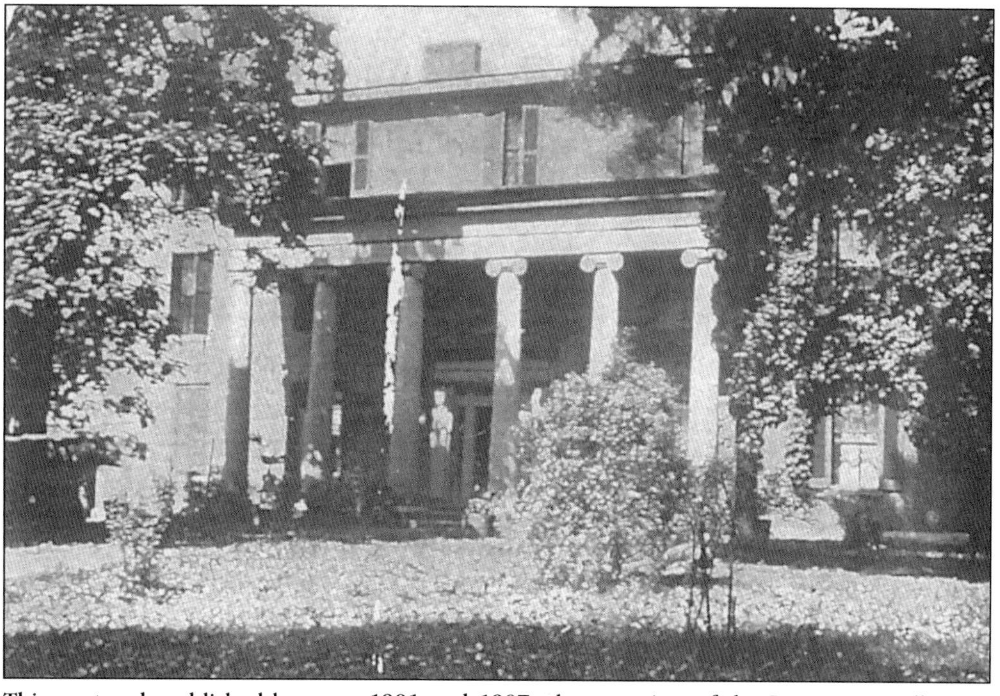

This postcard, published between 1901 and 1907, shows a view of the Beaumont College in Harrodsburg. It had originally been the Greenville Female Academy and one of the most prominent schools in Kentucky. Another postcard, published between 1930 and 1945, shows the same view of the Beaumont Inn, which was recommended by Duncan Hines. The Inn was advertised as having rooms with or without baths.

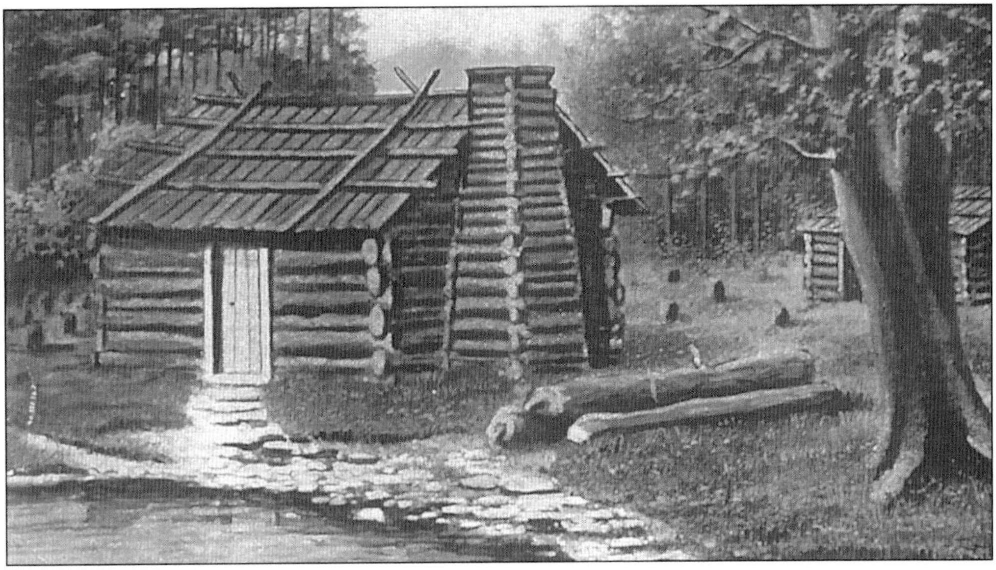

This picture of Kentucky's first cabin, built in 1774 by Jas. Harrod, had to be taken from a previous picture, this postcard having been published between 1907 and 1915. Pioneers came to Kentucky and laid out the town of Harrodsburg. After succeeding with the first hurried log cabins, next came homes of hand-hewn squared logs and later, Georgian and Greek Revival brick homes that later distinguished the town.

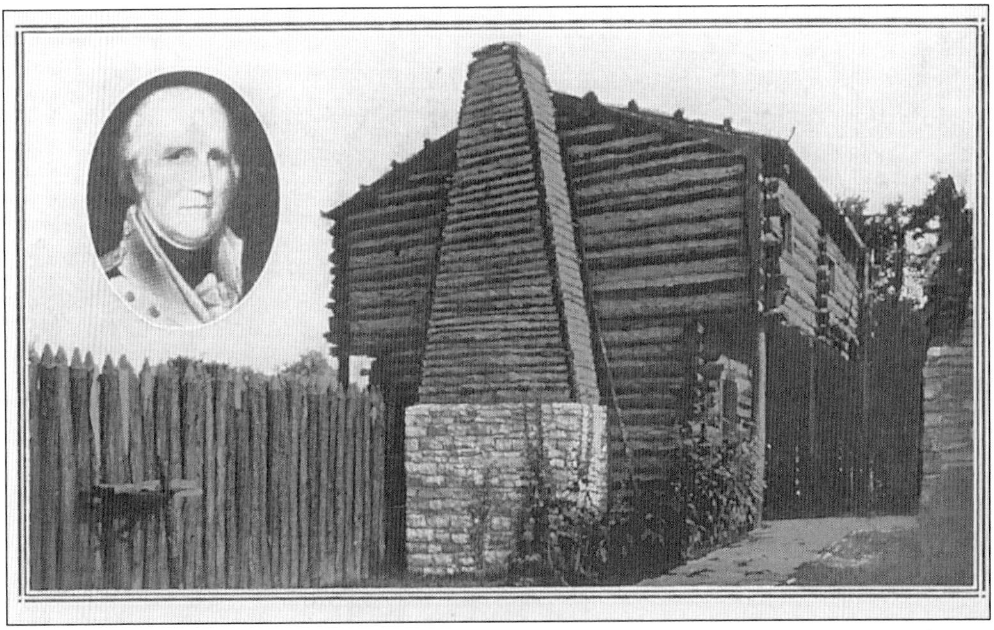

This postcard shows the George Rogers Clark Blockhouse at Fort Harrod, more currently part of the Pioneer Memorial State Park. Clark initiated the conquest of the northwest from this blockhouse in 1777. Also included in the Pioneer Park is the cabin in which Thomas Lincoln and Nancy Hanks were married on June 12, 1806. They were the parents of Abraham Lincoln, and this is all part of the Lincoln Family connection to "old Kentucky."

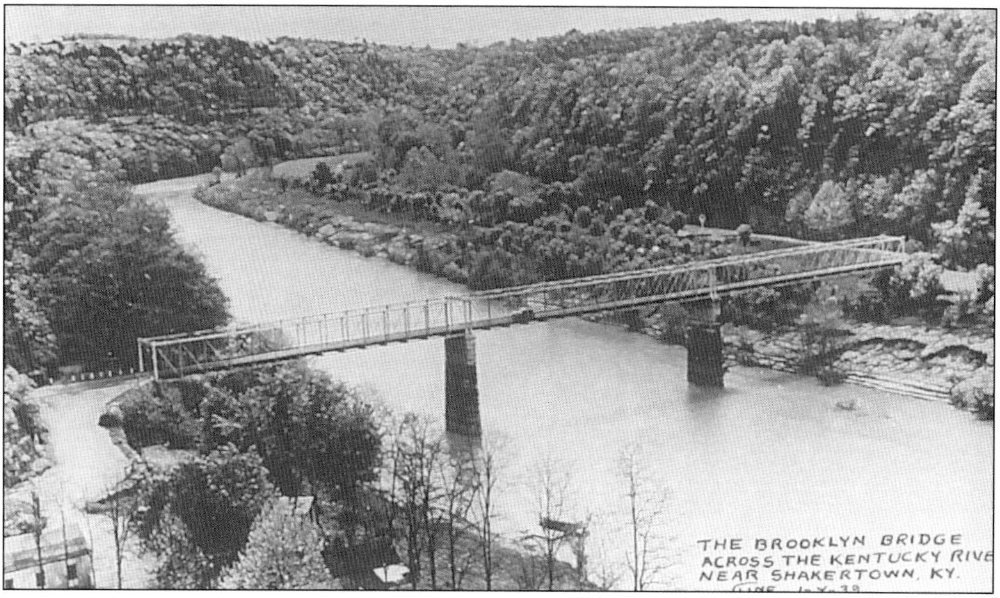

This is a photo view of the Brooklyn Bridge across the Kentucky River near Shakertown into Mercer County. The opposite side of this Brooklyn Bridge goes to Wilmore, in Jessamine County. The town of Brooklyn existed at this location, with a ferry, from 1845 to 1871. The town was destroyed by flood and fire by the late 19th century. The first Brooklyn Bridge was built in 1871 on what became U.S. 68.

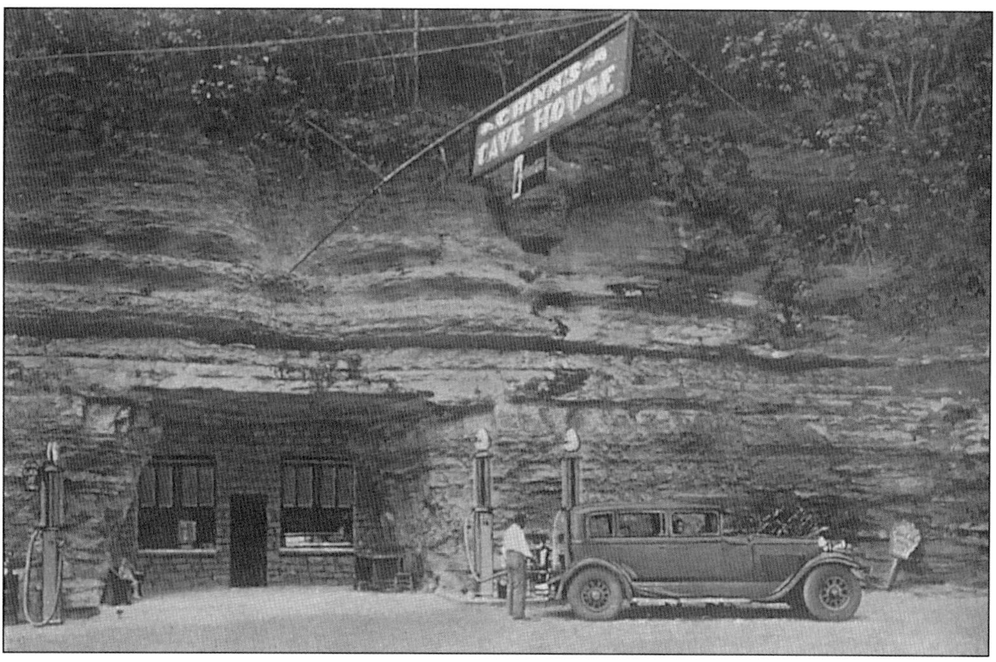

This postcard, published between 1907 and 1915, shows the Chinn's Cave House Gas Station. It was the most unique filling station in the world, being chiseled out of solid rock at the Brooklyn Bridge. It was originally a cave house, where refreshments were sold, and the cave provided refrigeration.

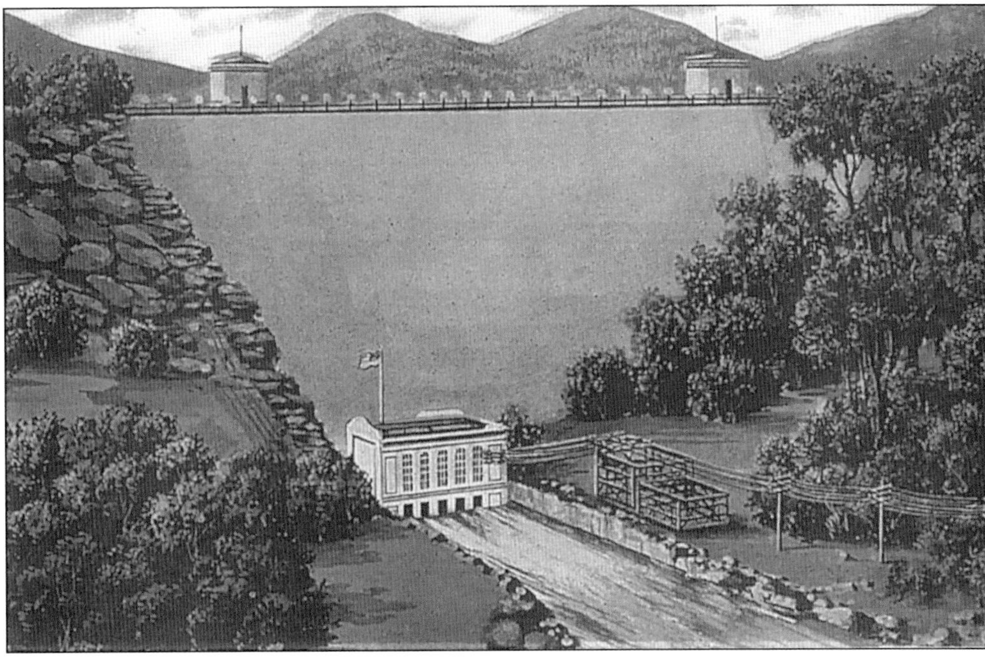

This is actually located between Mercer and Garrard Counties on Herrington Lake. This *c.* 1924 view of Dix River shows the Hydro-Electric Dam that was erected in 1924. It was formed by a wall of concrete built across the deep canyon valley of the Dix River. Hydro-electric power generated in the power house at the base of the dam was distributed throughout the Bluegrass region.

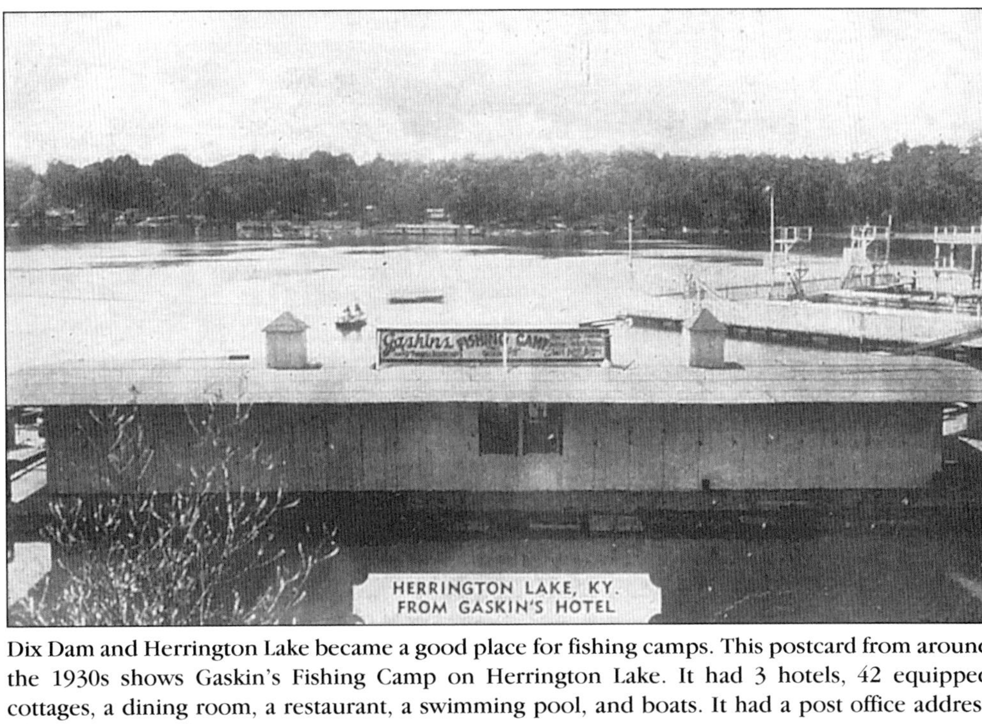

Dix Dam and Herrington Lake became a good place for fishing camps. This postcard from around the 1930s shows Gaskin's Fishing Camp on Herrington Lake. It had 3 hotels, 42 equipped cottages, a dining room, a restaurant, a swimming pool, and boats. It had a post office address of Burgin, Kentucky.

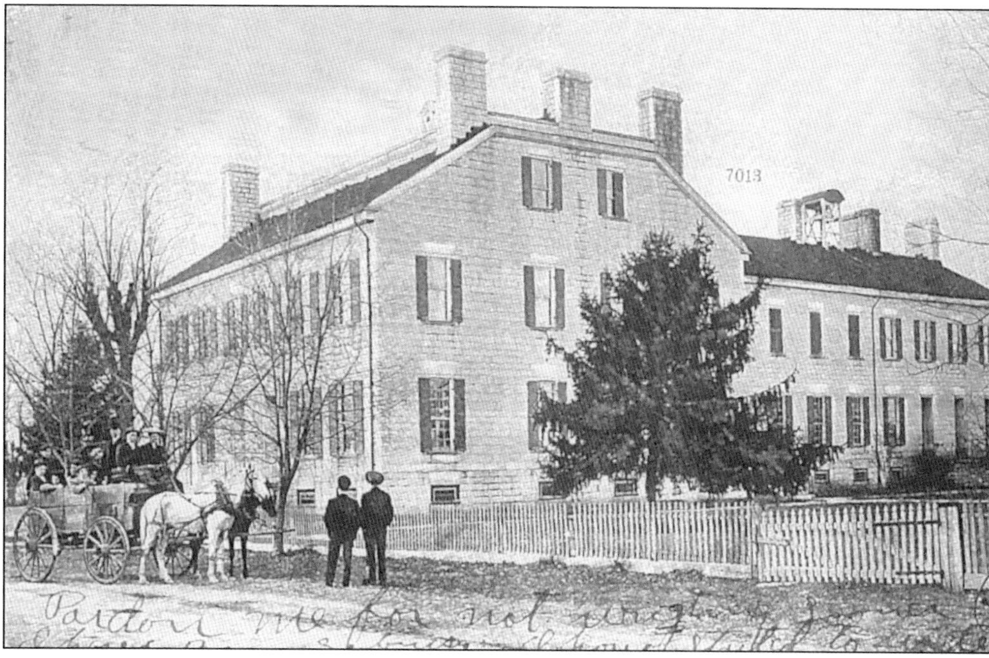

The next two postcards will focus on Shakertown in Mercer County. This postcard is postmarked 1907 and includes information about this women's building of the Shaker sect. There were originally 480 members but by the early 1900s there were 38 as they eventually died out. Marriage and intermingling between sexes was prohibited. This building was started in 1824 and took ten years to complete from hand-quarried Kentucky limestone.

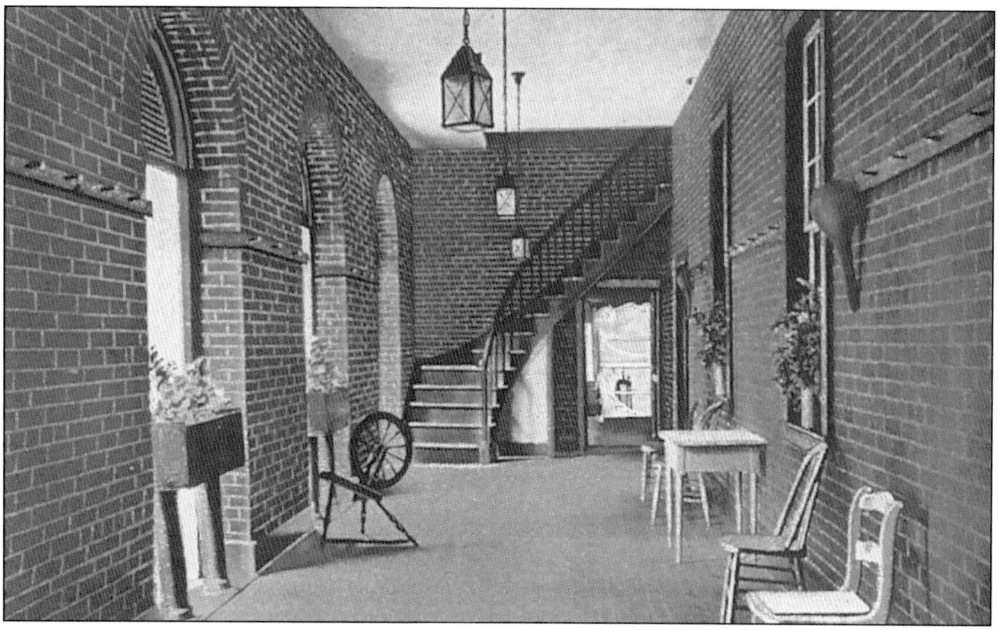

This postcard shows the Shaker Village guest house, called Spiral Hall Garden. The original Historical Shaker Village was founded on the principles of altruism, simple living, and hard work. Shakertown is now a significant tourist attraction after having been restored.

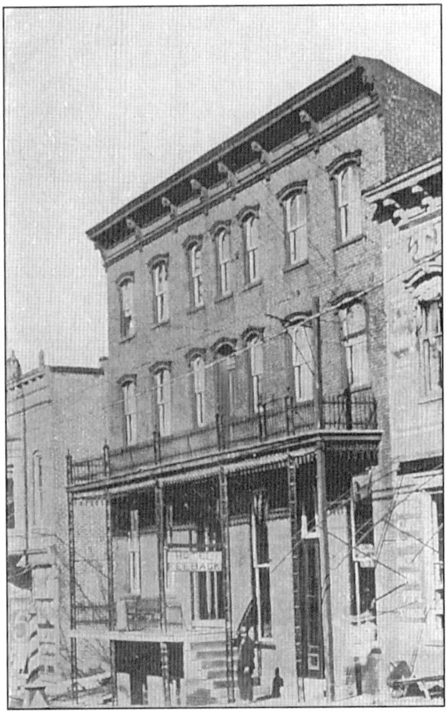

The next four postcards will relate to Nicholas County, which is on the northeast edge of the Bluegrass. This postcard, with a postmark of 1912, shows the Feeback Hotel in Carlisle, Kentucky. Notice the barber pole on the left and the man standing in the middle. This is a rare picture.

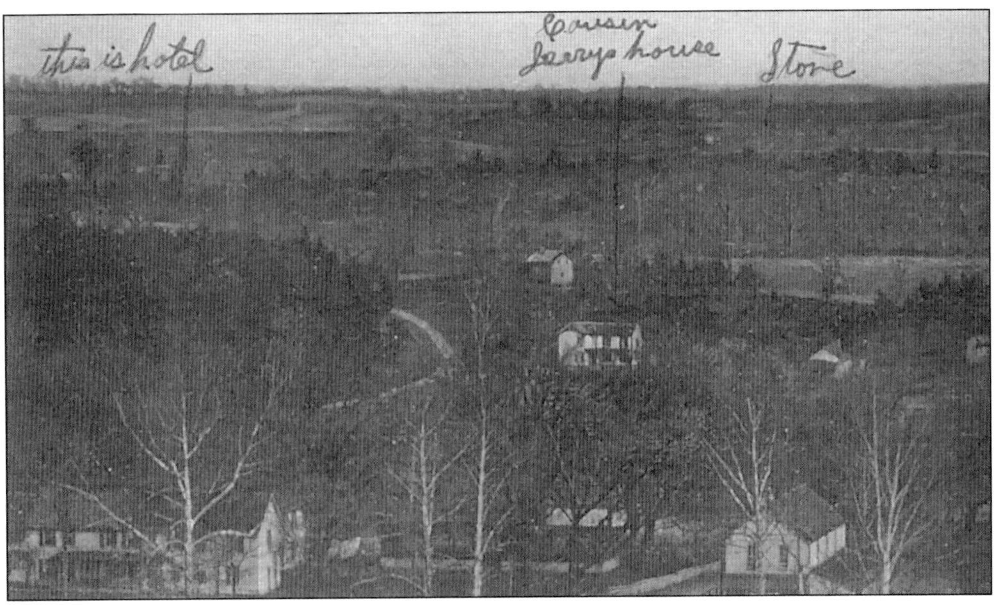

This postcard, which is faded and difficult to see, is a bird's-eye view of the famous Blue Lick Springs. What is more interesting, someone has drawn lines to show the hotel and "cousin Jerry's house." On the back is a long handwritten note that includes, "not a thing to do but rest in Cousin Jerry's nice sweet home, . . . so you see I won't have a thing to do but get well . . . I hope your pa's back is better, love to each of you, Mama." This postcard was postmarked from Blue Licks Springs in 1909. The lower Blue Licks Post Office opened in 1805 and operated as Blue Lick Springs from 1850 to 1919. The Springs was a popular spa during the 1800s.

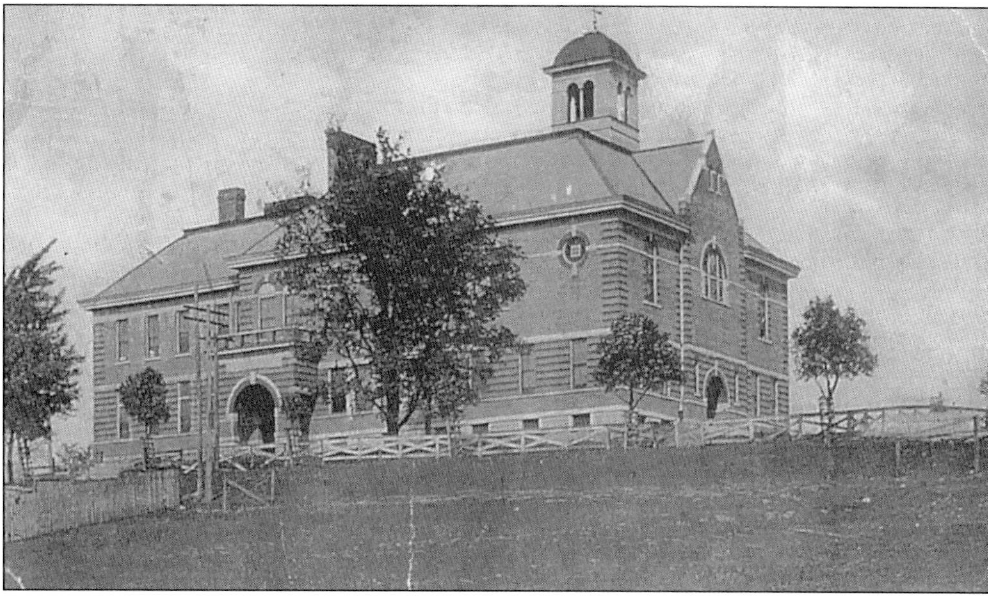

This postcard, with a postmark of 1911, shows the High School Building of Carlisle.

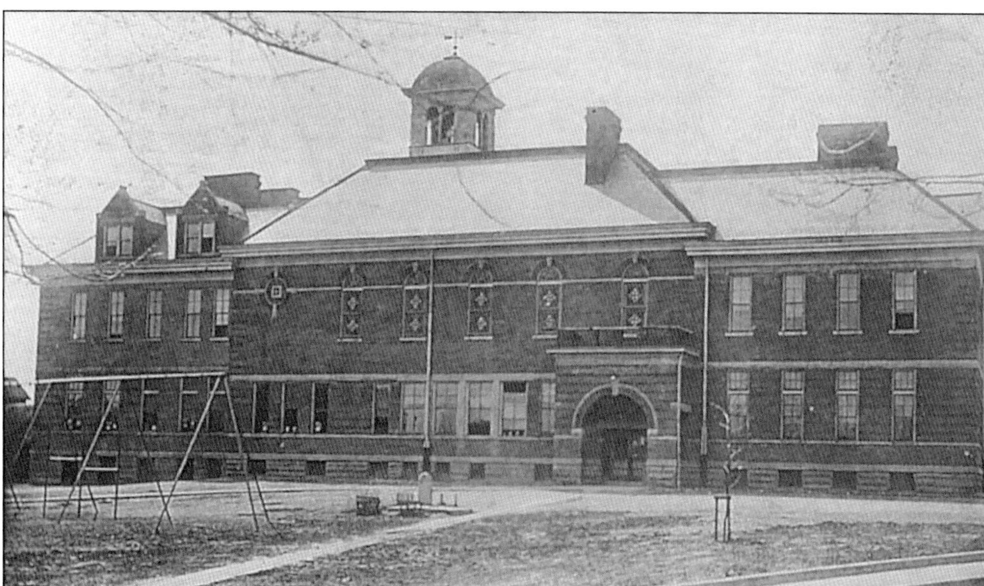

This postcard, showing the Carlisle City School, is similar to the previous card; however, it was postmarked 1937, a later date than the previous one.

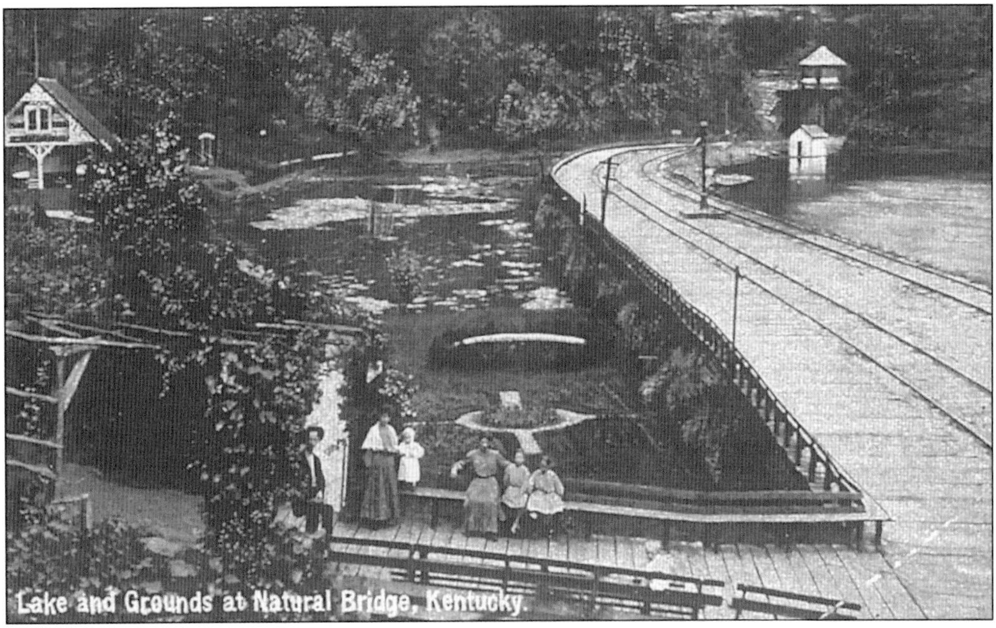

The next two postcards will be related to Powell County. This one, with a postmark of 1911, shows the lake and grounds of Natural Bridge, Kentucky. This is a great area for camping and seeing the beauty of nature near Slade, Kentucky. The area was known as Beaver Pond. A U.S. Post Office opened in 1849, and the area was renamed Stanton in 1852.

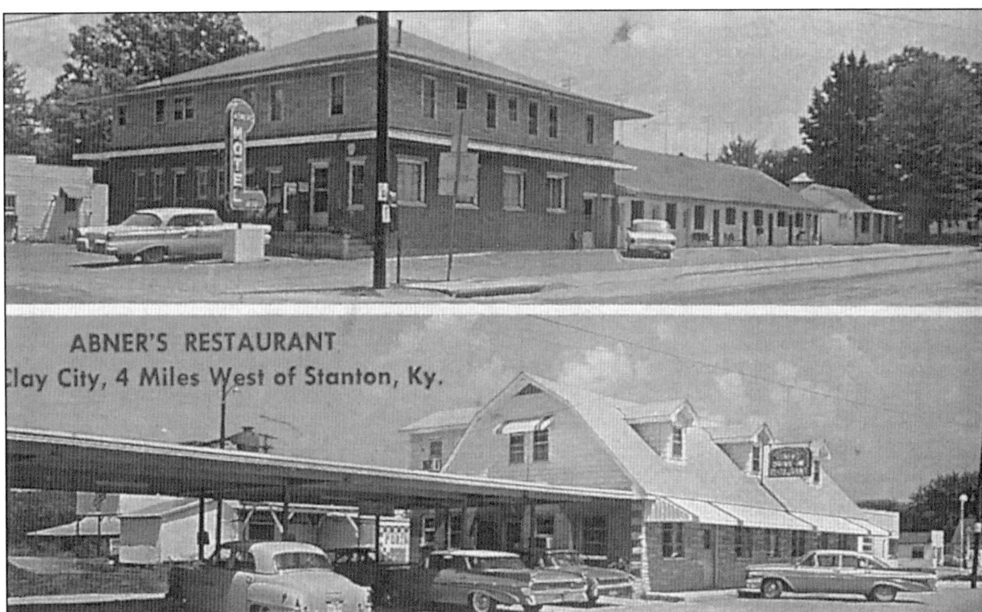

This postcard, published in the 1950s, shows newer buildings in Stanton, Kentucky. One is the Abner's Hotel, with 21 units and 10 furnished apartments. They are 14 miles from Natural Bridge, which is in the next county. The other is Abner's Restaurant in Clay City, which is west of Stanton. This is roadside America, with the drive-in restaurant and the motels, at the Mountain Parkway Exit and Kentucky State Highway 15.

Eight

Scott and Woodford Counties

This chapter will include old postcards of only two Bluegrass counties, Scott and Woodford. Scott County was named in honor of General Charles Scott, who later became governor between 1808 and 1812. South Elkhorn forms the south, southwest, and southeastern boundary of Scott County. Georgetown is the county seat and was originally settled in 1775 as McClelland's Station, then renamed Lebanon, and, later, incorporated by the Virginia legislature to Georgetown in honor of George Washington.

Woodford County was formed in 1788 and was the ninth county organized by Virginia before Kentucky became a state. The Kentucky River forms the entire southern and western boundaries, while the South Elkhorn Creek forms its northeast border. Versailles is the county seat, which was named after the city of Versailles in France. Another town, Midway, named for its central position between Frankfort and Lexington, was incorporated in 1846.

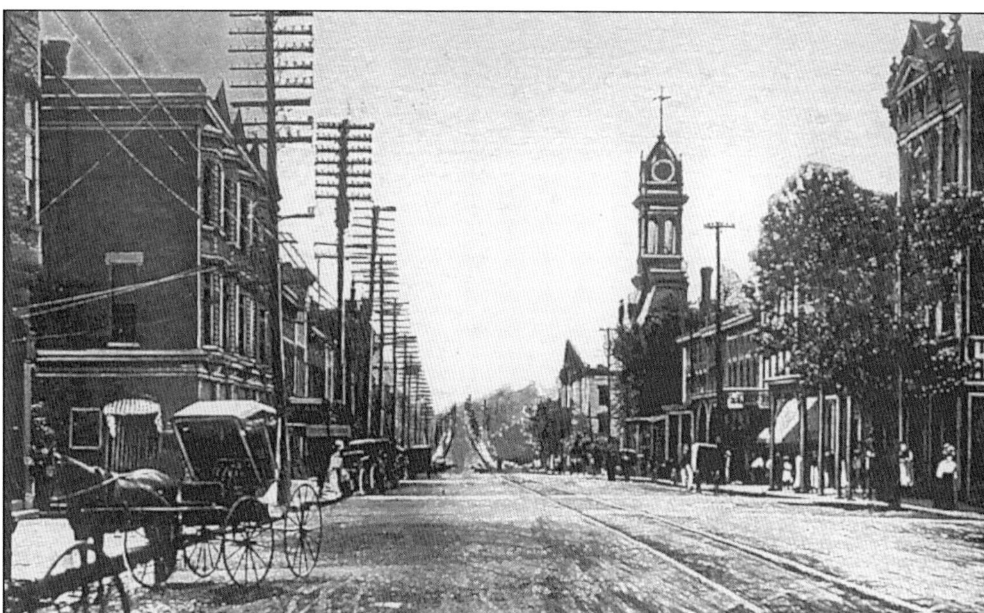

The next ten old postcards of the Bluegrass will focus on Georgetown of Scott County. This postcard, with a postmark of 1909, shows the business section and main street of Georgetown.

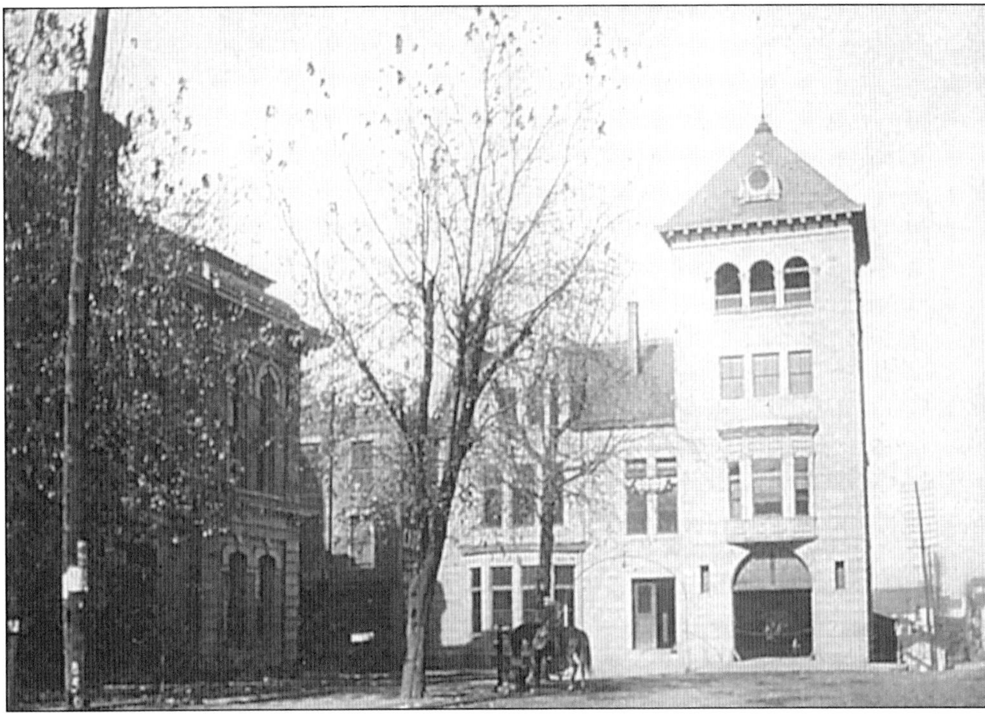

This view shows the city hall of Georgetown. Of the county's 200 historic landmarks, most are fine old residences or buildings in Georgetown.

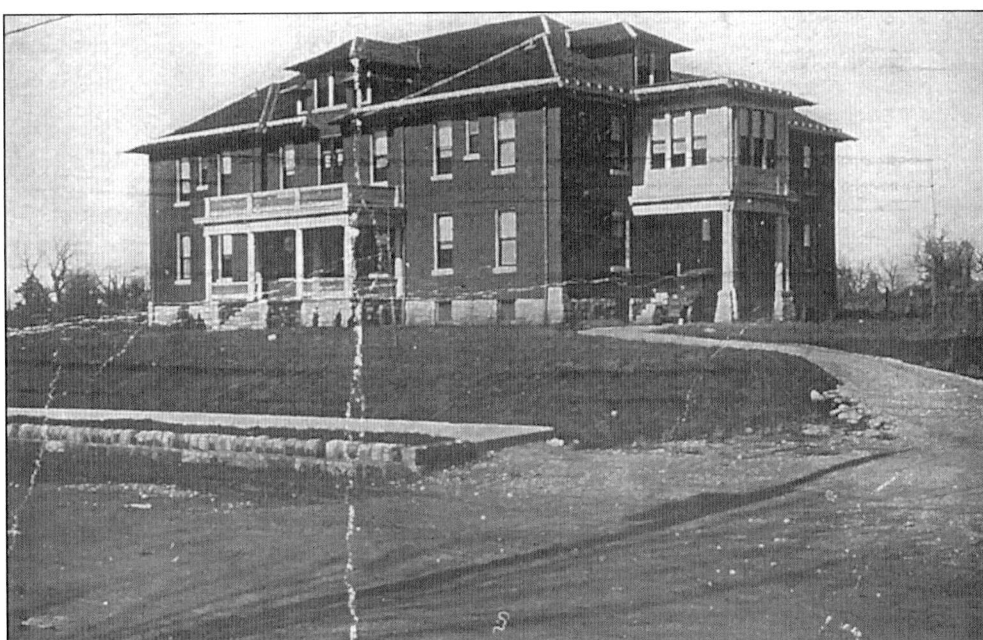

This postcard, published between 1916 and 1930, shows the John Graves Memorial Hospital in Georgetown.

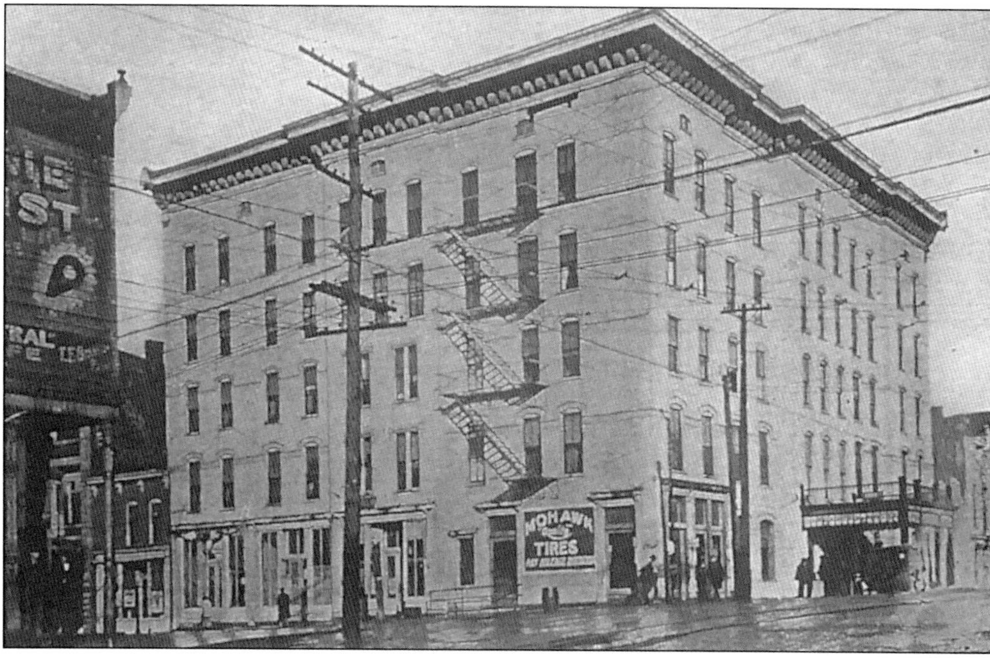

This view, taken between 1916 and 1930, shows the Lancaster Hotel in downtown Georgetown. Notice the advertisement for Mohawk quality tires on the side of the building, which says, "pay mileage dividends."

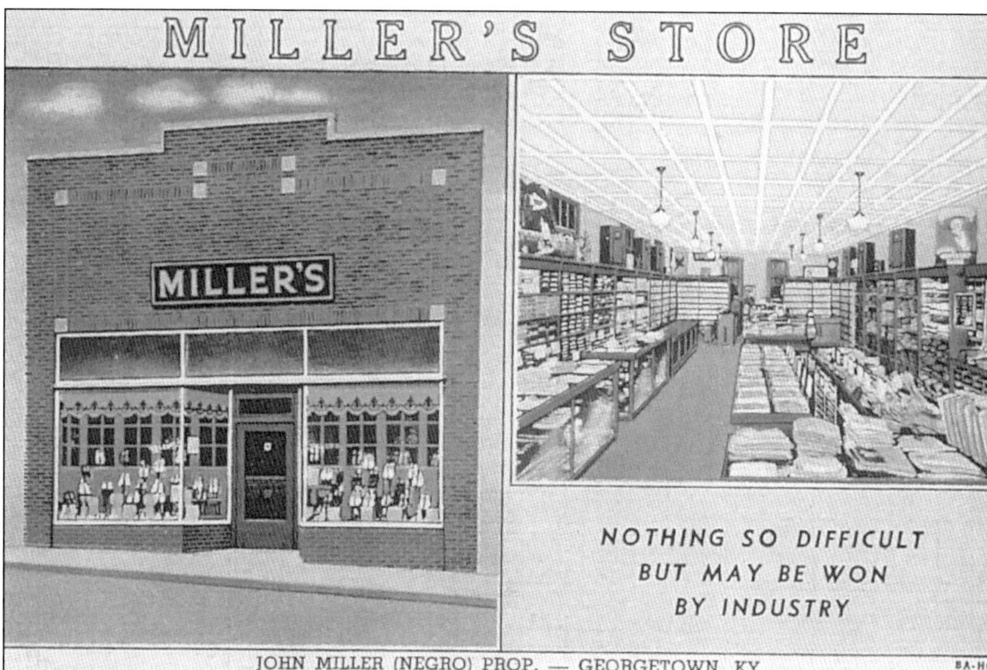

A view of Miller's Store, published between 1930 and 1945, shows the inside of the store with a slogan, with the proprietor's name and race printed on the postcard.

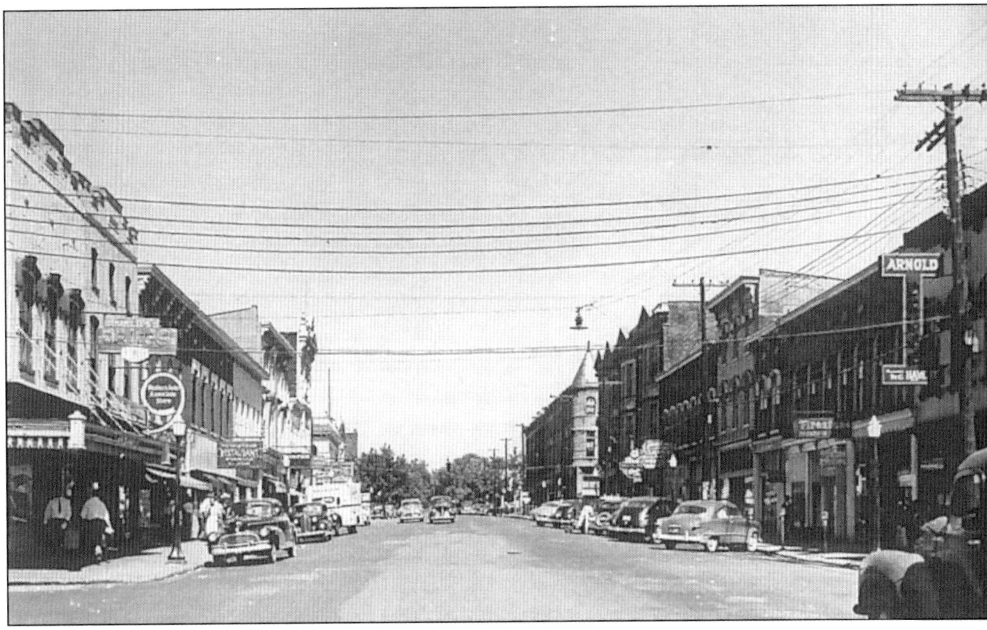

The next two views were taken at a later time period, between the 1940s and 1950s. This one shows the street scene in Georgetown showing the Western Auto Associate Store, Hamilton Drugs, and a restaurant all on the left side. On the right shows Arnold Drugs and a Firestone store.

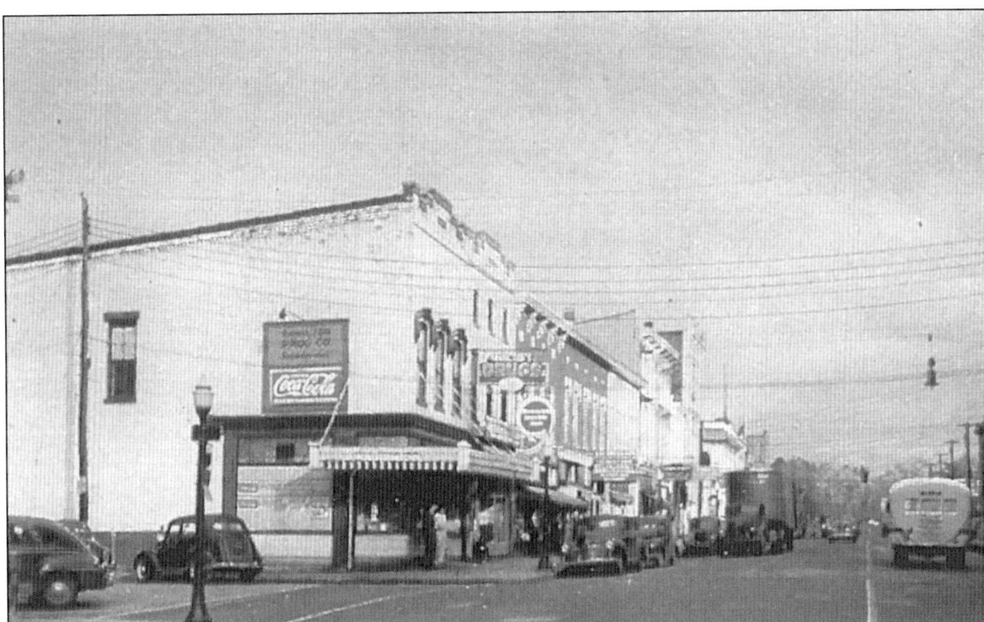

This view is similar to that of the Western Auto Associate Store, Hamilton Drugs, and the restaurant but does not show the right side of the street.

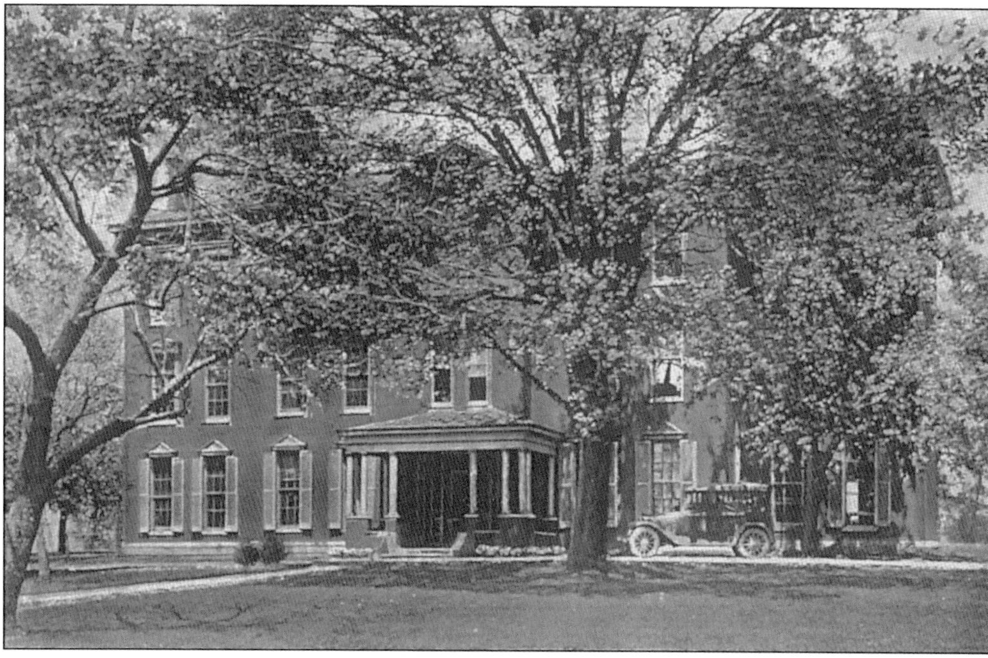

Both postcards on this page show pictures of Georgetown College between the time period of 1911 and 1930. This view shows Pawling Hall. Notice the automobile.

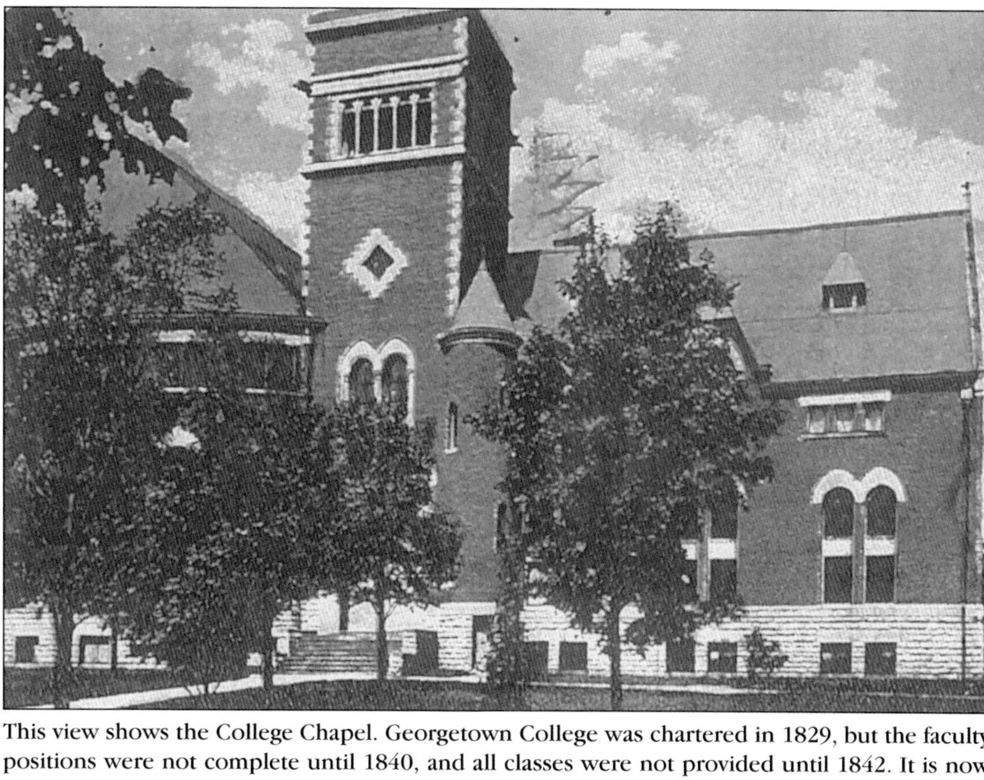

This view shows the College Chapel. Georgetown College was chartered in 1829, but the faculty positions were not complete until 1840, and all classes were not provided until 1842. It is now the second oldest Baptist College in the United States.

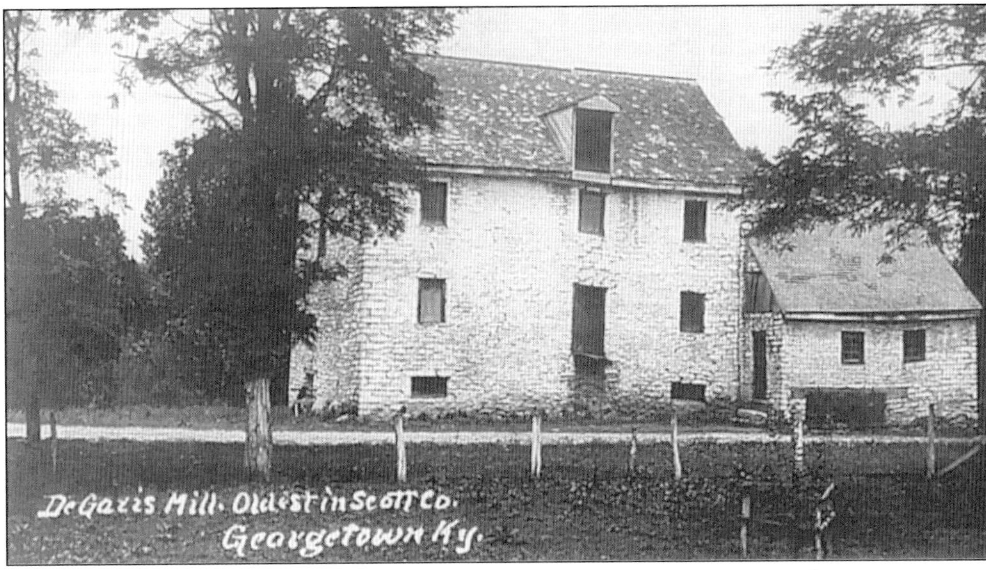

This postcard shows the DeGaris Mill in Georgetown, listed as the oldest mill in Scott County. The Weisenberger Mill on South Elkhorn is considered to be the last flour mill in Scott County. It is difficult to determine if these two mills are the same with different owner names or if they were two different types of mills. There was a John DeGaris, who bought a mill in 1854 in Georgetown, Kentucky.

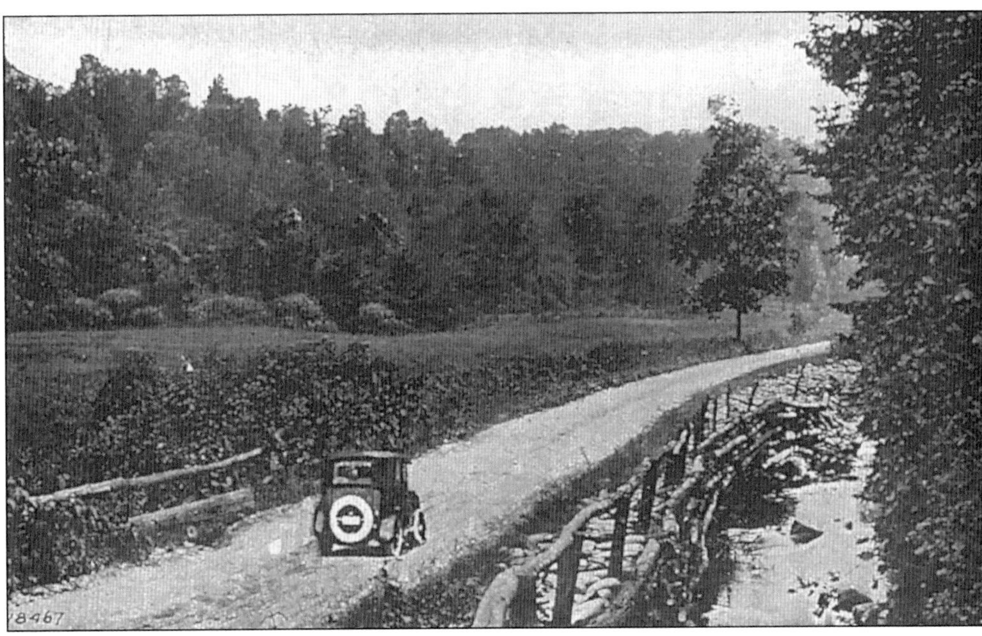

This postcard, published between 1915 and 1930, shows the landscape around Georgetown, with limestone rocks in the creek and a road of that time period.

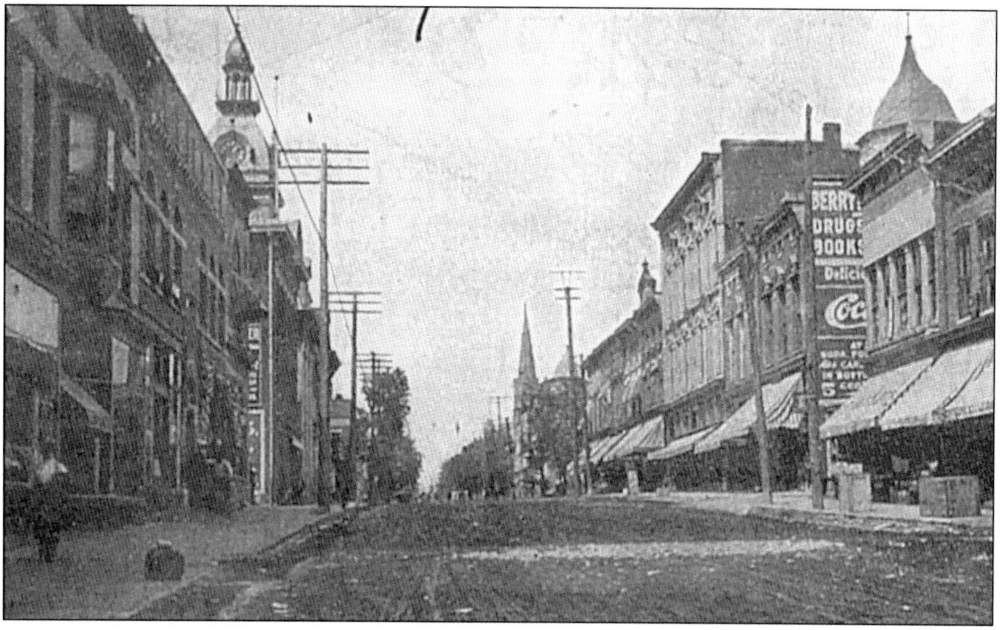

This postcard, published around 1910, shows the main street of Versailles, Kentucky. The courthouse cupola and clock can be seen on the left, along with two people on the sidewalk.

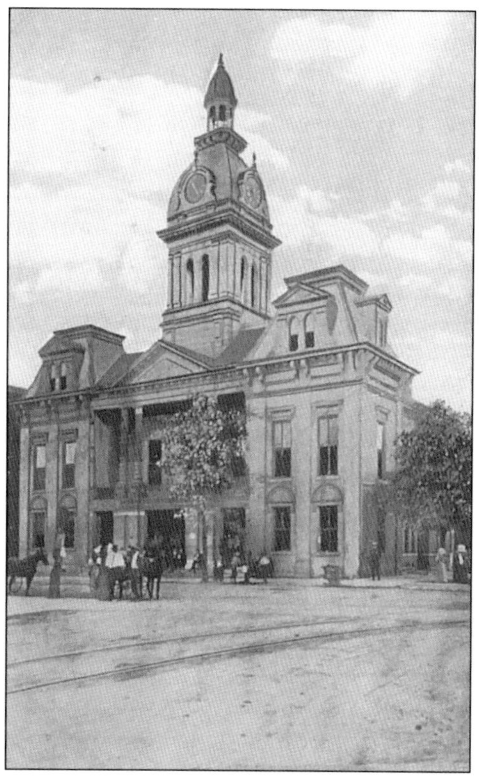

This postcard shows a *c.* 1915 view of the courthouse in Versailles. This was the third Woodford County Courthouse. It was built in 1809, with the cupola and clock being added in 1845. Renovations over the years have included the mansard-roofed towers and room additions. In 1965, the building burned, and a fourth and current courthouse was built, and it was dedicated in 1970.

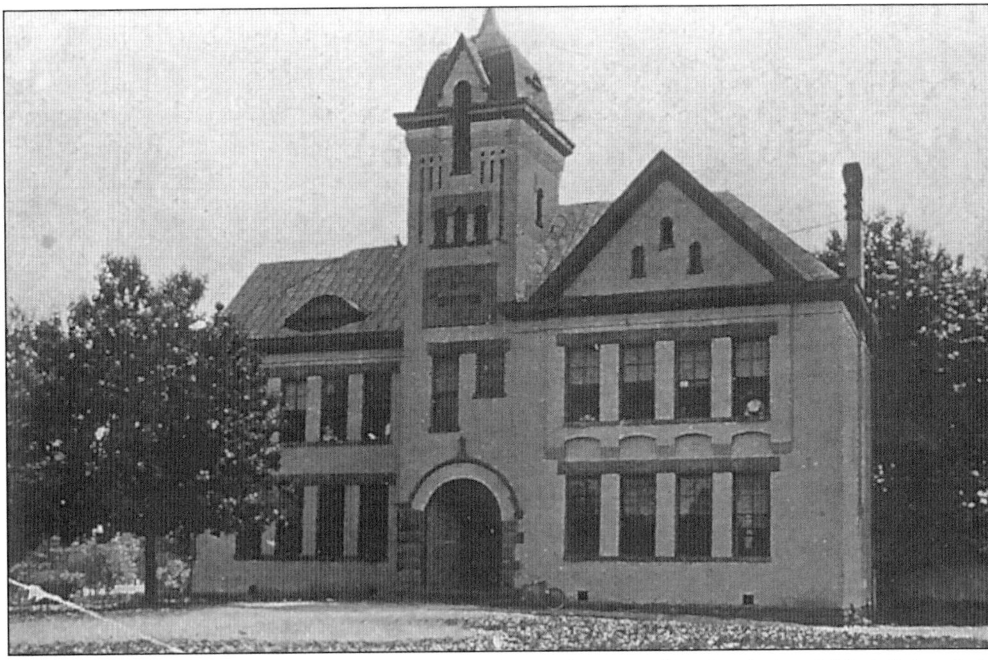

This view, published between 1915 and 1930, shows the Versailles Graded and High Schools in Versailles, at a time when both were combined.

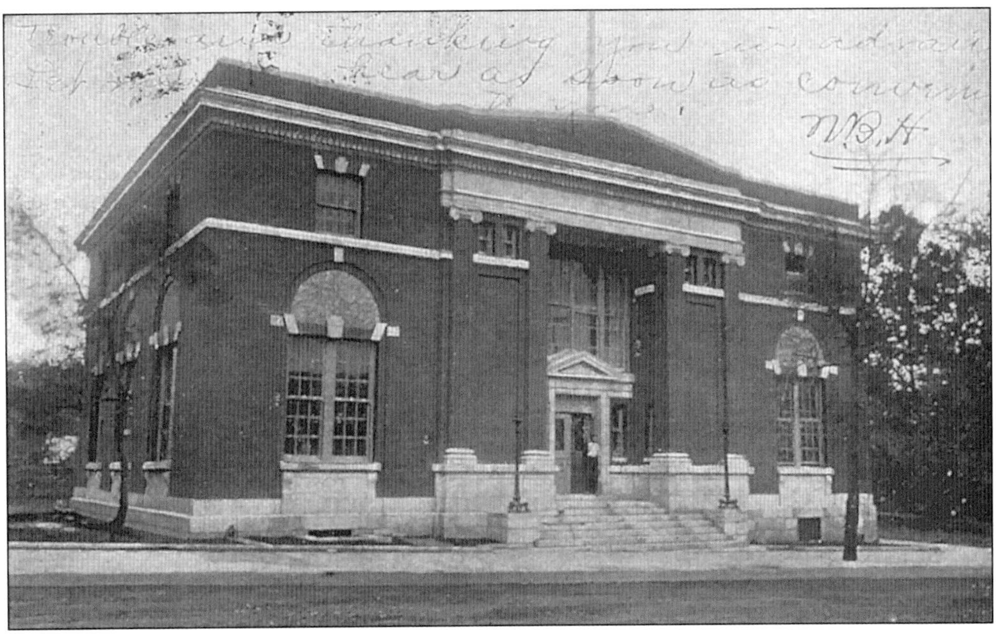

This view, with a postmark of 1913, shows the Government Building in Versailles, Kentucky. The Bank of J. Amsden & Co. in Versailles published some beautiful pictures demonstrating people saving money in 1911 and 1912. Those pictures were not included in this book, but the existence of that bank is significant to the history of Versailles.

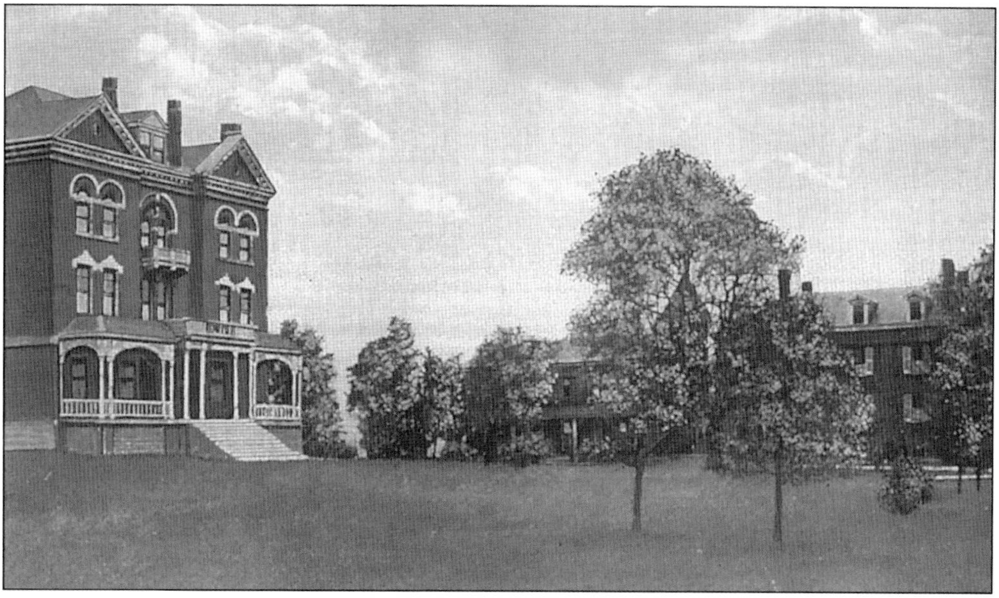

The final two postcards will focus on Midway, Kentucky, which dates back to 1795, when a log house at a point midway between Lexington and Frankfort was built. A town formed around the railroad and grew into Midway, Kentucky. This postcard shows the Kentucky Female Orphan School buildings and campus in Midway. It was founded in 1847. The building on the left, Pinderton Hall, was named in honor of one of the original founders and was built in 1859.

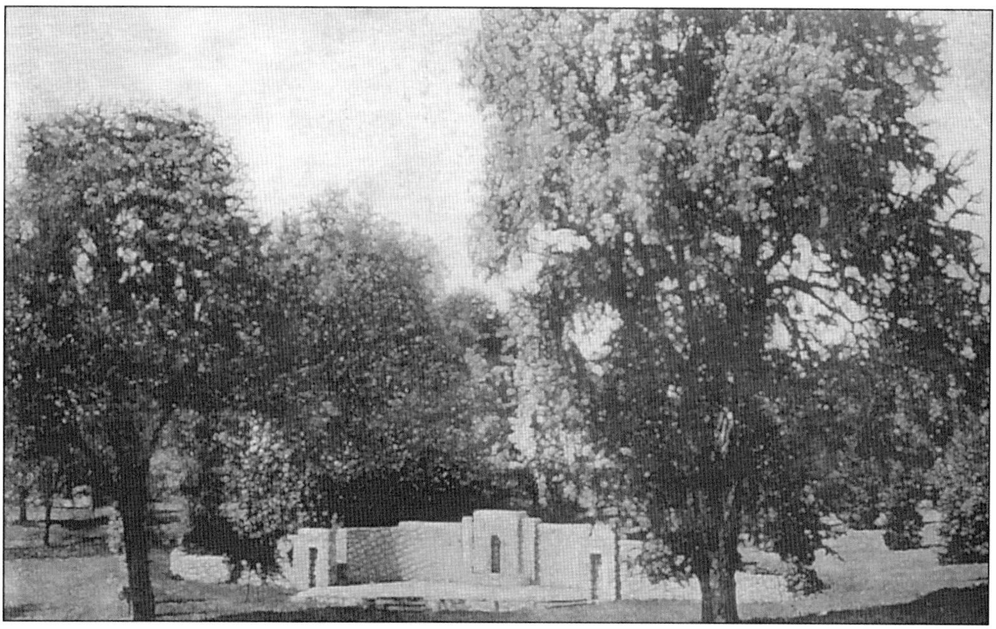

This view shows the Fannie H. Graves Amphitheatre as part of Midway Junior College. An earlier postcard (1936) of the same area shows this as an open-air theater on the campus of Kentucky Female Orphan School. The school claimed to be the only secondary school that chose students from orphan girls, and it was maintained by the Christian Church. It became Midway Junior College in 1949 and claimed to have a campus of 105 acres.

Index of Bluegrass Towns